Mentors, Masters and Mrs. MacGregor

Mentors, Masters and Mrs. MacGregor

Stories of Teachers Making a Difference

Compiled by
Jane Bluestein, Ph.D.

Health Communications, Inc.
Deerfield Beach, Florida

.**Library of Congress Cataloging-in-Publication Data**

Mentors, masters, and Mrs. MacGregor : stories of teachers
making a difference / compiled by Jane Bluestein.
    p. cm.
    ISBN 1-55874-336-7 (hardback). — ISBN 1-55874-337-5
(pbk.)
    1. Teachers—United States—Case studies.   2. Teacher
effectiveness—United States—Case studies.   3. Students—
United States—Quotations.   I. Bluestein, Jane.
LB1775.2.M46   1995
371.1'00973—dc20   95-576
                                                        CIP

©1995 Jane Bluestein
ISBN 1-55874-337-5 (paperback)
ISBN 1-55874-336-7 (hard cover)

All rights reserved. Printed in the United States of America.
No part of this publication may be reproduced, stored in a
retrieval system or transmitted in any form or by any means,
electronic, mechanical, photocopying, recording or otherwise without the written permission of the publisher.

Publisher: Health Communications, Inc.
              3201 S.W. 15th Street
              Deerfield Beach, Florida 33442-8190
Cover design by Lawna Oldfield

To everyone who has ever sparked a burning desire for learning, expanded someone's vision of self, made the world a little safer or in some tender way touched the heart and mind of a child.

CONTENTS

A Really Great Teacher Is Someone Who

A Really Great Teacher Is Someone Who 114

ACKNOWLEDGMENTS

I had no idea how enormous, not to mention paper-intensive, this project would be when I started. In the process, I received a great deal of help and support and wish to thank the following:

First and foremost, my gratitude goes to the nearly 200 individuals from all walks of life and many corners of the globe who responded to my invitation to share a story about their experiences for this book. I also appreciate the graciousness of those people who took the time to write back or call, even if they couldn't think of a story or didn't have time to participate in this project.

My thanks to the story evaluators who gave me feedback and suggestions based on the first 80-150 stories I received: Peggy Bielen, Susanna Bluestein, Syndi Ecker, Pat Freeman,

MaryAnn Kohl, Nancy Krivokapich, Judy Lawrence, Linda Sorenson and Sandy.

Thanks also to the hundreds of children who shared their ideas and to the teachers and parents whose kids sent in a large number of these comments: Susan Feder, Marjorie Eisen, Glenn Capelli, B. Weddell, Neville Helme, LaRue Davenport, Cathy Riley, Nancy Krivokapich, Byra Warner and Chris Simon.

To Jerry, who got stuck with a whole lot of the typing, transcribing and filing! I could never have done all this alone.

To Linda Sorenson for all of her international connections, and for her enthusiasm and patience when mine wavered or disappeared entirely.

And to my editors Christine Belleris and Matthew Diener who held onto this vision as this book came into being.

The Book

THE IDEA

Not too long ago, I was driving around with a friend who used to do construction work. As we were going through various parts of the city, he pointed out numerous buildings and structures he had helped create. Later that day, he noticed the ceiling in the store we were in was one that he had hung a few years before. Everywhere we went, monuments testified to this man's talents, energies and his contribution to the world.

As an educator for the past twenty-some years, I know that the evidence of my work is far more subtle. I am fortunate and grateful for the reinforcement that I have received—letters from former students, the applause after I've spoken to a group or a comment from someone who took a class from me a year or two ago. But there are no monuments for me to point to, no physical "creations" I can take credit for.

So many of the changes that occur when we interact with, influence and touch one another's lives happens slowly, interwoven with the impact of other events and encounters. Many of the seeds that we plant may not become visible to us for years, if ever. So we work on faith, and in the day-to-day realities of working with children, the community and "the system," that faith can sometimes wear pretty thin.

I work with teachers and parents throughout the world and have seen my share of burnout and despair, much of it grounded in the nagging doubt that the people involved are making a difference. So I wanted to write a book, to compile "evidence," as it were, that our dedication, the persistence of our efforts and the courage of our continued faith—not only in the children we live and work with, but in our mission as well—does, in fact, take hold.

I ended up with three primary goals for this book. The first was to reassure and remind anyone in contact with children that we can and do make a difference, even with seemingly insignificant words or actions. Second, I wanted to honor some of the people who have touched someone's life in a positive and significant way. And third—and to me, perhaps most important—I wanted to present a picture of positive mentorship, to show, specifically, what supportive, encouraging and nurturing influence looks like, to show how simple and practical these gestures can be.

MY SOURCES

I started this project by bouncing the idea off friends, acquaintances and especially other educators. A few weeks later, armed with overwhelming encouragement, excitement and support, I sent flyers describing the project and asking about a thousand friends and associates to tell me about their favorite teacher, the one who had the greatest and most positive impact on their lives. I followed up on dozens and dozens of these contacts with telephone calls, realizing that it would be easier for many people to just tell me the story as I recorded it, than it would for them to sit down and write it out.

I kept a tape recorder by the phone and another in my briefcase or purse. I asked people I met on the road to tell me about the best teachers they ever had. As a result, this collection includes the experiences of a number of people who sat next to me on planes, who clerked at the hotels I stayed in or who drove the occasional shuttle buses I relied on to get me to an airport.

I have stories from people who were in the audiences I addressed during the past year or so, from the salesperson who sold me my modem, from the guy who came to install another phone line in my office for the fax machine.

I wrote to several hundred "notables," asking for their stories. I called other speakers and authors whose work I respected. I called friends and friends of friends. I scoured magazines for articles about people in which the influence of a teacher was mentioned. I followed up on dozens of leads and lists of potential contacts that associates sent me. I put a request in my alumni newsletter and, after spending months figuring out how to do so, put the word out on the Internet. I wanted a variety of stories from people of different ages, different occupations, different parts of the country (and world) and different cultural backgrounds and experiences. I ran up astronomical telephone bills and spent more on postage in three months than I had in the previous year! These efforts led to many rewarding connections—in a couple of instances, with people I hadn't talked to or heard from in almost 20 years—and lots of new friends. And it showed me that there are people all over the globe whose lives have been touched by a teacher in the most wonderful ways!

THE KIDS

This part of the book came as a bit of an afterthought. On yet another airplane trip, I sat across the aisle from two children and their mother. It turned out that the mother had formerly been a classroom teacher and when I mentioned the book I was working on, her boys started talking about their teachers. I asked if they'd mind if I jotted down what they were saying, at that point realizing that I could include students in this project by asking them to tell me what they thought made a great teacher.

When interviewing students, I either asked them to tell me about their favorite teacher or had them complete the sentence, "A really great teacher is someone who . . ."

I had some help on this one, as a number of parents and teachers I met through the various channels previously mentioned were willing to collect responses from the kids in their lives and send them off to me. I ended up with ideas from students between the ages of 4 and 24 from all over the United States, plus Canada, Mexico, England, Western Australia, Indonesia and The Netherlands.

Despite some really sweet comments that emerged from my first ventures into this part of the project, I'll admit I was a bit cynical at first. I half expected most of the answers to be "gives us candy" or "lets us do anything we want to do in class." While I did get two "candy" responses and encountered a few middle-school-aged kids with attitudes—if that isn't redundant—I found the majority of the kids' comments to be sincere, constructive and, in many cases, rather sophisticated.

THE RULES

In looking for stories and interviews for this book, my first rule was that they had to be positive.

I had recently read a story in our local newspaper by someone who had been shamed and humiliated in front of his entire sixth-grade class, and then went on to say how much this experience had benefited him! I cringed the entire time I was reading this account and couldn't help thinking that if this teacher's goal had been to instill a sense of commitment and responsibility in this individual, she could have easily accomplished the exact same thing in a far less hurtful way.

I decided that I didn't want any "survivor" stories, no stories of abusive or mean-spirited behavior, regardless of how well the student may have recovered. Instead, I wanted examples of kindness, of inspiration, of support.

I started looking for stories about individuals who had, in some way, been an advocate for a child's reality, who validated a child's sense of worth or belief in self, who helped someone through a hard time, who taught someone to appreciate his or her own talents, abilities or uniqueness. I wanted to hear about people who had advanced someone's cognitive functioning, appreciation for some subject area, view of the world or progress toward a career goal.

I wanted to hear from individuals who, as a result of their contact with some adult in their lives, were inspired to reach beyond what they thought they could achieve or become, felt safe enough to take risks and try new things, or were guided in development of their personal standards, morals or value system. And I looked for stories of teachers who used specific educational or guidance techniques in the hopes that readers would be inspired to try the same, as such techniques might apply to their lives and relationships with children. In order to avoid a lot of editorializing, I screened out stories and interviews in which contributors focused on personal opinion instead of personal experience. And finally, I wanted to keep the stories, as much as possible, in the voices of the individuals who contributed them.

OH, ABOUT MRS. MacGREGOR

The inclusion of Mrs. MacGregor in the title of this book was inspired by Uncle Walter's grade-school teacher. (Her name was actually Miss McGregor—back then, teachers weren't allowed to be married—but we took some license with her marital status and last name so that the title would read a little better.) Her name came from a story Uncle Walter shared in response to hearing about this project I was working on. He wrote to tell me about the teacher who had made a definite impression—on his ribs, with a pointer! So much so that many years later, he was alerted to the fact that she had died by a sudden, stabbing pain in that general area of his body. Although this wasn't quite the positive nature of the stories I was looking for, I wanted to include her name, perhaps as a tongue-in-cheek tribute to a woman who obviously made a much greater impression on this highly literate and knowledgeable man some five decades later.

THE RESPONSES

I entered into this project with a few assumptions, one of which was that everybody had a favorite teacher—probably because I had so many. I was quite surprised at the number of people who replied to my requests for an interview with a willingness to help, but an inability to remember any teacher who had made a difference in their lives in positive ways. There were several people who stated flat out that there simply were no teachers they experienced like that, and others who could only remember the negative experiences of school. All, however, thought the book was a great idea and graciously wished me luck.

Some of the people who couldn't think of positive influences in their experiences with a school or university system had other people in their lives they wanted to tell me about. As a result, while the majority of stories focus on school-related experiences, this collection includes stories about the influence of parents, grandparents, in-laws, writers, counselors, tutors, neighbors, spiritual teachers, an AA sponsor and an Air Force commanding officer. There are also a few stories from teachers about students whose lives they influenced. The majority of the stories focused on a single teacher, or even a single interaction in some cases, although several contributors spoke of the cumulative effect of a number of teachers, or identified two or three influences, each of whom had his or her own impact.

Many of the stories I received arrived through the mail, fax or e-mail; however, the majority were given as personal interviews. During these interviews, I witnessed the impact of simply talking about these life-changing people and events. For many people, the experience was extremely emotional. More than a few men and women broke down while telling me their stories. For others, the process was very introspective, bringing up many of the "threads" connected to the experience or the context of the experience, particularly with regard to what was going on at home at the time.

Every now and then I saw the contributor go through an amazing transformation in the course of telling his or her story. I could often hear changes in voices, tone and language patterns, almost as though the person telling the story had "become" the age he or she was at the time of the experience.

This phenomenon hit home early in my story-collecting. A few months before he died, I was visiting my father in the convalescent hospital in Los Angeles where he spent the last year of his life. I started telling him about this project and he replied that he could still remember a lot of his teachers. Sensing an opportunity for another interview, I immediately fished my tape recorder out of my bag and turned it on. He lay back in his bed, took a deep breath and started to talk. As he described his teachers, I did a double-take. This fragile, bed-ridden, 78-year-old man had a smile on his face and a light-ness about him I hadn't seen in years. At one point, I would have sworn that he was no longer in that bed, in that room. He had drifted off somewhere—back to fourth grade, to his high school English class or to a baseball game with his school team. With pure geriatric aplomb, this same person who, at times, wasn't sure which coast he was on anymore, could recall where the father of one of his teachers worked or something he learned from a grade-school teacher nearly 70 years before. It was truly a thrill to watch. Even more signif-icant for me personally, the interview left me with the only recording I have of my father's voice.

MY TEACHERS

I'm one of those whose education, growth and personal development happened with the help of a number of people, including many members of my family. One of the greatest gifts my parents gave me was complete support for my inter-ests, particularly in the areas of art, music and various crafts. In addition to making available supplies, materials, equip-ment, instruments and the necessary classes or instruction, they never questioned my ability to excel at any of the numer-ous ventures I wanted to explore. As a result, I have a great deal of confidence in just about any endeavor I'm tempted to undertake and believe that, with very few exceptions, I am capable of learning and achieving almost anything.

Some of these early explorations led to an art teacher named Frieda Reiter, whose classes occupied many, many

Saturdays throughout my adolescence. Mrs. Reiter was the one who taught me to really look at the world, seeing beyond what my mind often thought it was seeing. She took our class to sketch a portrait of a 106-year-old woman one week, the fountains and statues in a park in Center City, Philadelphia, another. She had us paint the reflections in a silver pitcher and the textures of rotted fruit. For the rest of my life, I will never see the Philadelphia art museum, where we frequently went on our outings, and not think of her. While I don't do much with my art these days, her classes and assignments provided a much-needed sanctuary at that point in my life.

In seventh-grade social studies, my teacher, Mark Blasko, was young and cute and wore these neat tweed jackets with leather patches at the elbow. Knowing that year I was into creating crossword puzzles, he actually helped me sell one to a publisher of educational magazines for kids. Aside from being a terrific social studies teacher, Mr. Blasko has the distinction of being the only teacher I ever wrote to over the summer. Even more amazing, he sent a three-page reply that, 31 years later, I still have.

Mark Blasko and I are still in contact, and I'm fortunate to count him among my friends today. I am quite sure the amount of traveling I do now is directly connected to the geography lessons that so turned me on to wanting to see the world. To this day, I generally do well with maps and written directions, and on any trip I've ever taken, I am invariably the one who navigates.

There were others: Miss Bell, the only gym teacher I ever had in my entire school career who treated me with respect, even though I was one of the worst students in her class.

Or Michele Matzkin, whom I wanted to look like, talk like, dress like and generally *be*, even though, in ninth grade, I didn't think I could ever come close. She inspired me to continue studying French and to pursue my dreams, "no matter how impossible they seem right now." Her posters of Mont St. Michel eventually culminated in a dream-fulfilling trip there some 25 years later.

Or Dr. Southworth, my supervisor and instructor during my teaching internship, who told me that I was going to be a great teacher even after seeing me on the absolute worst day of my entire classroom career.

But perhaps the teacher I loved most was my kindergarten teacher Edith Mather. I don't remember a time that I didn't want to be a teacher, and after a day or two in kindergarten, I couldn't envision myself doing anything else. Mrs. Mather never seemed to mind that for weeks on end, despite dozens of other available activities, all I ever wanted to do was "paint at the easel," or that I was just about the only girl who ever wanted to play in the wood shop. She let me hum the Christmas carols when my parents said I wasn't allowed to sing the words. She was the one who took a poster I had painted of children at a playground to a school board meeting and, as a result, according to what she later told my parents, got the necessary funding to have a playground installed for us at the school that year.

Mrs. Mather never, ever yelled, although she did lose her patience with me once when I simply would not quit talking, and asked me to go to the cloakroom to wait until she was finished with her announcements. Arrogant because I honestly felt as though I were somehow above this kind of punishment, and furious that she kept interrupting *me*, I stormed off to the cloakroom uttering a few choice swear words to let her know that this five-year-old was not pleased! I remember Mrs. Mather calling me away from the now-stunned class, sitting on the piano bench so she could meet me at eye-level, and calmly proceeding to let me know that we just don't use words like that in kindergarten. In a million years I will never know how she kept a straight face, and in the end, she let me sit back down again.

When I was in high school, I tried tracking her down to go visit her but discovered that she had left the district. Many years later, after numerous unsuccessful attempts to contact her, a friend's mother discovered that Mrs. Mather had moved to another town in New Jersey, and sent me her address. More than 30 years after being in her class, I wrote her a letter, detailing some of my finer memories of her class. I sent her a copy of my kindergarten picture, as well as a copy of my latest promotional brochure, telling her how, because of her influence, I had decided to pursue my lifelong ambition to become an educator.

Later that summer, I received a letter from her son. He had been going through his mother's things and found my letter. He thanked me for writing and assured me that his mother had enjoyed hearing from me. My letter had arrived two weeks before she died.

If I had any doubts before I started this book, I am now completely convinced that we do indeed touch one another's lives. We are products of a lifetime of experiences, events, interactions, a word or a look—any of which can have a profound effect on who we become in life. How we act with one another matters because people notice and they remember and they sometimes carry these memories throughout their lives. I'm also reassured that no matter how many negative forces are at work in a person's life, it sometimes takes no more than one person, one act of love or acceptance or encouragement, to make a difference. More often than not, that person will never see, know or receive evidence of the impact he or she has had on us—unless we stop and say, "Thanks for making a difference in my life!"

Quid Pro Quo

A tribute to Mrs. Berland, my sixth-grade teacher
at Indian Mounds Elementary, Bloomington, MN

by Janet Stelzig Brunner

Though it isn't too likely you remember me
You must have known how strong your impressions would be;
By the love and creativity you spent to tool
My fondest memories of elementary school
Out of dozens of teachers, you were the one
Who gave to me what I love to share with my son.
The Boxcar Children, A Wrinkle in Time;
How to make nature, fun and learning rhyme.
I'm not rich or famous, or even especially
Unusual in any way most people might see.
Yet my life has a rhythm of which you are a part
And there will always be a grateful place in my heart
For someone like you who took the trouble to sew
A golden thread without knowing where it might go.
To fine linen, polyester, cotton, denim or lace?
The fabric of childhood is what clothed the adult face.
Along the way, so many have made their impression
And contributed to someone else's expression.
To mine you added spirit to wonder and enjoy
All that life has to offer and pass on to my boy
How living with an open heart and mind
Gives one strength, courage and wisdom to find
The world and himself in sweet harmony.
I want to thank you for doing that for me.

Funky Winkerbean

The Stories

I'm often asked what influenced me to go into education, and I always say it started with my first-grade teacher, Mrs. Fredrickson. From the first day of school at age six, I realized that I never wanted to be anything but just like her, and I've never changed my mind.

Every day when the school bell rang, I always knew where I'd find Mrs. Fredrickson. She was always at the door, greeting every one of us with what she called "an H or an H," a hug or a handshake. I always chose the hug. Most of the kids began with a handshake, but by the end of the first month everybody was going for the hugs.

On my birthday she came to my house and she bought me a Little Golden book. (I know why it's called a Golden book, because it's one of my most cherished possessions!) She was there for maybe five minutes, but to me it was an eternity!

I remember her being tall, with glasses at the bridge of her nose, but 30 years later I realize her appearance had nothing to do with the impact she had on me. The impact came from her personal touch, her personal caring and always her ability to make me feel like I was special. Every moment that I was in that woman's room, I felt like I was "Teacher's Pet."

And now whenever I talk to teachers, I tell them about her. Because when it comes down to how we really and truly can impact kids the most, it isn't in the curriculum or some program or kit. We can make such tremendous differences on our students' lives with our personal touch, by greeting them with "an H or an H," and by being a teacher who, like Mrs.

Fredrickson, can really make them feel special. To me, that's the whole secret to unlocking a child's potential—being there for them, letting them know that we believe in them. What a difference we can make!

Dr. Michele Borba, Educational Consultant and Author, Palm Springs, California

Of all my teachers, two had a positive impact. This isn't a big percentage, but then I was a disciplinary case—I was always a wise guy getting into trouble.

One teacher was Bessie Abramowitz. She was my home-room teacher in high school and she taught biology. She always used to say to me that if I could harness the energy I had, I could do anything in my life. If I would just harness the energy—I had no idea what she was talking about. I'd say to her, "Bessie, I got it harnessed! I got it harnessed!" Although I didn't know exactly what she meant, I somehow understood that she really had faith in me as a person. She exhibited that faith and spoke about it. She really encouraged me, telling me that someday I'd get in the right lane, and once I did, I'd go all the way.

When I became a celebrity, I went back and visited her class—to thank her. I told the class I was a poor kid sitting in the same seat they were sitting in, that I had the same dreams and the same worries and the same fears that they had. "But you could make something out of your life," I said, "because somebody very wise told me one time that if you just harness your energy, you can do it." I told them what "harness the energy" meant, and tried to encourage them. Bessie had passed it on to me and I tried to pass it on to her students that day. She was all tearful as I spoke to the kids. She's gone now.

The other teacher was Dr. Jacobs, who taught physics. I was a disruptive student, as I said before. I upset every class because I was always thinking funny. So we made a deal: He would give me five minutes at the beginning of the class to tell my jokes, to joke around, to do anything I wanted for exactly five minutes, then I had to shut my mouth for the rest of the period.

He would get up there as soon as the bell rang and everyone was in their seats. He would say, "Ladies and gentlemen, Physics 101 is proud to present the comedy styling and antics of David Brenner." And then I would do five minutes. He'd sometimes cut me off right in the middle of a joke! But I could use those five minutes however I wanted. I could make fun of him or do anything I wanted to do.

He knew how to harness that energy. He would have spent a lot more than five minutes getting me under control. All my other teachers tried for years with a lot less success.

Once on a TV show, I said that I hadn't been that great a student, and Dr. Jacobs, then in his late 80s, sent me a letter with a transcript of my class's grades. The transcript showed that I was one of only three students who got an A in physics that year. He wrote in there, "So you weren't a bad student at all."

David Brenner, Entertainer and Network Radio Show Host, New York, New York

I learned how to write in a class called College-Level English, which I took during my senior year of high school. On the first day of class, Mr. French stood up and said, "This is a college-level class and I will teach it like a college-level class. I will not mark you off for tardiness and I will not say anything if you are late. Just come in and sit down."

He wasn't about to make us come to class. We could miss every class day if we wanted; if we could miss class and complete the work, that was our business. He let us know that when you got to college, that was the way it was going to be. None of my other high school teachers were anything like that. He said, "This is the way I'm going to do it. You've got five weeks to write five perfect papers. You can do it any way you want to. You can hand in one a week and I will grade them and hand them back to you as soon as you're done. You can wait until the last day and hand in all five of them. You can hand them all in the first week and then I'll hand them back to you and you can do revisions on them. When you are done, you will have written five perfect papers." By the time that five-week period was up, I had written five perfect essays, and I knew why they were perfect essays.

The ability to put my ideas down on paper in a clean and concise way saved my bacon in college. In college, you have a few courses that test by "multiple guess," but for most of the work I did in college, I had to be able to write. Because of Mr. French, I never, in all my time in college, got less than a B on a paper—most of them were A's. Because of him, I knew how to write a paper.

Edward McNair, 34, Computer Salesperson, Albuquerque, New Mexico

In the middle of the seventh grade, my family moved to a new school district. In my new school, my English class had just finished studying prepositions and moved on to something else. I had not covered this material in my old school, but I was expected to somehow catch up. I told my new teacher that I hadn't learned about prepositions in my old school. She responded that I'd have to learn them on my own, but offered no assistance or materials to help me.

I wrote a letter to my previous English teacher, asking her to recommend a book with the information I needed. She immediately responded with a 20-page handwritten paper, teaching me everything I needed to know about prepositions, with diagrams and exercises as well as the title of a book I could find in the library. She even gave me her phone number if I had any questions!

It was a brilliant letter because it not only taught me prepositions, but it also showed what this woman would do for a student. She saw me as a real person in need, and she was really willing to be there for me. She gave me what I needed, and she did this in a way that I felt like I deserved. I visited her many times over the years and always thanked her for that. She was always surprised at my appreciation. She didn't think she was extending herself—she was just being a teacher.

Lynn Collins, 47, Professional Speaker, Consultant, Counselor and Author, Albuquerque, New Mexico

I deal with lots of people who are confronting life-threatening illnesses, so at workshops I will often say, "Which mottos do you live or die by?" I ask this because many people grow up with incredibly negative messages. They expect the worst to happen because of things their parents often repeated or mumbled when they were younger. It's like a hypnosis session: The parent keeps repeating a message to this little child until it becomes a part of the child's life. So if anything good happens, they expect something bad to happen. They go through life expecting adverse situations and circumstances.

I realized only later in life why I was not like that, by talking to my parents about what I had learned from them. My mother told me that when my father and she got married, he was not looked upon too nicely by her parents. He had lost his job, and in order to confuse her parents, he would get dressed and leave the house looking like he was going to work but he would just sit at the unemployment agency all day. One day he called my mother to say, "Rose, I have two offers. One is a civil service job, which is very secure, and the other is with Paramount Theatres, which is not secure but I might advance. What should I do?" (I always pause there and ask, "What do you tell somebody at that moment?")

My mother's answer was the only one that I think is appropriate. She said, "Do what will make you happy." Now, what does that do to you? It makes you get in touch with your feelings, your desires, your happiness. It's not being selfish. It's exploring how you want to contribute to the world and what you want to do with your life, and doing what will make you happy. I realized later that the same was done to me. They didn't agree with me wanting to be a doctor, but they never said, "Don't do that," or "We can help you more if you become a lawyer or a plumber, or if you play a violin." It was, "You want to be a doctor? Okay. Be a doctor. If it will make you happy, be a doctor." I never grew up worrying that I wasn't pleasing them.

I also heard my father say something nice about me when I wasn't in the room. I realized later that this was probably one of the most powerful things he could have done for me. He was complimenting me on my potential and saying that I could be successful at anything. I was a little kid in the next room and he didn't know I could hear him. When you think about it, to hear your parents say nice things about you when you're not there, you know they must mean them.

The third thing, which I think was the most important, was the way my parents responded when something negative happened. I can remember as a young man coming home after not being accepted to a college, or when some girl wouldn't go out with me. When I was upset about all these terrible events in life, my mother and father's view was: "It was meant to be. God is redirecting you. Something good will come of this." I can remember as a kid not liking that answer! I would have been happy if everybody were miserable, and they all wailed and moaned. But hearing "Something good will come of this," led me to go to my room, sit at my desk and look up and say, "All right, God, what is gonna happen? What do I do now?" Ultimately, over the next day or week or two, God would always tell me that a new girl would appear or I would go to a different college or whatever, and it always worked out. So I began to have this faith in life and in this intuitive aspect, to not judge events but to see how they direct you and help you find your way and your path.

Later in life I realized how important that message was. Often it is the difficult way that ultimately is the one that rewards you. My concept of life became "Life is a labor pain."

If you're actually giving birth, it's worth all the difficulties. Whether you're talking about going through surgery or literally being in labor or putting up with certain things, it's your choice, not somebody else imposing that on you. In this very subtle way, my parents taught me without preaching—they just lived it, and helped me give birth to myself.

Dr. Bernie Siegel, 62, Surgeon, Author, Teacher, Woodbridge, Connecticut

He came from Yale University, to teach at my Catholic high school. When he showed up, I was in tenth grade. Our bodies were raging with hormones and we couldn't think of anything but girls. He gave us some direction and helped us see that there's more to getting something on a date than what was under her sweater.

He wrote on a chalkboard "SINGOD," which meant "Sin is not giving on a date." And of course all the guys looked at each other and snickered and said, "Yeah, it's a real sin, you know!"

He was talking about giving 100 percent to someone when you're with that person. For example, you shouldn't read your newspaper at breakfast. You should really connect with the person you're with. That has really stuck with me. In class we would do things like reflect the sun off our wristwatches to the teacher's forehead or put ice cream bars in his drawer. He was such a cool guy that some of the kids would want to break his spirit, but he hung in there.

I got a sense of peace just talking to him. I was one of the more outrageous kids in his class, and he would spend time with me, just sitting in his Volkswagen and talking. He was just a good ear, a good soul. He was like Sidney Poitier in *To Sir, With Love*. He was an exceptional guy and I can't think of anyone who had a greater influence on me back then.

Life is more precious having known him—like having a brush with death without the trauma. Because of him I reach out more to people. I'm more accepting and more tolerant. He gave us that guidance without much fanfare, helping us realize that we can be easy with people, that we can be patient, accepting and loving.

*Matthew Bertoni, 44, Masseur, Ironworker, Treeworker,
Minister, Ann Arbor, Michigan*

When I was in third grade, my music teacher noticed me. She smiled at me and acknowledged my existence. This was unlike my other teachers or my parents. That impression has stayed with me throughout my life.

Anonymous

During my senior year in high school, I had been sick with bronchitis and missed two weeks of school. When I returned, I had to make up nine tests in one week. By the last one, I was really out of it. I remember looking at this test paper and not knowing any of the answers. I was a total blank. It was like I had never heard of this history junk before.

It was after school and I was the only one in the classroom. The teacher was working at his desk and I was staring off into space. "What's the matter?" he asked. And I said, "I can't do this. I don't know any of these answers." He got up and he came over and he looked at my paper and he said, "You know the answer to that! We just talked about it in class yesterday. You answered a question I asked about that." I said, "I don't remember. I just can't remember." He gave me a few hints, but I still couldn't remember. I realized I was on overload, and my straight A's in history were now a thing of the past. I looked at him and I said, "Look. You're just gonna have to give me an F. I can't do it. I feel too bad." He reached down with his red pencil and I watched him, certain he was going to put an F on my paper—I mean, there was not one answer on this test! But he put an A on the top.

I said, "What are you doing?" And he said, "If you'd been here and you felt good and you'd had time to study, that's what you'd have gotten. So that's what you're gonna get." This guy really did recognize that I had been operating out of excellence all the time I had been in his class, and that I was telling the truth. My mind was a blank and I was willing to take the F, because that's what I deserved. But I didn't have to.

I then realized that there are people out there who will give you a break once in a while. It was empowering. It was like he was saying, "I know who you are, not just what you do." That's an amazing gift to give somebody. I will be grateful to that guy till the day I die. I thought, "That's the kind of teacher I want to be."

Lynn Collins, 47, Professional Speaker, Consultant, Counselor and Author, Albuquerque, New Mexico

I had my all-time favorite teacher in third grade. Miss Johnstone was funny, intelligent, young and outgoing. She had everything in her power to really change a child's life and was especially talented at getting us motivated in school. Our class was Miss Johnstone's very first class—we got her straight out of college. We all really bonded with each other.

One of my classmates from back then ran into her about three months ago. When she saw me afterwards, she excitedly described her encounter: "You know who I ran into? Miss Johnstone! And she remembered all of our names, each and every one of us in the entire class." My friend said that Miss Johnstone took about 30 minutes of her time, wanting to know exactly what happened to each one of us. Did we all graduate? Who didn't graduate? Had anyone passed away? Where were we? Anything, everything. It had been 19 years since she had been our teacher and she still remembered everybody because, she said, she had such a strong bond with us.

I remember one day when I was in third grade, Miss Johnstone looked at me and said, "You know, you're going to be something one of these days. I don't know what, but whatever you pursue, you are gonna be great!" I don't know if that was a general statement or just the naïveté of a first-year teacher, but she obviously felt something was there.

In later years, any time I was tempted to deviate from school and pursue other goals or take a bad turn in life, I always thought back and remembered what she told me that day. That statement always stays with me and many times has helped me stay on track.

Guadalupe Diaz, 28, Administrative Assistant in Programming, TI-IN Network, San Antonio, Texas

I certainly couldn't have done it without her. Though there have been many individuals in my life who have had a strong effect upon my view of the world and who have served as mentors, none have shaped my future more than an elementary-school special-education teacher, Miss Hunt.

I was the youngest son of a very large Italian immigrant family. We spoke Italian in the home and English was a second language to me. My parents carried their Italian heritage across the sea, and in many ways I was different. I preferred opera to popular music. I knew Italian fairy tales rather than those read by my neighbors. Our food was different. Our view of life was more full of joy of the moment, passionate behaviors and deep family ties.

Though I saw all of these things as decided advantages, I fear that our school psychologist saw me through different eyes. My English language skills were low and my view of the world was radically unrealistic. He classified me, after the usual tests, as mentally deficient and recommended special class placement.

It was in the special class setting that I encountered Miss Hunt. She was caring, warm and wonderful. She paid little, if any, attention to labels such as "retarded." She saw us all as children with rich possibilities and unlimited potentials. She helped me to love learning and created an unforgettable loving, accepting environment for us all. I was soon blossoming: reading, writing, sharing and expressing my uniqueness in a myriad of positive ways. She nurtured my mind and my psyche and encouraged me to be proud of who I was.

After several months in her class, she insisted that I be retested. Much to her joy and my despair, I tested out of her class and into a regular classroom. But Miss Hunt's door remained forever open to me. She continued to encourage me and to convince me that there was a wondrous life ahead of me.

I cannot help wonder what might have become of me if I had not encountered Miss Hunt. What she taught me in a short period of time has remained with me all my life, especially my professional life as a teacher. For years I attempted to find her, but to no avail. I wanted very much to thank her and to express the wonder in the life knowledge she shared with me. But I know that with Miss Hunt, it didn't matter. She was a lover, and love is certainly its own reward.

Leo F. Buscaglia, Ph.D., Author, Glenbrook, Nevada

He was a natural science teacher in high school. He had a Ph.D. Both he and his wife were teachers and both were extremely enthusiastic about what they were doing. He brought a lot to class, a lot of hands-on experience. During the summers, he used to go to Africa and work with the game preserves.

He brought a lot from that experience into the classroom to share with us. Rather than just standing up in front of the class and saying, "Okay, this is the Serengeti, and lions and hyenas live here," he would tell us instead, "One night we had a pride of lions circle the encampment and we felt lucky to get out of there with our lives." He brought stories about setting up a weather station, that sort of thing.

A lot of times you get to high school and teachers just get into the theories of what's going on. This was more real. I think this was what sparked my interest in natural sciences and led to a degree in wood science.

Chris Murray, 34, Truss Designer, Cedar Crest, New Mexico

I came from a background of verbal abuse and had very low self-esteem. I was very withdrawn as a child and do not remember most of my teachers. I felt that they did not like me. The one teacher I had who really does stand out was Mrs. Keener, my tenth-grade English teacher. I remember looking up at her at the beginning of the school year, and looking at her long beautiful fingernails and her perfect hair, and thinking about how someday I would like to have fingernails and hair like Mrs. Keener.

But as I grew to appreciate this teacher in other ways, I realized that she noticed something in me that no one else did—that I spoke English very well. I was raised in the South in an area where sometimes people did not speak properly. But for some reason, my pronunciation, my accent and my grammar were always better than average, and she took an interest in me because of that.

Nobody ever told me I was good at anything, and she did! She used to say, "Oh, I love the way you pronounce that," or she would tell the class, "Listen to the way Rosalee pronounces that word." She pointed me out in a positive way, and was actually the first person in my life to ever do that. This was the only high school course I took that, when I left, I felt that I had really learned something, that I was really interested in the subject—all because a teacher took a special interest in me, because she saw something in me. She gave me something for the first time in my life that I felt I was good at.

And look what I became—a radio talk-show host! Who could imagine the amount of influence she had on what I became!

Lee Mirabal, "Ageless," Nationally Syndicated Radio Talk-Show Host, Entrepreneur, Mother and Wife, Chicago, Illinois

My very first teacher, aside from my parents, was my sister. She was two years older than I and would teach me every day whatever she learned in school that day. I idolized her and waited for her to come home from school so that I could learn about letters and numbers. Her enthusiasm was contagious. She was born to teach and everybody seemed to know this somehow. She even had me spelling "antidisestablishmentarianism," the longest word in the English language, I think, by the time I was only four! What she impressed upon me was curiosity, confidence in my learning ability and a capacity to expand my awareness that has served me my whole life.

There are several other teachers I'd like to thank, each contributing significantly in my life's unfoldment and maturity. I really liked Mrs. Janet Taylor, my fifth-grade teacher, because I felt that she liked me and that when she looked at me, she was both acknowledging me as I knew myself inside and seeing something that I could grow into someday, like watering a seedling. I liked her reflection very much. I knew that it was genuine. When I walked into the room, I could feel her light up and I'd light up, too. She indirectly taught me that I could do this, in turn, for others.

Then there was Mr. Warren Mullen, my art teacher in high school. He was very laid back and spacious. He just created a space for people to be creative. He was very open in an otherwise closed-minded school. Being a teenager was very difficult for me, and he probably kept me from either flipping out or dropping out completely.

In chiropractic school, I had this wild anatomy teacher. He

was teaching on so many levels at once. The school board really had a hard time with him, I think. But I thought he was one of those rare individuals who was born to teach. He not only knew his subject matter back and forth, but could make anatomy so creative to learn. I went from being extremely timid around a cadaver to becoming his lab assistant and teaching dissection! That is all his influence, and my respect for him and the subject, too.

He would ask provocative questions, but he would also throw out these one-liners like, "When I was in college, I was so poor I couldn't even afford to pay attention." Things like that. I would write all of his side comments in the margins of my notes. They kept me awake and laughing, usually. He would also say things like, "Consciousness does not need form to function." Whoa! And then he'd be onto the next thing. If you caught it, you caught it. He'd diagram anatomy, systematizing it into what he called "manageable units." These days, when I have a lot to do, I look at my work in terms of manageable units, thanks to him. Some days, well after I was no longer in his classes, I'd sit in just because it was such a treat. Others would, too. He comes through occasionally when I am teaching and I just smile to myself.

Another favorite teacher was this spiritual wild card named Joe Miller. Now Joe was an ex-vaudevillian and his method might be called "crazy-wisdom." He would do anything to get people to open up, usually through laughter, and just when all defenses were dropped, whoosh! He would shoot in some lightning bolt that would change your life, whether your mind caught it or not. He was offered titles of honor from all kinds of traditions, from Zen to Sufi, but he wanted to remain title-free, just Joe. His wife, Guin, was at least as potent a teacher as he, but she taught by her presence and remained pretty quiet. She held the space for the whole show to happen.

Chronologically, my next favorite teacher was a friend

named William. He has one of the greatest minds I have ever encountered, just fantastic! Over a period of ten years, directly and through his example, he taught my mind the art of attunement, subtlety, depth of perception and the capacity to articulate. He is a wordsmith and has the great gift of giving something its rightful and exact name, thus activating what had before only been latent. I will be forever grateful to him for taking my dull mind from fog to ever-clearer functioning, and for teaching me the blueprint of my life.

With my current teacher, teaching is really an art, with consciousness as the medium. He not only answers a question, but he answers the person who asks the question as well. He has an extraordinary capacity to be precise in his use of English, which is not his original language—more precise than almost any American I've met. He is a teacher's teacher. As a result of his perceptiveness, skillfulness and example, he is like a spiritual surgeon, teaching a way of living and natural unfolding that is deeply satisfying and fulfilling to the soul.

Dr. N. Susanna Bluestein, D.C., Chiropractor and Counselor, Albany, California

My sixth-grade teacher was a gentleman farmer. He farmed just for the fun of it. He was big and he was tough. This was at a small school in Martinsville, Wisconsin, with only 69 kids in it. This teacher knew everyone's families and was friends with all the parents.

I remember one time when I was having a problem with

my lunch. There was a kid who kept coming up to take my apple. My mom was always asking what was wrong, what was wrong, but I couldn't bring myself to tell her.

This teacher helped rescue me. He got me to talk about what was going on. He spoke to my parents. And the next day, we waited for the kid to come up to take my apple and when he did, the teacher was right there. He had been watching from a little ways away.

The reason I liked this teacher was that he was very fair with everybody. He didn't play favorites with anyone. Even this kid who was messing around with me got a fair shake from him. I mean the kid was punished, but then that was it.

Everybody liked this teacher. Even though you'd get in trouble with him sometimes, you knew why you got in trouble. I learned from him that you can be very fair and strict with people and still be very likable, and that's always stuck with me.

Scott Kalscheur, 24, Hotel Receptionist, Aspen, Colorado

My sixth-grade teacher, Mr. Butler, was an older man and a wonderful teacher. If we finished our work early, he would tell us stories of how he imagined the future would be for us as adults. He would say things like, "One day, you're going to be able to pick the television programs you want to watch, but you'll have to pay for them." This sounded bizarre to us in 1968. We thought he was crazy!

I also remember him telling us, "You're going to be riding on trains that go 200 miles per hour." He also said things like, "Probably by the time you are young adults, the United States is going to be running out of some resources. We're going to have problems getting enough gas and oil to run our cars." Now, this was when gas was something like 26 cents a gallon! Again, this sounded nuts to us at the time, but it certainly doesn't now.

Upon telling us these things, we would get really excited and make our own predictions about the future. He always kept us thinking about what was going to happen down the road. What was the world going to be like? What did I need or want to be doing in the future? How did I fit into the world of tomorrow? That kind of thinking remains with me today. Mr. Butler helped me immensely in making responsible decisions, in seeing cause and effect and in understanding my responsibility as a member of the world community.

Karen Sides, 37, Director of Education, TI-IN Network,
San Antonio, Texas

I'd always had fairly good teachers growing up, but this one struck me as a really caring person. I was a yearbook editor, and though this wasn't the most difficult subject or a tough program to get into—I mean, it's not a physics class or anything—for me, it was a challenge. This was the teacher who asked me to be an editor and gave me two partners to work with.

The greatest thing about this man was that he really gave us a lot of freedom. He respected us, and we respected him. Being the middle child between a very smart sister and a very smart brother, I needed the confidence he helped build, just by the respect he gave me. He saw me as an intelligent person. In addition to a very positive teacher-student relationship, we also had a friendship that was really nice.

One day, when we were going to a yearbook conference, this teacher told us that there was going to be a writing contest. He said, "We need to pick a couple of people to enter this contest." He chose this student who we all knew was a great writer, and he picked me.

I didn't want to do it. I knew there was no way I could compete with this other student. Well, it ended up that I won the entire contest and I owe it all to this teacher. There is no way I ever would have stepped into this TV business had I not felt like I had the confidence, and that's where I got it. I know it came from him.

Robyn Nance, 24, News Anchor, Reporter, Photographer, Quincy, Illinois

Probably the teacher that had the most impact on my life was a professor I had at the University of Wisconsin, Whitewater. He was definitely a curmudgeon, but he was also a scholar and thinker. He'd been the former dean of students and vice chancellor during the late 1960s, when

Whitewater was in turmoil. He had been fired from the job because he didn't handle it properly. Because he had tenure, they put him back in the classroom.

He was assigned to teach several education courses. Most people avoided him because he was so conservative, so bitter and so intense about some of the experiences he had had at the university.

The first course I took with him was called Major Achievements in Education. We looked at events like the G.I. Bill and Sputnik and how they changed education. I was one of only eight people in the class. That man had his heart and soul in what was important in education. You could tell that he really wanted education to make a difference in people. Everything else was really superfluous. He had a genuine interest in people earning power through education.

I'll never forget this teacher because he consistently challenged me in what I thought. I was a liberal graduate student and I had all kinds of great ideas. He'd get right in my face and he'd say, "Aaron, do you really believe that? Do you really believe that we want a society where all people are equal?" He challenged the concept of "political correctness" long before the phrase was being used. He feared that future society would be where people are politically correct and have no deep-seated beliefs. He was worried that people would not say what they wanted to say. So when I defended my ideas and gave my heart and soul to an argument, he'd put his hand on my shoulder and say, "If you really believe that, stick with it. I don't agree with you, but it's important to believe in what you feel."

He was my instructor for two more courses. In Philosophy of Education, there were four graduate students. Normally a class like that would be canceled, but all four of us, who had had this teacher before, had written to the dean to keep the class going. Every Wednesday night, he and four liberal students would challenge each other about every idea in education. Through that class, he probably changed more about the way I talk to people and teach people than any other person I've ever met.

The best thing he ever said to me in that class was, "The philosophy of education is that no matter what happens, something in you has to change. If you have been changed by contact with another person, that has taught you something." You may not agree, you may be coming from completely different places, but he really believed that any contact with another person could change someone's belief about anything. That was what teaching was about—and everything was a learning experience.

In The History of Education, we got to know each other very well. There were about 40 kids in that class, because it was a required course. He'd say, "Now, Aaron, I understand that you're probably thinking that it is not a good idea having corporal punishment for kids. Why don't you present to these other people your liberal beliefs about corporal punishment. I know you can articulate this well." What that said was that even though we were on totally different philosophical planes when it came to our beliefs, he respected mine. The respect was mutual. When we got into very heated discussions in class and some students became disrespectful of his old-fashioned beliefs, there wasn't a time when I hesitated to defend him. Toward the end of every class there was really a mutual appreciation for what one another believed and what we wanted out of life. Sadly, that was the last course he ever taught. He retired after that.

I felt so fortunate to have studied with him, as no adult except for my father has had more impact on me than that professor. I disagreed with everything he stood for. He was former military. He grew up in the Depression. He was tough. He was ornery about the way things had turned out. And yet at the same time, he deeply believed that educators could make a difference.

Aaron Trummer, 41, High School Principal, Union Grove, Wisconsin

This lady taught in Dover, Massachusetts, near Boston, and may still be there, for all I know. She was my creative writing teacher in high school during my sophomore or junior year. She had a real love for creative writing and, I guess, all creative expression.

I was a lousy creative writer. I'm an engineer, really technical. When I'd try to write, everything had to be perfect, so it would take me about a year to write a sentence. She'd say, "Just write. Just write whatever comes out." I can do that now, but I couldn't then. I was a little bit more closed, I guess, in my ability to express myself. But she started me thinking in that direction. Somehow, she got us all subscribed to *The Atlantic Monthly* for the year. The stories in there were so great, I really enjoyed reading them. I still love *The Atlantic Monthly*, even though I don't have the time to read it now. There's a warm spot in my heart for that magazine and for her, for the door she helped open. I hope that kids today are getting the same kind of thing. I don't know if it happens everywhere, but it was real important to me because it enriched my horizons far beyond just the three R's.

Bob Drake, 38, Applications Engineer, Dunwoody, Georgia

The summer of my seventh-grade year we moved from California to Oklahoma. My father passed away two weeks after we moved. We didn't know anybody. I started school, and you know how horrendous 12- and 13-year-olds can be. I was quiet. I was overweight. I was the new kid. And I was dealing with the feelings of losing my father on top of everything else. For the first few months of school, I didn't have any friends. I went to school, went home, went to school, went home.

I had always been pretty good in English, but I was one of those kids who kind of disappeared once I got in class. One day in class, instead of doing my assignment, I was writing poetry. My teacher walked by, looked down and asked me quietly if she could read what I was writing. She didn't get on me about not doing the work she had assigned. She read my poem and she praised me for it, telling me that I had done a good job. Then she asked me if I had any more, and told me that she would like to read them. I said yes and the very next day, I brought in all the poems I had at home, written out as neatly as I could. She said, "This is very good. I would like to use you as an example. Could I put some of these on the board?"

I had no idea what she was going to do, but she took all of my poetry and typed it up. She put up pink letters that said "A Star is Born" and put "Sue Culver" underneath it. A lot of the kids didn't even know my name, so they were going, "Who's Sue Culver? Who's Sue Culver?" At that point she asked me to stand up.

It was really wonderful on one hand because I was finally recognized and the kids knew who I was. I was embarrassed a little bit, too, but that embarrassment went away immediately at recess, when I was asked to join some of the other girls.

Jana Sue Culver, 29, Seventh Grade English Teacher,
Ponca City, Oklahoma

I went to Brooklyn Preparatory School, which is now closed. It was a Catholic school run by Jesuits. While at Brooklyn Prep, my Latin teacher, Thomas Bermingham, a future priest, played a significant part in shaping my life and my philosophies. He took an interest in me, and two or three afternoons each week we would spend 40 to 45 minutes talking about something he'd told me to read. He had a particular interest in the Roman poet Virgil and asked me to read Virgil's *The Aeneid* in the original Latin with him. Father Bermingham questioned me and challenged me to develop feelings not only for the precision of words, but also for the subtle shadings of Latin. The adventures of Aeneas seeped into far corners of my mind, into my feelings about what is true and honorable and important. They helped shape everything I have since become. I don't think anybody can get a handle on what makes me tick as a person, and certainly cannot get at the roots of how I coach football, without understanding what I learned from the

deep relationship I formed with Virgil during those afternoons and later in my life.

***Joseph V. Paterno, Head Football Coach, The
Pennsylvania State University, University Park,
Pennsylvania***

Teaching is a process of seduction: the teacher seduces the
pupils toward himself or herself, and then redirects that
seduced attention toward the subject matter. It requires a
tremendously strong and engaging personality to pull it off. I
learned this from one of the late Paul Goodman's books. He is
one of my intellectual heroes.

There were two teachers in particular who embodied these
qualities. One was a teacher and guidance counselor in junior
high school who was hilariously sarcastic, and the other was a
teacher of New Testament in seminary. Both of them had
absolutely pure form, true senses of humor about the world
and themselves and life and everything they came into contact
with. It was that humor that got me, where I learned that
almost all learning can be fun and funny.

This is certainly being substantiated by current wellness
research about how laughter releases all those little endorphins
to run through your body. What those teachers were doing was
essentially getting their classes high on humor endorphins.
And they did it in the context of their subject matter. So you
found out you could get high on New Testament history, in this
case. It works!

My other favorite teacher trick came from a science teacher our son had in high school. He said, "The thing I really do is not teaching, but remembering." The way it works is this: Let's say Sammy makes a comment of some sort on Monday about the subject the class is studying. And then by about Thursday, why, Susan over there says something and the teacher says, "Wait! Do you remember what Sammy said about that exact same issue on Monday?"

Now, of course, Susan doesn't remember it, and on top of that, Sammy doesn't remember it—he doesn't even remember he opened his mouth—but all of a sudden he realizes that he must have said something worth listening to. And so the teacher says, "Sammy, say it again." And Sammy goes, "Uh . . ." And the teacher says, "Now what you said was . . ."

So Sammy starts realizing that he's had thoughts that were worthy of keeping and remembering, and suddenly he just shines and glows all over. Susan and others in the class have a new respect for Sammy, too. The teacher consistently did this. He made it a point to remember one thing that every student said in every class. He did this every day. And by remembering what every student said, he taught them to respect the value of their own thinking. It was the most exciting thing. I mean, it's a trick, it's a technique. But it's a cheap trick, and it works!

Larry Rood, 53 ³/₄ , Book Publisher, President, Gryphon House, Inc., Beltsville, Maryland

My Greek teacher was a small, soft-spoken man. On the first day of class, he said, "Now if you pass my class, you'll be able to make it through any graduate school in the country." He said, "I am a tough teacher, but I'm fair. This is how my grading works: 100 to 96 is an A, 95 to 90 is a B, 89 to 80 is a C, and anything below 80 is failing." I nearly had a heart attack!

But then he said, "I will do everything in my power to help you succeed." In class, if you couldn't get it, he would sit there with you until you understood the information. You could even call him at home from 7:00 until 9:00 in the evening, and you could ask him anything and he would help you out. But he was tight on that grade. He felt that if you could get over this hump, you'd know the information. He was there for you. I had a lot of teachers who set difficult goals for us, but they weren't willing to help—it was just sink or swim. His thing was, "You will swim the English Channel, and you can't swim halfway because you will drown. When you swim the English Channel, you have to swim all the way across. If you want to do this, I will help you, but there is not going to be an easier way to get there." He didn't make it easy, he just helped you.

This professor, let you know exactly what you were in for right from the beginning, and he also gave the option to bail: "If this is not for you, you don't need to be here." He wanted you to make it. I ended up getting a 95 percent, which is the highest percentage I've ever scored in a class. He taught me that I could accomplish a difficult task, and not to be afraid to tackle something just because it was difficult.

Edward McNair, 34, Computer Salesperson, Albuquerque, New Mexico

This was how I learned that teachers are human, too. In high school, we were going to a vocal competition where you had to sing classical songs. There were certain stipulations you had to follow, one of which was that one of the songs had to be in a foreign language.

Prior to going to the competition, we were given four weeks to prepare. Well, I had a lot going on in my life at that time, and I didn't prepare as well as I should have. So when I went in the room to perform for the adjudicators and the audience there, I forgot some of my German. I'd been taking German at the time, so I threw in anything that I could think of in German, not knowing what I was actually saying. As a result, I did not receive the terrific critique that I had always been given at past competitions. I felt awful.

On the way home, we stopped to have lunch. We were all told to go inside, and to just forget about what had happened that day—it was over. Our teacher was proud of us. "Don't worry about it because you did your best," he said. That was all he expected.

I commented that I wasn't that hungry and I was just going to stay on the bus because I was tired. So everyone got out, and right when the door closed, I burst into tears. I knew I could have done better, but I had just not prepared. I put my head down and sobbed.

The next thing I knew, I felt a hand on my back and I looked up and there was my teacher. He had big tears in his eyes, too. It was nice to see that a teacher was human, that he was not afraid to cry in front of his student. That was a very touching moment in my life. I appreciate him for showing me his feelings, because now it's not difficult for me to let the kids I teach know that I care. I have feelings and I can show them, too.

Beth Raby, 29, Elementary Music Teacher, Ponca City, Oklahoma

I met Sister Helena when I started working on my master's degree at Incarnate Word College in San Antonio. My degree program was in multi-disciplinary studies with concentrations in English, sociology and religion. At the time, my personal life was in a shambles and I was an emotional wreck. To top it off, I was very intimidated by all of my graduate classes because my background was in fine art, painting and drawing.

Sister Helena was my professor in contemporary poetry. I was terrified of her class because it was filled with students who had spent lifetimes studying literature and creative writing. I seriously considered dropping out of the program only a few days after beginning. But Sister Helena had this way of talking about poetry, about writing and about the life-force of good literature that was so inviting. She put everything into a kind of spiritual context. She managed to touch the light inside of me that few people have been able to do.

As she continued to reach me and as her words continued to make me look at things in ways I never had before, I became more vocal and more willing to contribute to the class. This was very frightening for me. After speaking out the first few times, I half expected the other students to laugh at me for just now discovering something they had discovered years ago, or for displaying a high level of naïveté. After all, art majors aren't always thought of as being the most intelligent people around! But every time I said something, Sister Helena would always make a positive statement and even said she was glad I was in the class because I brought a unique perspective. She would take my comments and insights and restate them in a way that made them seem very special.

However, no sooner had I built my confidence in being verbal in class, than I found myself confronted with having to complete a writing assignment. Again, I felt terribly intimidated. This time, I felt comfortable enough with Sister Helena that I told her how nervous I was about the assignment. She told me that if anyone in the class could write a paper with some depth and meaning, I could. She said because of my varied background, I would be able to bring insightful commentary into my writing. She really encouraged me and made me believe I could do it. She pushed me to do well and provided whatever assistance she could.

This happened back in 1984, and now I'm a published writer. I don't think I would have considered writing if it had not been for Sister Helena. I owe a lot to her. To this day, I remember her saying, "Now Karen, when you go on for your doctorate . . ." and I thought, "Are you kidding? I don't even know that I can make it out of this master's program and you're talking doctorate!" Well, here I am today, preparing to defend my dissertation in a few weeks. Sister Helena will be a lifelong friend. She's been an incredible mentor and role model. I only hope I can give back to others as much as she's given to me.

Karen Sides, 37, Director of Education, TI-IN Network, San Antonio, Texas

The teacher who made a difference for me was Mr. O'Regan, in eighth-grade math, who gave me a noogie if I failed to give him the correct answer. This is why, to this very day, I know that *pi* is the ratio of circumference to diameter. Not that it matters.

Dave Barry, Author and Columnist, Miami, Florida

A REALLY GREAT TEACHER IS SOMEONE WHO . . .

. . . isn't serious about everything.
. . . treats everybody equally.
                    Matt, 13, Seal Beach, California

. . . gives prizes if you get a certain amount of points.
                    David, 9, Seal Beach, California

. . . doesn't make you scared to ask a question.
                    Dorothy, 10, Edmonds, Washington

. . . lets you do projects with her.
                    Rosie, 4 ³/₄, Katy, Texas

. . . lets you help her.
                    Brent, 9, Katy, Texas

. . . asks the students what they want to learn.
                    Summer, 16, El Cajon, California

. . . has a personality and loves to learn and share
what he or she has learned.
                    Choral, 16, El Cajon, California

. . . treats students as equals, and has no qualms
about teaching them and learning from them.
                    Bonnie, 15, La Mesa, California

. . . is kind to you and helps you when you're in trouble.
                    Jacqueline, 9, Pasadena, California

. . . doesn't treat you like you're in the military.
Krystle, 11, Toronto, Ontario

. . . doesn't lose her temper.
Mike, 9, Toronto, Ontario

. . . helps out with school events—and even includes her own family.
Deborah, 20, Albuquerque, New Mexico

. . . can let the students have fun yet still have a strict workplace.
. . . gives a variety of assignments.
Ankur, 15, Albuquerque, New Mexico

. . . is strict about stuff like when you have to have your homework in.
Hailey, 8, Albuquerque, New Mexico

. . . isn't just your teacher—she's also your friend.
Jessica, 9, San Juan Capistrano, California

. . . takes pride in their teaching.
. . . lets kids cooperate and work together in groups.
. . . doesn't break the rules.
. . . doesn't leave you out if you're quiet and shy.
Maria, 14, Salem, Oregon

. . . explains things to you.
Erin, 10, St. Louis, Missouri

. . . makes you feel better if you're hurt.
          Ben, 10, St. Louis, Missouri

. . . gives you candy when you're good.
          Ayesha, 7 ½, Indianapolis, Indiana

. . . gets your interest and keeps it.
          Eric, 21, Ithaca, New York

. . . allows you to go on tangents because that's
usually where you learn the most.
          Kristian, 18, Chicago, Illinois

. . . lets all the kids play together.
. . . never yells at us.
          Kristie, 10, St. Louis, Missouri

. . . learns along with us.
          Ronnie, 14, Bernalillo, New Mexico

. . . is understanding and can compromise.
          Devin, 12, Yonkers, New York

. . . can see potential in you and encourage you to reach it.
. . . can bring a group of students together as a team
but still appreciate individual differences.
          Letty, 20, Ciudad Juarez, Mexico

. . . is fair to all the kids.
. . . makes learning interesting rather than just reading things out of a book.
          Erica, 11, Beardstown, Illinois

. . . keeps you in line and is firm, but still lets you have
fun.

> Stephanie, 10, Belleville, Illinois

. . . is nice.

> Jessica, 7, Shiloh, Illinois

. . . gives no homework on Fridays.

> Megan, 8, Alhambra, Illinois

. . . teaches me.

> Natalie, 6, Alhambra, Illinois

. . . helps you out and doesn't ignore you if you need
help.

. . . is real interested in you and in making you a better
student.

> Mark, 13, McKees Rocks, Pennsylvania

. . . lets the kids do tricks once in a while.

. . . lets us play games in the classroom, like "Duck,
Duck, Goose."

> Luke, 6, Cogan Station, Pennsylvania

As soon as you asked me about my favorite teacher, what leapt to mind was my first-grade teacher, Mrs. Gooler. She saw right away that I was a real reader. She encouraged me to get my first library card. I started reading a book a day. I'm 40 years old now and I've read a book a day for almost 40 years. I'm a real lover of libraries because of her. I now make posters for the libraries to help them raise money.

Back in school, I was one of those gifted kids that they didn't know what to do with. There weren't school programs at that time for gifted kids, so I was kind of desperate and bored in this class. This teacher was wise enough to see that I was a little actor. She would have me go to another class with a book and announce, "Susan's going to read to the class."

I mean, I loved it! I wasn't at all shy. I would act out the parts. This teacher was one of the first people, besides my mother, who really made me want to have more teachers. I certainly had some bad ones, so I knew the contrast. Whenever there was one that didn't work out too well, I would think of my first-grade teacher. She kept in touch through the years and wrote postcards to my family. She helped my brother, too. He's a real reader because of her. I'm sure I wouldn't be a writer, sitting at the American Booksellers Association Convention with four published books, if it weren't for this teacher. What could be more powerful than that?

SARK, 40, Author/Artist, San Francisco, California

I was totally terrified of going from elementary school to junior high. My English teacher, Mr. Riggs, was also in charge of our homeroom. Some friends of mine told him to look out for this little lost kid—that was me. On the first day of school, I was walking down the hall, lost and looking for my homeroom. He stuck his head out the door and saw me coming up the stairs and down the hallway, and he said, "Hey, Chavez—in here."

I never forgot the guy, and I followed him to another junior high school later on. That man always stood out in my mind because he knew he was looking for some lost kid. He did that with all the kids. He was always real well liked, and congenial with everybody. He took the time! I knew at that point that I was not going to be just a number, just a body that was there. And I knew that there was somebody who would take the time to help.

John Chavez, 45, Universal Technician with US West, Albuquerque, NM

The person I think of immediately was my high school coach and math teacher. He wanted you to become comfortable with mathematics. He did not want math to frighten and scare you off. The year that I spent with him in tenth grade was fabulous. He was a master motivator. He had a sense of humor that was incredible, and he wanted all of his students to succeed. Everyone who had him as a teacher felt the same way. At our ten-year reunion, the only teacher's name that came up from anyone was his. His students had never forgotten the life lessons they had learned from working with him.

I can remember I made an incredible screw-up in a game. It was just one of those tenth-grader-playing-varsity-football kind of mistakes. When I went back to class the following Monday, I really felt awful. He pulled me aside and he told me this fabulous story about life's mistakes and how you should learn from your failures.

I think that he was the only teacher I had who talked about failure as a gift. I think for a coach in the middle of the 1960s—a time when coaches could be pretty Draconian— bringing that kind of insight into a teacher-student relationship was really phenomenal. He could coach exceptional talent out of his players. He took them to greater and greater levels of performance and was able to transmit his expectations without yelling, without screaming, without casting guilt. While other coaches could make you feel like you were beneath dirt, I never, ever saw him berate a player or a student in class. It just was not his way. He was a magical person.

It was through his lessons in life, through his spirit, and certainly through his voice as a teacher that education and academics became very important to me. He taught me that education is something that cannot be taken away from you. He also taught me that everyone is special and everyone has ability. I think this is why I've been successful as a teacher, and as a student of teachers and as a teacher of students. I share stories about him with my education students because he was genuinely a special person, and because I want them to know this man as a model educator. I've remembered a lot of his little sayings and phrases. He always comes back in my mind, his voice and his face. Even in my darkest hours, he's always there.

Richard Biffle, Ph.D., 44, Professor of Education, Salem, Oregon

My junior high teacher was a young woman who loved the poetry of Walt Whitman. She recited from her memory all of his poems, many of which I still remember. After learning that I was in love with mathematics, she pointed her finger at me and said, "You are going to be an engineer." And that's something, of course, that I did become.

We also had an English teacher who had a wonderful, elocutionary voice. She took the parts of everybody in Shakespeare's plays and performed for us. She was extremely good. She also was the chairman of the committee that handled the scholarships for the schools. She was the person responsible for my receiving one of those scholarships. Had I not received that scholarship, I would not have been able to go on to college. Although I wasn't the most brilliant boy in the school, she thought I had a lot of potential.

Several years later, she was thrilled that I had done well in my college work. "I knew it all the time!" she said.

Stanley Lukoff, 80, Retired Engineer, Wilmington, Delaware

Betty Dresner was the one person who could really tap into people's talents. She was the Activities Director at the Jewish Community Center in York, Pennsylvania. Even if you didn't seem to have any talent, she always found some way to involve you, some way for you to participate and produce. And she made you feel good about yourself. She was extraordinarily gifted in that way.

Betty always set up things for people to do that pushed the limits of their creativity and their talent, and somehow they always managed to do a good job. She'd never actually give you a direct compliment, but she still had a way of communicating a tremendous faith in your ability. She wouldn't come out and say, "Oh, I think you're wonderful. I'm sure you can do this." But by simply and confidently giving you the job, she expressed an assumption of your capability, along with the expectation that you could—and would—do whatever she asked. She got people to produce way beyond what even they imagined themselves capable of doing. She'd ask them to do these impossible things as though there was no doubt in her mind that they could do them. And they did! It was amazing. People who didn't seem to have much going for them could still feel special and would achieve great things.

Lynne Gordon DeWitt, 40, Music Contractor, Pacific Palisades, California

I love talking about this! My favorite teacher taught a poetry class when I was in college. She is a writer, a poet and an activist of sorts. I have many favorite teachers, but she's the one who has given me the most power to be myself.

I was involved in her first class, called "The Politics of Female Childhood." She told me that whatever was in me, and whatever I believed, was the truth. She gave me permission to recognize my truth, to tell myself this truth over and over and to share it with others. This experience gave me the strength to exist, to create and to change.

She made a really big impact on me. No one had ever validated my reality like that. Instead, all my life I had been told, "Hush up the truth," "Don't say what's going on," "That's wrong," or, "Oh, you don't think that." This teacher gave me the courage to take that first leap in believing in myself, and learning to trust myself was definitely the most important lesson in my life.

Elizabeth Riva Meyer, 25, Creative Director of a Publishing and Art Company, San Francisco, California

Two years ago when he was in second grade, my son, Danny, had a really special teacher. Danny went into this class with really low self-esteem. He's considered Gifted Learning Disabled and the year before had a really awful experience with a very regimented teacher. But his second-grade teacher was different, and her impact affected all of us.

She used a lot of hands-on activities and creativity in the classroom. This woman had an inner sense of what children need and knew which accommodations to make for each and every child. She had an ability to get down to their level. Toward the end of the year, she made Danny the star of a play that the class put on. We didn't think he could ever learn a whole script, but he learned something like 40 lines and was so excited. What can I say? She was incredible. I mean, she turned my son around. He went into her class very timid, but he certainly wasn't timid by the end of the year!

There's an emotional impact that goes along with having a learning disability, particularly if you're bright. You know you're smart, but you can't get it out. This teacher's methods and her creativity allowed Danny to "get it out." For example, if the class was doing a unit on Viking ships, instead of giving out ditto sheets and other seatwork, she'd have them build models of these ships and sail them. Her influence impacted our lives at home, too. The previous year, things had been very difficult and emotional because Danny was upset all the time. This teacher made everything easier. She touched all of us.

Donna Evens, 39, Small-Business Owner, Potomac, Maryland

I remember my seventh- and ninth-grade art teacher because she took a personal interest in all the kids who were supposedly considered the "dummy" kids. She made us aware of who we were, and she made it clear that nobody in her class was a dummy.

She honestly answered our questions, straightforward and to the point. If we had problems in the class, she'd take time out in her class to show us how to do it. She got us to work with our hands. She taught us history by clay-working. She had us build houses and models of all the different things that we liked. I knew I could do better than just going into a factory to work. She put the adventure in me.

Larry Wood, 42, Truck Driver and Fleet Manager, Santa Fe, New Mexico

When we moved to Paola, Kansas, I was four years old and it was time for me to go to school. Since I already knew my ABC's and how to tie my shoes, they put me in the first grade. I was reading on a second- or third-grade level, but I had this great teacher who encouraged me to read and knew I was really bored when it came to "See Jane run." Whenever reading time came, she sent me down to read to the kindergartners, which I did while all the rest of the first-graders did "See Spot run." She was really instrumental in spurring me on and encouraging me to get my education, even at that young age.

We stayed in that particular town from first through fourth grade. This teacher used to check on me and make sure I was doing okay. When I was in fourth grade, I had a teacher who said, "Well, C is an okay grade." When my first-grade teacher found out, she stressed that I still needed to excel, even if the teacher was satisfied with an average grade. She always wanted me to do the very best I could do, and C wasn't the best I could do.

Britt L. Casey, 39, Psychologist, Alton, Illinois

In my junior and senior years in high school in Paterson, New Jersey, the outstanding, classic, Sherwood Andersonesque character was a Miss Francis Durban, who was a huge lady weighing perhaps 250 or 300 pounds, of immense girth and humor, who dressed in blue dresses with lace around the neck. She taught Walt Whitman by reading him aloud with tremendous enthusiasm, in particular the lines, "I find no fat sweeter than that which sticks to my own bones . . ." (and I have to paraphrase the rest: "the odor wafting from my body . . . admire my own armpits . . . breasts . . . feet . . .").

I still remember Francis Durban's smell wafting across the classroom on hot May days. There was an awful body odor from such a sweating mass of fat. Somehow, repulsive as that was, her cherubic round face, half-smile, and huge-girthed laughter were miracles of pleasure and energy that imprinted Whitman on my head forever. Her presentation of his humor and self-acceptance was decisive in turning me on, not merely to his sympathy, not merely to his empathies, not merely to his range, but also to his humorous intelligence.

I had home teachings of all poetry, including Whitman, particularly, from my father. Whitman was on the curriculum in high school, too, so I knew something, particularly "When Lilacs Last in the Dooryard Bloomed." But Francis Durban specialized in the self-acceptance poems in "Song of Myself."

Allen Ginsberg, Poet, New York, New York (Reprinted with permission from **Teachers and Writers Newsletter,** *January-February, 1986.)*

36

My scholastic life began in the same one-room schoolhouse that my dad had attended through eighth grade. My experiences were a little different than his, though. Instead of there being more than 30 kids in the school, there were no more than 15 when I began in first grade, and only nine students when the state of Minnesota closed down all the country schools for good four years later.

I believe that those five years of school prepared me in a unique way, however. You see, I am a Montessori grade-school teacher and my classroom consists of students in third, fourth and fifth grades. I am very comfortable with the multi-grade levels and in fact, it felt kind of funny when I taught a single grade level years ago—even though, as any teacher can tell you, there is enough variance in ability level in a "regular" classroom to keep a teacher very busy trying to figure out how to teach to all the children. I really enjoy having children of different ages in my classroom; it makes us seem more like "family." Plus, the fact that I keep children in my room for three years also enhances the relationships I have with my students. I'm sure that having spent the first five years of my school experience in a similar situation helped me form a feeling for the classroom that has made having students of varying ages and keeping them for a number of years seem normal. In fact, anything else feels quite separated and somehow unnatural.

I had one teacher in particular who made a very strong impression on me. To this day, the way she related to us as students influences how I interact with my students. Mrs. Malm was our high school choir teacher. She had taught college choir, and I think that when she taught us, she expected the same quality. And she got it. She elicited this level of performance from us, not only from having us for choir every day, but also from the voice lessons that offered personal contact with each of us every week. When Mrs. Malm talked with us, it was just that—talking with us, not at us, as teachers do at times. She didn't try to be anything other than a "regular person" around us and didn't feel the need to maintain distance out of fear of losing control. She talked to us and cared about what was going on with us. It's been many years now, and it's hard for me to remember specifics. I just know that when I think about how she interacted with us and remember how that made me feel, I know that I want my students to feel the same caring attitude coming from me.

Diane Bjorstrom, 38, Elementary Teacher, Alton, Illinois

Before I became an author of art idea books for children, before I started my wonderful publishing company, before I was a parent and long before I knew the true meaning of the words disappointment, fatigue and ache, I was a first-year kindergarten teacher in Ferndale, Washington, teaching Lummi Nation children from the uppermost corner of the Pacific Northwest. I was a dynamo! I don't know if I could ever teach that way again, with the depth of caring, creating, planning and individualized teaching. I loved each child as if he or she were my own. I could have taken any one of them home at any given moment and raised them to maturity with the devotion of the best of any mother!

Looking back on those days of youthful exuberance, I recently wondered if any of it had made a difference to those quiet, brown-eyed, beautiful children with the shining black hair. Did any of them remember? Did any of it matter at all? My remembering took me back to the highlight of my teaching years, the time we called "Thursday Dinner." Every Thursday I brought two students to my home for dinner. We knew each other in a different way after they had been in my home. We had new warmth, love, respect and a personal attachment I've never felt with students before. And truthfully, it was just plain fun! After school we would plan our menu, go to the store and buy the food and then drive to my home. The kids would then play outside for a while, watch some cartoons and then prepare the meal. Creamed corn—the favorite choice for nearly three months! I tried to talk them into anything but creamed corn, but how they loved it!—and fried chicken, mashed potatoes, peas. After dinner and washing the dishes, the kids played with my dog, wrestled with my husband, jumped in my beanbag chair, colored or played quietly, and then, tired and content, settled in the car for the long ride back to the reservation.

Last Thursday, I sat in the Department of Licensing waiting for my 16-year-old daughter to hopefully pass her driver's test, and saw a familiar curve of neck, hair color, glasses and posture sitting in the chair in front of me. The warmth I felt was like seeing a dear friend.

I said with mock stern reproach, "Albert, have you finished your work?" As he turned, the warm smile I remembered from 20 years earlier greeted my eyes as Albert said, "Mrs. Kohl, I knew that was you!" We had a big hug, chatted a bit and then Albert asked, "Do you remember when we came to your house for dinner? Remember when me 'n Lance played with your dog and then you let us sit in your giant beanbag chair? Me 'n Lance still think that was the best thing we ever did in school."

Yes, Albert, I remember. Me 'n my husband think that was the best thing we ever did in school, too.

MaryAnn F. Kohl, 47, Publisher, Author, Educator,
Bellingham, Washington

I went to fourth grade in Philadelphia in 1966. My teacher, Mrs. Gilmore, was a tough African-American woman from Germantown, the hard side of town. She was just as tough and rough and as gifted as a teacher could be. And she never let you be lazy. She never let you space out in class. And she never let race be an issue, even during the 1960s when race issues were a very big deal. She was always concerned with individual abilities and kept her focus on students as individuals. Even though there were 40 kids in her classroom, there were never any "back of the class" kids!

Mrs. Gilmore helped me learn to respect people, to listen to people and to not "judge a book by the cover." Because she never did.

Dave Lovald, 36, Sales Manager for a Music Company, Montpelier, Vermont

When I was in the ninth grade, my English teacher insisted that everyone in the class write a short story. Much to my surprise some days later, he informed me that I had a talent that I really had no idea I had. He said that my short story was much better than anyone else's and he encouraged me to write. However, in the 1950s it was considered very effete to be artistic, so I became what I thought of as a closet writer. I continued to spend the vast majority of my time playing high school sports and hanging out with my friends, using writing as a therapeutic activity, although I could not have defined it as such at the time. Like most teenagers, I had not only a hormonal insurrection taking place, but all kinds of other psychological events making life somewhat complicated, making the passage difficult. So writing was a wonderful outlet for me that I otherwise did not have.

I didn't really take myself seriously as a writer until I got to college. When I got to the University of Miami, I took an advanced comp class my first semester. I was with a teacher, Dr. Grace Garlinghouse-King, who was about to retire, a very Victorian woman. I asked her one week if instead of writing the assignment that she wanted us to write, I could write a short story. She cautiously said okay, and I delivered it to her a week later. That night, she called me at one in the morning. I heard this sepulchral voice on the phone saying, "I can't teach you anything more about writing. I'm passing you on." This was a really extraordinary event in my life, because at that time I thought I really would like to be a writer but I was afraid to hope that I might be one. So this Dr. King really changed my life.

She passed me on to the man who ran the creative writing program at the University of Miami. His name was Fred Shaw. And as I found out very quickly, Fred Shaw had an exceptional reputation among the people in the Miami area who fancied themselves as writers. To get into his class was a coup. You had to win your way into his class. So Dr. King set up a meeting for me with Fred Shaw. He told me that based on this story, if I wanted to put up with certain things for about a decade, he thought that I could become a writer.

And so he quite simply became the most important and influential person in my life, after my parents. He pretty much taught me the few things that I know about writing, and there are really not a lot of concrete things about learning to write. In fact, the first thing he always told his classes is that there are only two ways to learn to write: You read and you write. And you teach yourself. No one is going to teach you.

I came to see creative writing classes, both the ones I took from him and the ones I taught for a quarter of a century afterward when I became a teacher, as therapeutic outlets for aspiring writers. They create a forum in which you can hear your work and, often, get useful feedback. They tend to be very congenial at the most basic level because you have a whole bunch of people who are as frightened as you are and you can often get a certain kind of support, if not acclamation, for what you're trying to do.

Fred said, "You're out there on your own, but if you will apprentice yourself to yourself for about a decade and write for at least an hour every day, and if you can learn that writing is rewriting, and if you can learn that it is an undertaking much like a job as opposed to an inspiration, you might become a writer. You can't sit around and wait for inspiration to strike; you sit down and you write every day. It doesn't matter what you write, but you write every day."

He had the unique ability to make me feel as if I truly had the ability to be successful and, at the same time, he made it clear that he would not pull any punches with me. A couple of times, he really devastated me by telling me that something I had written was atrocious. At the time it was very hurtful, but I learned to get over it very quickly and move on, and to try to improve what I was writing. That may be the most important ingredient about him for me as a teacher, that he could stroke and he could also strike. I knew, therefore, that when he told me something, I could depend on it.

He told me once that I was the most talented young person he'd ever seen, and that meant a great deal to me. It was really the stamp of approval that allowed me to go to my parents and say, "I'm going to drop out of pre-med and go into English and pursue a career as a writer. I'll give myself until I'm in my early 30s to see if I can do it." And to their eternal credit, they supported me in all ways, financially, morally, spiritually, right to the point in my early 30s when I began to be successful.

I wrote hundreds of thousands of words for Fred during my college career, and even when I'd used up all my courses, I kept coming to class and taking my stuff to him, and I spent a great deal of time with him. It became clear that he hoped I was going to become the writer he had not.

He was my mentor, no doubt. He sent me to New Mexico State, which was where he taught as a young man. Fred called the then-department head, who was a lifelong friend of his, Dr. Newman Reed. Dr. Reed told me that there were no jobs open, but that if anything should change, he'd let me know. I was happy because when I finished graduate school at Stanford, I really didn't want to teach anywhere. I wanted to go to Europe and bum around for a year and write. Fred said he thought that was foolish, that I was about half-way through my apprenticeship and I should get a teaching job where I would have time to write and also support myself. He told me to stick with it and not go off and indulge myself.

But since there were no jobs, I planned to go home for the summer, get a job of some kind, earn some money and take off. Two weeks later, I got a call. I was about ready to leave Stanford and start driving home. Somebody on Newman Reed's faculty found out she was pregnant and she was going take a leave, and did I want to come and interview for this job?

I didn't but I said, "Sure." It was on my way home, or what I thought was my way home. I thought in the geographic morass of my brain that New Mexico was where Utah actually is. But anyway, I got AAA to route me correctly and when I arrived, I thought, *There's no way in hell I can possibly live here.* They had cows on the campus, for God's sake. I told Newman Reed, "I'm just not sure about this. I'll let you know in a couple of weeks."

My father said it seemed to him that I should go for at least a year. How could it possibly hurt me? He was right, of course. Fred had gone out of his way to get me the job. So I came back here and have been here now for 28 years. I kept sending stuff to Fred and I was always in touch with him.

Sadly, Fred died right before my first play opened in New York. But I know he was proud of me and believed in me.

I still communicate with his wife a couple of times a year, and to this day I carry him with me. I always credit him with the things that I offer my students and tell them that whatever I can tell them concretely about writing, I got from him.

Mark Medoff, 54, Playwright, Screenwriter, Novelist and Professor, New Mexico State University, Las Cruces, New Mexico

I encountered my first memorable teacher in kindergarten. One day, a friend playfully asked me to turn around. I complied. He kicked me. I punched him in the stomach. He wandered around the room moaning.

The teacher stood over me and spoke in a loud, stern manner: "Mr. (my last name), BLAH, BLAH, BLAH." I don't remember the rest. I just remember that she actually called me "Mister." I learned that even though, from her perspective, I had done something terribly wrong, I was still accorded the distinction, even at the age of five, of being called an appellation similar to an adult: "Mister." I was impressed and have remembered it ever since.

Anonymous

I had a fifth-grader named Eddie who came from a severely disadvantaged area. Although he had been a severe discipline case in fourth grade, when he came to my class, I made him the class monitor whenever I left the room. By the end of the third week of school, he had changed so much from this experience, along with a great deal of positive reinforcement.

I cover a chapter on drugs three times during the year. One day, right after the holidays, we were relating "drug experience" stories during "Drug Awareness Week."

Eddie said, "I was walking along the canal when a car with three guys drove up and offered a little package of white powder to me."

I asked, "What did you do?"

Eddie answered, "I took it, of course."

I was about ready to turn loose with a lecture about the evil of drugs, but I paused to ask, "Why did you take it?"

He answered, "There were three guys in the car, and they were high on drugs. If I didn't take the package, they might have got upset and who knows what they might do. I told them thank you, and they left."

I asked, "What did you do then?"

Eddie answered, "I threw it in the canal."

I was so proud of Eddie.

Eulogio (Izzy) Izaguirre, Elementary Teacher, Alamo, Texas

I had quite a few really good teachers. One that I had in fourth or fifth grade, Miss Candy, used to say, "An empty wagon makes the most noise." It meant that people who talk a lot or make the most noise make the least sense. She was an old lady, as well as I remember, and she was a good teacher.

In high school I remember my gym teacher, Mr. Spangler. He was very, very fair, but also very strict. I learned that you couldn't con your way in class, that you had to come up with the goods. You had to do your assignments. You couldn't con your way along. He was the baseball coach and the football coach. I played baseball for him. He was also very, very honest in his marks.

We had Mr. Glazer. I remember his father had a luggage store on York Street in Philly. He was also very strict, but also very fair.

I remember my English teacher, too. His name was Eliot Lester. He went to Hollywood as an advisor in a movie with Edward G. Robinson. He wrote a story that was portrayed as a movie. He was a man that I eventually got to be good enough friends with that he invited me out to Hollywood to play a part in a movie, but I never got there.

He was a very, very good teacher. He used to chew on pretzels, and if he had any left, he used to throw them at you, 'cause you know how kids are. He used to throw them at us like he was taking target practice. It was a lot of fun. These were all good teachers. They got your respect without bullying you.

Irving Bluestein, 78, Retired Salesman, Los Angeles, California

I recall my first positive school experience just like it was yesterday. My sister and mom taught me how to draw a house using colored pencils and a ruler, so I drew one for my first-grade teacher. She thought it was magnificent and put it on the bulletin board. In fact, she called several other teachers in to see it hanging there.

This was a big deal because in those days there was no such thing as self-esteem in the curriculum and it was rare to have anything but writing papers put on the bulletin board. When I mentioned this to my 75-year-old mom the other day, she said she remembered teaching us to draw the house. And you know what—I can still draw the same house, but probably not as well! Little did I know that I would be writing art books for kids some many years later. So, you never know how early experiences influence a life. Thanks, Mrs. McGrail!

Jean Potter, Author and Educational Consultant, Former Acting Assistant Secretary of Education, Charleston, West Virginia

In growing up, I never felt quite comfortable with my position as a middle child. It always seemed that my brother, who was three years older, had all these privileges and permission to do things I wasn't allowed to do. And my sister, who was three years younger, was babied and had more privileges than I had. I felt very left out and I became very rebellious at a young age.

Some of my cousins started using drugs, and when I was about nine or ten years old, I became their guinea pig. They literally started pouring drugs into me, and I became very confused and very unhappy. When I was 12, my mother was diagnosed with multiple sclerosis. When my mother got sick, I really felt abandoned. Before I was 13, I left home and went to live with my girlfriend and her family.

I certainly had a very poor self-image. I felt worthless and I believed that nobody loved me. My family let me go and they didn't show any indications that they wanted me to come back. I think I left because I wanted my family to say, "No, Elizabeth, come home." But they didn't. They let me stay out of the house. I started working with a social service agency that set me up to work in my high school. They connected me with a guidance counselor, who was also a teacher, when I was 14. For the next nine months we worked very closely on self-esteem and abandonment issues, and I developed a strong trust in him.

I was doing pretty poorly in school. I was more involved in taking drugs and going to marches in Washington because of the Vietnam War. Between the walkouts and sit-ins, my school grades were very bad. As a matter of fact, I was what was called "Circle 65," which meant that my teachers passed me on ability, but I was marginal, very borderline.

One morning I walked into this guidance counselor's office and looked at the top of his huge desk, and every square inch was covered with schoolwork that I had done from the time I was in second grade! Everything that was in my file was in front of me. I looked at him and I said, "Doctor, what is going on—why do you have all these things here?"

He said, "Elizabeth, I've been spending all morning going through my records and examining your test scores and the work that you've done, and I'm very confused!"

And I said, "What do you mean? What are you confused about?"

He said, "You're 'Circle 65,' but do you realize that every test you've taken, including your IQ test, shows that you're in the top 10 percent?"

I was amazed. "Do you mean I'm smart?" I asked.

He said, "Not only are you smart, but you can be anything that you want to be! You have the capacity to be anything. Just believe in yourself. Look at my desk. You can do it, you've already done it! You just forgot. You have the capacity and the intelligence to achieve great things in life."

Well, that turned around my life. Because the next semester, I got straight A's. From a "Circle 65" to a 90 average in every single course I took. It completely and totally changed my life.

There are other parts of this story that I don't think he banked on. I eventually returned to a very sick and very dysfunctional home, and I ended up dropping out at 16 and traveling around the country for a year. Three months before my class was to graduate, I took the GED and literally had my diploma in hand three months before my class graduated.

I went to community college for the summer semester. One day I walked into the State University of New York in Stony Brook, where they were interviewing prospective students. You needed to have a grade-point average of at least 90 to 92 percent, with SAT scores somewhere in the neighborhood of 1200 or higher to be accepted.

I had an interview with a woman in the admissions office. We sat down and I laid it out for her. I said this is my life, and this is how I've done it, and this is who I am, and she stuck out her hand and said, "Congratulations, and welcome to

Stony Brook! I have the capacity to allow people to come in who fall into the category of either disadvantaged or extenuating circumstances."

She said, "I believe in you. I know you can do it and I'm going to bank on you. I've interviewed 10 people this week, and I didn't hear what I hear in you. You have a zest for life and enthusiasm and desire. You are going to make it!" I had a 4.0 average from Stony Brook, I transferred to Hunter College and graduated magna cum laude, then went on for my master's degree in counseling and human development.

There's definitely a connection here between my counselor in high school and what happened afterwards. Somewhere along the line I got the message that he gave me— that I could do anything. I proved that by turning around and doing phenomenal work. I needed this man to tell me that I was smart and I could make it. And when he did, my whole life really turned around for me.

He certainly, completely, totally and absolutely changed my life. In one minute's time, he showed me—in black and white, with a diagram and a schematic so I could not discount what he was saying—that I had everything it took, I didn't need to get it from anywhere else, and I could count on my own resources. He said, "I believe in you. Now it's time for you to believe in you!"

Liz Sterling, 36, Broadcaster, Boca Raton, Florida

Don Hake was a behavioral research psychologist and university professor, amongst other things. He was also my next-door neighbor, and became my parents' best friend over time. I was a high school freshman and initially got to know him and his family as their babysitter. As time passed, he clearly became my earliest mentor, and one who played a pivotal role in my academic, and subsequently career, choices.

This relationship began with him lending books to me and a curiosity on his part about my thoughts after reading them. I remember his kind face, smiles and interest. The message was "You count," and "What you think matters." A day I'll always remember involved my accompanying him to his research lab. I was a high school junior by this time. The lab was located on the grounds of a state hospital in southern Illinois. That day was a school holiday, and I recall being thrilled upon his invitation to "come have a look at the lab." Although much of his research involved animals as subjects, he was also interested in applied work with humans, unlike a number of his colleagues. His research focus had shifted into the area of cooperative and competitive behavior, with obvious human applications.

He clearly did not fit the stereotype of a "rigid behaviorist." He had a big heart and a genuine interest in the welfare of people. He also helped my own parents lighten up a bit, and no doubt provided them some guidance and reassurance about raising a teenager in the 1960s. He also liked my friends and helped create social opportunities that included us. He was always interested in what we thought or had to say about a variety of social, political and other issues. It was obvious he enjoyed us.

The following year, he helped me get a part-time job, as a high school senior, in a vocational rehabilitation training center. Later, as a college undergraduate, I was offered a behavioral research assistant position, no doubt largely on his recommendation. After that, a glowing recommendation from him accompanied my graduate school application. The list goes on.

I owe him much for all of the support and encouragement he offered in those early and scared days. My only regret is that by the time I was ready for graduate school, he had moved on to another state and university system. Still, he taught and offered me so much more than I realized at the time.

I am sad to have not had, or taken, the opportunity to tell him these things in person. Don died in his forties, suffering from a heart attack while jogging one day up a hill in West Virginia. Since then, I occasionally have imaginary conversations with him about a variety of subjects. I hope he had some inkling of the importance of his early guidance and friendship. He was quite a role model, an inspiration and a very good friend.

Emily Stafford, 42, Therapist and Program Director, Albuquerque, New Mexico

There are two things that I remember about third grade. One is that three over one equals three—my teacher was big on that. The other is once when I was asking for help, I was leaning over my teacher's desk and she shut my fingers in her drawer. That hurt, really hurt!

She said she was sorry, and I know how much she was sorry because every time that she saw me after that, even when I had grown and graduated from school, she always stopped and took my hand and looked at my fingers and said, "David, I did it accidentally. I really did. I didn't mean to do it." We shared a little laugh about that. She always cared and she always remembered. And so I have to remember that teachers have a memory for things that go well, and teachers have a memory for things that go poorly. But in either case, this teacher cared about me, not just in third grade, but throughout my life. What a lovely person!

Dave Friedli, 37, Project Director for Drug-Free Nebraska, Lyons, Nebraska

Miss Julia Coleman was my school superintendent and teacher when I was a child, and she greatly influenced my life. She taught all of her students to seek cultural knowledge beyond the requirements of a normal rural school classroom. As a school boy who lived in an isolated farm community, my exposure to classical literature, art and music was insured by this superlative teacher. I will always be grateful for all she taught me.

President Jimmy Carter, Atlanta, Georgia

I went to a very large high school. I wasn't a very good student, although I was considered smart due to the results on my standardized tests. My grades were pretty poor because I wasn't very attentive in most of my classes, except for cabinetmaking, which I liked and specialized in.

It was 1967 and the teacher I had for 11th-grade social studies was rather cynical, I suppose. You certainly couldn't describe him as being remotely hippie-like. He seemed to me to be very elderly—he must have been in his late thirties, possibly early forties. He was balding and smoked a cigar, and had an unlit one clenched in his teeth much of the time. He was very sharp-minded, and he was the first person who taught me that you didn't necessarily have to believe what people in positions of authority told you. This was an incredible revelation to me.

On some level, he also liked my rebellious streak, although he quashed it when necessary to maintain order in his classroom. He encouraged my questing nature, encouraged me to ask questions, encouraged me not to just accept what people in authority said, encouraged me to read about subjects I was interested in—I was a good reader but very disorganized—and I would say that he had a great influence in my life.

He showed me that really good teachers did exist. I had heard that the way he taught was more similar to the way courses were taught in college than in high school. He took quite a Socratic approach, questioning rather than telling. Certainly this was one motivation for me to go to college. I was lukewarm about college, but if some of the teachers were like this guy, college sounded pretty good.

He sparked my interest in learning and study. I wouldn't say that he made me cynical, but he made me realize that you didn't have to take on faith what anyone was saying, including him. In terms of my intellectual development, I owe this man a great debt.

David Harp, 43, Writer, Public Speaker, Musician, President, musical i press, Montpelier, Vermont

I had three teachers I'd like to tell you about. The first one was my literature teacher in ninth grade, Mrs. Whipkey. The reason she made quite an impression on me was that no matter what story we read, she brought it to life. She would go over each sentence and give us her idea of its meaning. It was the most incredible thing, because after her discussions, every sentence meant something different from how I had originally perceived it! I actually saw it live in my head. I saw the story being played out, and it was always very passionate once she explained it.

Ever since then, whenever I read, I always think that maybe there's a lot more to the story than how I'm understanding it, and as a result, I read things a little more in-depth because of that experience. I think, "Well, maybe I could read that line again and perhaps get something else out of it."

The next teacher, Mr. Swartz, was the one I had in tenth-grade math. He looked at each person as they walked in the class with such a look in his eye that you knew you were being recognized, which to me was not common in high school. He always made a comment to you whether it was, "Interesting shoes you're wearing," or "Oh, you're wearing your hair down today," or "What did you do today?" It was always something that made you feel special.

He told stories and drew connections between math and real-life situations. Like he would relate math to poker and taught us how to play poker in his math class! By the end of that year, I felt that everything had to do with math. It was as if there was an underlying math to everything in life. It made me realize that no matter what the subject—history, English, math, literature, art—it's all connected somehow. That idea clicked for me in his class.

He also related to us in very warm and personal ways. I still remember him saying how he'd eat a can of tuna fish at night. He would just eat a plain can of tuna fish, and it stuck in my head 'cause I didn't know anybody that would open a can of tuna and just sit there and eat it for a snack. He was a very kind, loving person.

The other teacher was my tenth- or eleventh-grade art teacher, Mr. Mullen. Everybody really liked him. One day I was doing my artwork as usual and I was very immersed in what I was creating. I overheard him saying, "Now what do you think Cheryl is thinking about?"

I looked up and he had his head on his hand, leaning against the table. Here was a teacher asking the other students what I was thinking about, like, "Cheryl—she matters!" I found it flattering. I had always been introspective, and this teacher actually noticed that there was deep thinking going on in my mind. In that moment, he touched a little of the core of me.

Cheryl Cramer, 34, Executive Recruiter, King of Prussia, Pennsylvania

Every year I debate whether to send my high school coach a Father's Day card. I don't know how he would take it because the last time I saw him, I wasn't in such good shape.

In 1969, the year after I graduated, I got into some trouble at the Atlantic City Rock Festival. I had never tried LSD before and at this festival, I did a four-way hit of purple mescaline, which is usually enough for four people. I expected to get off after a few minutes and when that didn't happen, I did some chocolate mescaline. A little while later I did some more acid because I still wasn't getting off. And then I got off pretty good!

At that point, I was pretty sure I was never coming back. After diving through a window and severely injuring my arm, I ended up fighting a whole bunch of police in the middle of an intersection. By the end of the day, I was in pretty deep with the Atlantic City Police Department.

Someone called my old coach, who was the vice principal of my school back then. When he heard what had happened, he drove all the way from Johnstown, Pennsylvania, to Atlantic City. He talked to the police and got them to let me go. All he asked was that I get a haircut, 'cause I had long hair at the time. I did what he asked but I haven't talked to him since.

When I was still in high school, he was my gymnastics coach and my mentor. Although there was another guy at the school with the title, my real guidance counselor was my coach. He also taught in a private gym after school and I went in there all the time to learn. I ended up being an instructor and teaching little kids gymnastics two days a week. Whenever our gymnastics team traveled for competitions, he took us in his car. He was like a dad to me.

Garry Reighard, 43, Survey Party Chief, Lantana, Florida

A REALLY GREAT TEACHER IS SOMEONE WHO . . .

. . . doesn't give a lot of homework the last week of school.
                    Laura, 10, Cogan Station,
                    Pennsylvania

. . . instead of just teaching, she does fun stuff when
    she teaches.
. . . uses games to teach things like capitals or math.
                    Allison, 10, Pittsburgh, Pennsylvania

. . . lets us do other things like play cards, do sports,
    or do arts and crafts.
                    Jason, 14, Pittsburgh, Pennsylvania

. . . listens to everything you have to say.
. . . spends time going over things with you.
. . . stays after school to talk to you.
                    Steve, 12, Cherry Hill, New Jersey

. . . likes me.
. . . says hi to me when I come in.
                    Hannah, 5 ³/₄, Cherry Hill, New Jersey

. . . can entertain while she's teaching.
. . . won't put you down for not knowing stuff.
                    Graeme, 15, Lethbridge, Alberta,
                    Canada

. . . can understand our music and our language.
. . . jokes around with us, even when he's teaching.
. . . plays basketball with us.

. . . can explain things a different way when we don't
   get it the first time.
. . . keeps explaining things until everybody gets it.
. . . lets you go ahead once you understand something.
                    Rasa, 14, Rochester, Michigan

. . . lets us do projects instead of tests to show that
   we understand things.
. . . lets us check our own papers.
. . . talks about his family and what he did on the
   weekend.
. . . has discussions about different things when some
   people agree and some people disagree.
                    Aimee, 11, Rochester, Michigan

. . . checks our papers at her desk while we're watching
   so we know which ones are right.
. . . pretends to not know stuff so we help her figure it out.
                    Nathan, 8, Reading, Pennsylvania

. . . has discussion days where everybody participates
   so they understand what's going on.
. . . gives individualized help before or after school or
   during lunch so that nobody feels embarrassed
   about getting special attention in class.
                    Aaron, 15, Aurora, Colorado

. . . is flexible in terms of schedule.
. . . lets you work the way you want to with an assignment.
                    Lily, 11, Corrales, New Mexico

. . . has guest speakers.

. . . really gets into her work.

. . . trusts us with her stuff, even her purse.

. . . does really fun projects that she puts a lot of work into.

. . . goes to workshops to learn new things.

. . . lets kids plan things themselves.

. . . compliments our ideas.

. . . calls your parents and tells them how you're doing, for good and bad.

. . . gives you her number if you need help.

. . . makes sure we have enough time to get things done.

. . . lets us decide things when they're appropriate and when she goes along with them.

. . . is willing to try new projects with the class that she hasn't done before.

> Sierra, 12, Portland, Oregon

. . . helps kids when they're not getting something.

> Lonnie, 10, Lincoln Park, Michigan

. . . takes you on field trips.

> Wanda, 13, Lincoln Park, Michigan

. . . teaches from your needs, not hers.

. . . figures out when you're not learning by one method, and finds different ways and uses different things to help you learn.

> Maria, 13, Kahului, Maui, Hawaii

. . . takes us out to play.

> Kara, 11, Las Vegas, Nevada

. . . lets me bring show and tell.

. . . gives us free play when we do all our work.

> Brandon, 8, Las Vegas, Nevada

. . . teaches us like we're his own kids.

. . . never sends us to the principal's office.

> Danielle, 14, Fairview Park, Ohio

. . . has ideas and things you can do, not just book learning.

> Sarah, 13, Knoxville, Tennessee

. . . is funny.

> Matt, 12, Pensacola, Florida

. . . is always nice about wrong answers.

> Lauren, 9, York, Pennsylvania

. . . does his or her work from the heart.

. . . loves the subject so enormously that he or she can get you really interested.

. . . gets you to enjoy the subject and want to do the work because you like it.

> Laurence, 19, Utrecht, Holland

. . . does not look upon students as toddlers or lazy scamps.

. . . knows how to present his subject in an original manner so that it is a pleasure to attend his lessons.

. . . lets pupils have a say in making his homework when he is sufficiently interested to do so or feels he needs the exercise.

. . . is not rigid in sticking to the rules.
. . . doesn't send one to the headmaster for being too
far behind with his homework.

Jeroen, 20, Utrecht, Holland

In my sophomore year of high school, I had a teacher for Spanish II who was originally from Spain. She was a tough teacher and she didn't give grades away, but it was actually fun to go to her class. She cared so much about her students. On the first day of class, she said to us, "This is the only day that I will speak English," and from then on, she would not speak English to you. If you asked her a question in English, she'd reply in Spanish, and you'd be like, "What's going on?" But it made you want to know what she was saying. This became one of the only classes that I would actually do my homework for, and almost looked forward to going home to conjugate my verbs, study my vocabulary and read the dictionary!

See, Spanish I was a really large class. We went in and the teacher wrote our notes and vocabulary on the board for us to copy. I hated Spanish I with the absolute biggest passion of my life. I didn't feel challenged there. It was just that I had to meet that foreign language requirement.

I'm not by any means a driven student. I mean, I've always done just enough to get by. But in Spanish II, I had a teacher who totally encouraged us to do our best and I pulled an A for all four quarters. I was so proud of myself! She and I became really good friends. Every year I go back to Tucson and see her because she has made such a difference in my life. She taught because she loved to teach. I hated school, but I fell in love with Spanish because of this teacher. I went on to Spanish III and Spanish IV in high school simply due to the fact that she also taught Spanish IV, so I knew that I could get her again senior year. And now I'm in the pre-law program, in political sciences, at Eastern Illinois University, and I have a double major in foreign language. What I really want to do is practice foreign law, maybe in Spain or Mexico. I think that would be really neat, incorporating my love of politics and my love of Spanish.

Tony Salaz, 18, Student, Hotel Bellman and Driver, Fults, Illinois.

Sister Cephas was my religion teacher in ninth grade, and she laughed at my jokes. If I told a story, she responded. She made me feel important in that class, and she appreciated my humor. For a student who was rather serious most of the time, she made me feel like I had a good personality, and that always remains with me.

I had one teacher in 1970, at Villanova, who taught a library science class called "Storytelling in the Elementary School." She recognized me with her smile and laughter. One day she encouraged me to tell a story to the class that I had told her in private. As in my religion class, this experience gave me status as being somebody who was worth listening to.

Recently, I saw that teacher at a library meeting where I was speaking. I wrote her a note and I passed it across the table. In it I said, "You probably don't remember me because it was 25 years ago, but you made me feel so good in that class." I could just see tears in her eyes, and she tucked the note in her purse. She really appreciated me sending her that little note.

The impact of these two teachers was clear when I started teaching. I'd look for the child who was shy or fat, for someone who had never been a teacher's pet, and I made a conscious effort to make that child important for the year. I had them help me with the bulletin board or gave them the extra errands to do. I looked at those kids and thought they would never be the one that someone else would pick. I wanted to make sure that at least in my class, they knew they were special.

Patricia Gallagher, 43, Mother of Four, Author, Richboro, Pennsylvania

The home that I grew up in was somewhat chaotic. As a child, I was inarticulate and didn't have people around who wanted to listen to me. But I had an uncle who played a big role in my life. When he visited, he taught me how to pick a subject, how to learn everything I could about it and then how to speak. He actually used to practice with me. He would assign me a subject, and then when he would be traveling through our town, he'd come over and he'd be my audience. He'd listen to what I had to say and then he'd give me new ideas. From him, I learned how to be able to speak and get some kind of feedback, how to get a result.

In school, I had a teacher named Mrs. Mett who polished the skills my uncle helped me develop. She taught me how to speak publicly. Mrs. Mett came into my life in about ninth grade, and she spent hours with me helping me learn how to speak, how to project myself, how to put ideas and concepts together. She believed in me, and the two things she gave me were time and encouragement. By the time I was in tenth grade, I was winning state awards as an orator. I continued all throughout high school to win oratorical and speaking awards. Of course my entire career in the last 15 to 20 years has been in public speaking, as well as in all the therapy work that I've done. These individuals were very important to me as mentors. They gave me something through which I could create a sense of manageability: I knew that if I could have the opportunity to speak, I could make things happen.

The other influential teacher in my life was Mr. Halos, who taught me about economics and business. I started learning from him in the ninth grade. He taught these wonderful classes! I could have sat in his classes day and night. He taught me how to avoid debt, how to increase passive income, how to put a business together, how to make business decisions. No one had ever taught me about these things. As a matter of fact, when I went to high school, which was 30 years ago, nobody really thought that much about economics or business. Mr. Halos had such good concept's which were considered somewhat outrageous at that time. He was anti-credit cards, he was anti-borrowing and he believed that all bills should be paid on time. I remember listening so carefully to him and thinking, "He really has good ideas and I really believe what he is saying." As I grew older, I found myself going back and remembering what he had to say and managing my life to a great extent with what I'd learned from him. I have since gone on to develop three different companies, and my most recent business has been a very successful national company. All of my graduate training was in therapy, counseling, addictions and so forth, so all of my business learning really came from Mr. Halos. I took every class that he offered. In many ways I feel that I got an MBA from him in high school.

I would say that in both of these areas—speaking and business—I go back to those high school learnings. I feel that I have profited so much by having good teachers that now it's important to me to become one. In the last two to three years I've been training a team to take over the kind of therapy work that I've done, I've been training some people in business ways, and I just recently did a workshop on women and finances. What's important for me now is to able to share many of the gifts that were given to me.

Sharon Wegscheider-Cruse, 55, President of ONSITE Training and Consulting, Rapid City, South Dakota

I took an undergraduate course in geology at the University of Colorado to fill in my liberal arts requirements. I still think about that course because of the professor. He really made us think. Normally, you would just go in and regurgitate information: "This is what volcanism is . . ." and "This is the theory of plate tectonics . . ." and so on. But Professor Reynolds' approach was different. He would give us a photograph of an area, say in Yellowstone National Park, and ask us to reconstruct the geology of that area from "day one" to the present. We not only had to justify our geological history, but also demonstrate how it fit into the overall history of that part of the country. For example, you couldn't have volcanoes in an area where there was never any seismic activity, and you couldn't have sedimentary deposits where there was never a sea or lake bed. You had to write a geological history and it all had to fit in together. It was as though he were giving us clues to this great mystery and we had to solve it based on those clues. This made geology exciting. I got a D in that class, but it was one of the best classes I ever took.

I also took an ancient-history class from Professor Rawlins. Going into his class was like going back in time, as though we were actually in ancient Athens, for example, short of being dressed up in original costumes. He made it that clear, that real for me. He had a sense of humor when he was talking about and describing the famous characters who lived back then, whether it was Herodotus or Alcibiades or Solon or whomever—he really developed those historical characters. They weren't just dry names in a book; they came alive for me in that classroom. When he described battles, like the battle of Salamis with the Persians or the land battles between the city states of Sparta and Athens, I felt as though I was actually there. I could see myself there! I was one of the Athenian hoplites, my shield on my left hand, interlocked with the guy next to me, surging into battle! He was an amazing history professor because he really loved and enjoyed history. He was one of the very few teachers that could convey that passion, at least to me as a student.

I'm a humongous procrastinator, and normally I'll put off reading assignments until the last minute; but in Rawlins' classes, I would read ahead just so I could keep up with him, and maybe try to get a little bit ahead of him to try and anticipate what he was going to talk about. Oh, it was a joy! I took every class with him that the university offered. He could have had four one-hour classes every day and I would have gone to all of them. Professor Rawlins is the one who turned me on to ancient history. I ended up taking as many ancient history courses as I could, and it was primarily because he had made ancient Greek history just come alive for me. I probably could have sat and listened to him talk about anything. He brought an enthusiasm into the classroom that was absolutely contagious.

If I had one wish, I would want everyone with three or more working brain cells to take a class from one of these guys, especially Professor Rawlins. I never wanted to miss a class, even though they were usually morning classes. I normally thought a 10 a.m. class was way too early, but I even took 8 a.m. classes from him because they were that good.

For me, when I look at professors like Rawlins and Reynolds and use them as standards for other teachers I've had, the rest have a tendency to drop off quickly. Reynolds took something that was initially as dry as hundred-year-old paint and made me see just how dynamic a planet the earth is and was and will be. And Rawlins literally brought history alive for me. Give me a cold night, a warm room and Plutarch's *Lives of the Noble Greeks*. It's amazing what that does for me!

Don Johnson, 46, Associate Business Broker, Westminster, Colorado

In so many of my college courses, I'd see the yellow notes dragged out on the lectern and read to us over and over again. But Brother Jim Zullo wasn't that way at all. Dr. Zullo is a psychologist, a Christian brother, and he teaches at Loyola University. He had quite a reputation here in Chicago for being a good therapist and an excellent teacher. Yet as we walked into the classroom the first day, he was sitting there greeting people, saying "Hello," and helping us to acclimate ourselves to the new world of graduate school. It was very disarming to realize that despite this great reputation and all of his knowledge, he was so warm and accessible.

His first approach to this class was to find out about us: where we were at, what we needed to do and why we felt we were taking this course. We spent a lot of time talking about what we thought the course was about, and he threw his two cents in. We discovered that he was not just piecing the course together as we went along, but he was actually integrating a lot of the information that we were concerned about into how he would eventually deliver the course. He spent the weekend collating the information he got from our discussion and planned the class accordingly.

This course was on adolescent psychology, counseling the teenager. In it I learned that this person, Dr. Jim Zullo, the engaging personality, was actually interested in us as people. This realization made his degree and his reputation even more profound.

I discovered that I could listen to him all day long—he's one of those lecturers who just has a magical way of speaking. He talked for part of the class, engaged us in discussions and offered individual time with people who needed it. He'd focus in on individual issues and concerns that people had. He was always available after the hour was over. To him, you weren't just a number, which is kind of rare in this day and age, particularly at a university the size of Loyola. He was teaching a number of different courses, doing therapy, writing books and doing whatever else he was doing, and still managed to spend quality time with us. He said to me, "You put people first and find out where they're at. Do a lot of listening, and put your agenda and all of the rules and regulations on the side until you find out what you're dealing with and who you're dealing with."

I try to do that here with the teachers. We talk about that a lot, too. They say, "We have an agenda. We have 13 chapters to cover!" And I say, "Wait a minute! Are we teaching the curriculum or are we teaching the kids?" I think he's been somewhat of an inspiration for me to not be so rushed and hurried, to be more of the kind of person who says, "I've got time for you. No hurry."

It's easy to think, "This is wasting time, let's get on with the real work!" Well, the real work was getting to know people, developing a relationship with the class, and eventually he had everybody on board. He practiced on the class what he was teaching. He actually lived a lot of what he was teaching. He is still a great lecturer and a genuinely well-rounded guy who is very easy to listen to. I don't know if you can teach a teacher to be that way. He definitely made a difference with me.

Father Jack Daley, 47, Priest, Rector of Quigley Seminary, Chicago, Illinois

I had a special ed teacher, in seventh grade I think it was. My wife had her, too. She treated me with a lot of kindness. She always encouraged me. She cared a lot. She had this thing about wanting us to succeed in life. She was just great, you know? She was real loving and compassionate. At that time I needed somebody like her 'cause I was having a lot of trouble as a youngster, you know? So I needed somebody like her to understand where I was at.

After I graduated and after I got married, my wife and I used to go to her house and talk to her. She was always happy that we were still married. People thought that our marriage would not last, but we've been married over 26 years.

There were other things about this teacher that made her special. She was the only teacher I ever had that never criticized me or accused me of stuff. I always felt safe in her room. Up until that point, I didn't trust anybody. This was the place where I learned how to trust.

Joe Chavez, 45, Albuquerque, New Mexico

I had this English teacher twice, once in junior high and again in high school when he changed schools. He was bright and a little bit on the cocky side but very interested in the kids, just a really good teacher.

There was an incident where another teacher in the school made an anti-Semitic remark to me. This was an older woman who could never get used to the fact that it was not okay to give tests on the Jewish holidays. She continued to do it. If I brought it up to her, she'd say things like, "This country was founded on Christianity and you people are just gonna have to get used to it." So I told this English teacher what this older woman had said to me. He was livid. And he went to the principal. I never did find out exactly what happened as a result, but that woman never made a remark like that to me again. And it was because he had that reaction that

I knew I should never put up with that kind of behavior from authority figures.

Now I have to say that I knew that anyway, because I grew up in a community where there were very few Jews. I was always very aware that I was a member of a minority group. It wasn't an enormous problem, but there were sometimes remarks made by friends and classmates who didn't know I was Jewish or thought that I was "different" than other Jewish people, as if that were some kind of compliment. So they'd say it in front of me, thinking I wouldn't care. I had always known this was something that I needed to not put up with from my peers. I was never the kind of kid who kept my head down and my mouth closed about that sort of thing, and my parents always encouraged us to speak up.

So it wasn't as if I would have just slunk away anyway. But the fact that he stood up for me and said, "This is unacceptable, this cannot be permitted to go on," showed me that it is possible to make institutions responsible, and that you have to hold them to certain standards and not permit them to ride roughshod over you, even when there is a power imbalance like the one between teachers and students.

Sally Kalson, 43, Journalist, Pittsburgh, Pennsylvania

When asked to write about my most "memorable" teacher, a number of people crossed my mind. Like my first-grade teacher who was also a Holy Roller preacher, or a seventh-grade teacher who distributed 45s of his rock 'n roll records (this in 1962!) before disappearing in mid-year, or a Spanish teacher who made learning fun with lots of games, skits and other interactions "en Espanol," or a freshman college English professor who depth-charged my whole way of thinking and view of the world at age 18. And there were others, but one person keeps coming to mind. This person was my aunt, whose dream was to become a doctor. But in rural Virginia in the 1930s, she was discouraged, as women didn't become doctors then—they became teachers. So she became a biology teacher, despite having a degree in English, and taught high school biology for 43 years. She gave me my first book, as well as hundreds of others. She also gave me my first classical record, my first camera, first artist's easel. . . . I watched her pore over books on a wide variety of interests—always several at once—and listened to her extensive music collection, and by listening to her talk about her travels throughout the United States and Europe, I traveled vicariously myself. Every summer until I left home, she spent most of her teacher's vacation next door with my grandfather, sleeping late, constantly swigging down sweet iced tea and reading most of the night.

Years later, when she was blind from diabetes, she still read constantly, with her special tape and record players and recorded books for the blind. She always worried that some were abridged or edited and she might not be able to "read" the entire book. She listened to the TV, kept up with current events, and showed a zest for life until the end. It was her early influence that gave me a lifelong enthusiasm to never stop learning, to keep an open mind and read, read, read!

MaryAnn Glynn, Photographer, Faber, Virginia

I spent twelve of the happiest years of my life in the Catholic school system in Philadelphia. Those were the years of the "old religion" days and I was taught by nuns all through school. There were no lay teachers in those days, with the exception of my high school gym teacher.

Those nuns were tough. You learned and learned well and for some children, it was too frightening not to learn. I didn't always like the regimentation and the discipline, but the traits I learned served me well later in life. In the 1950s and early 1960s nobody talked about alcoholism in the family. Many children lived under those conditions, but a child would never admit that his or her parents had a drinking problem. I was one of those children, and school was a safe haven for me in an otherwise crazy, chaotic world. My parents weren't abusive, but their disease caused them to be emotionally neglectful. Any encouragement or self-esteem I had as a child can be attributed directly to the nuns and priests I came in contact with on a daily basis in school. I was an A student and on the honor roll most of the years I was in school. However, when I graduated from high school, I married and retired into a very abusive lifestyle for the next ten years.

At 27 years old, with four children and no money of my own, I moved into an apartment and went out job hunting. This is when I realized just how much of an influence my teachers had on me. I got a job based solely on what I had learned during those 12 years of school. The typing and bookkeeping skills had stayed with me, despite the years of turmoil and just trying to survive. More important, the social skills I learned came into play during interviews. I knew how to act, dress and present myself in the best possible light. I was a lady, albeit a desperate one. I had learned the assets of punctuality, neatness, responsibility and loyalty. If I didn't feel good about myself in any other ways, I knew I was a good employee and over the next 20 years, I advanced to the very good position I have today.

I'm sure the nuns who taught me saw an outgoing, clever child, with an eagerness to please and a smile always on my face. They couldn't know that inside me was a fearful little girl who looked to them to be both father and mother to me.

I will always be grateful for my education. It gave me a life and helped me provide for my children. I cannot think of any specific nun who did more than the others. Collectively, they gave me the best they had to offer and ten years after graduation, I reaped the rewards of their dedication.

Rosemary "Mickey" Macklin, 50, Office Manager,
Philadelphia, Pennsylvania

I hate history. I've always hated history. I always thought that it was a useless subject. But my junior year, I had this teacher who was brand new to our school. The way he taught history was so much fun. I think this is the thing I like most about teachers, when they make learning fun. I mean, it's not just going in to get a lecture and "Here's your homework" and getting out of that classroom. This teacher would dress up in traditional clothing and come to school, say, in an all-leather suit and moccasins to teach us about Indians. The one story I remember most is the way he taught us about Paul Revere's ride. He had this podium and he started making the sound of a horse trotting and kept it up as he went through this whole story. In the middle of his lecture, all of a sudden, he stopped and he said, "Uh-oh! There's a fence!" And then the horse jumped the fence. I mean it was totally bizarre—but that's what made him special.

Most people thought he was an absolute psychotic freak. But he was so unique that I'd think, "Wait a minute. Maybe I should stop and listen to this guy." Because it was never just history. He always included a joke in there. Whether it was the Constitution or the Boston Tea Party, he always incorporated the lesson into his jokes. It made me remember whatever he was teaching. His lessons stuck in my mind more than just some guy talking to you about the first Constitutional Convention and writing three pages of notes on the board and giving you a test on Friday. It never was like that with this teacher.

If you really think about it, history is probably the easiest subject you'd ever want to learn. I mean, you learn the same thing from kindergarten till however long you go to school and take a history class. History is the same, no matter what. The Constitutional Convention can never change. It's always going to be the same story, you know? But it depends on who's telling it. And that was the thing. This teacher was a great storyteller, and that's what I think history is, the story of our civilizations. If you can tell that story well, you're going to get people involved by thinking about what you're saying and actually remembering it. You can make it fun!

Tony Salaz, 18, Student, Hotel Bellman and Driver, Fults, Illinois

I work in a classroom, and I do remedial work with selected students while the teacher teaches other subjects to the class. I love it because she's very funny and she's very warm to the children. She has a bulletin board that has wrapped gift boxes on it, with a statement like, "Give a Gift to Another." During the week, the children each write something nice about another child, and then they pick from the box and read the different things that the other children wrote.

When she teaches, she uses a lot of manipulatives and just makes every lesson personalized and interesting. She doesn't just say, "Open your book to page so-and-so." She will use different kinds of objects, like blocks or an overhead projector, or she'll be dramatic and act out something. She uses a lot of humor in her teaching, and I find that interests the children.

She is also a wonderful disciplinarian because she knows when to joke but when to be serious as well. She runs a very tight ship, and she stresses that the children should be nice to one another. I see that there is a lot of maturity in those children. They can do many tasks independently. Still, there's a lot of order in her room, a lot of structure. But she does give them the freedom because they're mature enough to be independent. Also, there's a lot of cooperative learning and group work, which is fun, and the children are able to participate in a quiet way. I mean, who wants to work where the atmosphere is out of hand, and where you don't see learning actually taking place? She lets the kids know what their limits are. She devotes her whole life to it, and it takes a lot of energy.

Just because I've worked in her room, I feel that the greatest thing that a teacher can do is to make children feel important and help them do the best that they can do. I try to give that to my remedial students, and I try to build their self-image. If they don't understand something, I try to not make them feel bad that they don't understand it. We can't always control everything with a child, but I think that we do have an impact on molding behavior and that we have the ability to make learning easier and more fun. I know that children can learn and enjoy themselves and have self-discipline. From working with her, I've tried to be more creative and more humorous. I've tried to be less controlled—to still show discipline, but to be more relaxed with the children. Personally, this experience has helped me realize how much we can be an influence on children's lives.

Lois Romm, 43, Basic Skills Teacher, Homemaker, Cherry Hill, New Jersey

Dr. Roslyn Terborg-Penn, head of the Graduate History Program at Morgan State, is my most memorable teacher. I've taken at least six different courses with her. She had a definite impact on my college career. She is a strong, independent person and I admire that. She goes about doing her thing and not bothering too much with the politics that take place on a college campus. She was also the first published author that I met.

Back in college, she brought out the best in me. Every now and then I had the tendency to get bored with school—sometimes it became too easy and I would lose interest. She was always there to say, "Look, Kevin, you're messing up," in a way that I understood.

I'm originally from the Virgin Islands, and when I came to Baltimore I was 17 years old. I guess in a sense Dr. Penn became almost my "education mother" away from home. I was quiet, did my work and got my grades, but I was never particularly outgoing in class. I came from a different culture. I spoke with an accent. So I kept quiet and to myself in class.

In Dr. Penn's classes, part of your grade came from classroom discussion. I received a B the first time that I took one of her courses because I never participated. If I had participated, I'd have received an A.

Dr. Penn let me know, "Look, Kevin, you have a lot to say. You're intelligent. Speak up. If you don't, you're going to continue getting B's in my class." So I started participating in classroom discussions in Dr. Penn's and my other classes and I haven't stopped talking since—because of Dr. Penn. In fact, being in her classes has enabled me to speak at conferences in front of hundreds of folks and conduct lectures in classrooms. It doesn't bother me in the least. I even look forward to public speaking.

Dr. Penn is still at Morgan State, where I'm working on my master's degree. She still gets on my case when I need shaking up, and when I do something well, she lets me know. She has definitely had a positive impact on me, more than any other teacher or professor that I've come in contact with during my educational career. Thanks, Dr. Penn.

Kevin Mercer, 28, Director, Project 2000, Baltimore, Maryland

I met Betty Hatch at La Belle Modeling Agency in Santa Barbara, California, where she was my mentor and instructor in the 1970s. I was in the ninth grade or so, and I didn't have a whole lot of self-esteem due to my ethnic background, which didn't really fit in with Santa Barbara. Until I met Betty, there was no one in my life to say, "Yeah, you look okay. I want you. You fit in wherever you are." I didn't get a whole lot of inspiration and empowerment at home, as an African-American woman or as a woman in general. I was very much neglected in that regard. But Betty was able to allow me to learn the tools of the modeling trade, and to be able to get up in front of people and walk and sell things in a way I had never really done before. I learned to articulate myself by taking several classes that were offered through her school. Before the commercial-acting class, I was not able to even get out a simple sentence without stuttering and stammering and just shaking in my boots because my diction was so bad!

I didn't have the self-esteem to sit up and take charge in front of an audience, but through her classes I was able to get the confidence to do exactly that. I took the talent I developed and the tools I learned through Betty into many new situations. I am now able to go forth and be a leader and a healer in a lot of different ways because of this. I'm able to teach children and have taught at different modeling schools. I was also able to model for Lawrence Ferlinghetti, an internationally known poet and artist. I was able to articulate myself with artists in that kind of venue through my artistic modeling career.

As a fiber alchemist, I incorporate fashion concepts, principles and ideas when I work with fiber. Having a sense of how to work with clothes and color, and knowing how to sell clothes—these skills are encompassed in the fiber art that I make. All of the skills I learned were very trans-ferrable—the confidence, the poise, how I stand, how I look, my body language, all those things that sell me today. They helped me create my career.

April Martin Chartrand, 30-something, Fiber Alchemist and Administrative Assistant, San Francisco, California

My first-grade teacher was a friend to everyone in the class. She encouraged me to get great grades and enjoy school. This started the momentum that continued throughout my school career and has stayed with me ever since.

John Heavin, 33, Rental Car Agency Operator, Rock Springs, Wyoming

Back in the early 1950s, kindergartens were few and far between in the average public school. Instead, most children spent their early childhoods in close contact with their mothers, sometimes attending a nursery school for a few hours once a week, or playing outside with neighborhood friends. Kindergartens did not become commonplace in the public schools until early in the 1960s or late in the 1950s.

When I started school in Longmeadow, Massachusetts, it was also a common practice to "skip" children who showed talent, intelligence or maturity. Due to a mysteriously high score on a verbal IQ test, I was placed in first grade at the age of 4½. Imagine my shock! A year or more younger than everyone else, with no group experiences, no understanding of what school and friends were about, and no understanding of maternal separation!

I cried through most of the year until my teacher, a stern woman who had lost the joy of teaching somewhere along the way, told me to stop crying for my mother, that I couldn't go home because she wasn't there. "What! Not home! Where else could she be?" I stopped crying, but I did not stop being miserable. I had been yelled at—yes, yelled at!—by this teacher for using my thumb to help me hold my place when reading out loud. As the year finished, school seemed more like a punishment than a joy. We had no art. No music. No stories. No talking. No frivolity or creativity. Or so I remember. I do remember enjoying the weekly "banking" of my 50 cents, but that wasn't enough to make me want to return in the fall.

But after one of those summers we recall as children that seemed endless to the point of pain, I was ready for second grade at the age of 5½. Because I was also physically immature for second grade, I struggled to see the chalkboard and the smaller print in the books. I was tested and then given glasses with red plaid frames, which I diligently polished when I should have been paying attention. I don't even remember wearing them. In fact, the only thing I seem to remember about second grade was that I took to telling on other children who misbehaved. I remember the teacher saying, "MaryAnn, we do not tattle in second grade." However, since I didn't know what "tattle" meant, I kept on telling on the naughty kids, hoping the teacher would like me, since she obviously didn't like my performance in class or much of anything else I was doing.

One day she came to me and said she was sending me back to first grade. Even a poor student who is academically tuned out for the most part knows what that means. Teasing! Ostracism! Flunking! After several days, the decision was made and I was escorted back to grade one, but this time to a different teacher's class. I was frightened, defeated, confused and feeling the choice was out of my control, that I was at the mercy of adults who didn't know what this all really meant. I clung to my mom, whom I didn't really miss so much anymore, but looked to for rescue. "Honey," she said, as she crouched at my level, "you'll love this class. The teacher is really glad you're going to join her today. If you don't like it after one day, we'll see about some other plan. I promise." I was doubtful but relieved that someone was feeling what I felt. After all, I had already experienced first grade at its worst and didn't know how anything might be different.

I entered the classroom and first of all noticed something with a bright flash of light and of recognition . . . THE ALPHBET! The alphabet was on the wall above the chalkboard! I knew those letters! This was looking pretty good. Then the teacher said, "Oh, boys and girls, here she is. MaryAnn has joined our class and is going to be the math helper because she is so good at math. MaryAnn, here's a desk just for you, right next to Susan, who will be a new friend to you. (And she was! She stayed my best friend through eighth grade.) We're so glad you are here."

Well, you could have knocked me over with a dandelion seed! No one had ever been glad to see me that I had noticed. No one had ever complimented me or made me feel useful or special. I forgot all about second grade, was never teased and became a motivated, happy student and even a good reader, writer, artist, athlete and leader.

This new first-grade teacher made the difference to me that day when she said, "You are valuable. You matter. You are wanted." I will never forget her for that.

MaryAnn F. Kohl, 47, Publisher, Author, Educator, Bellingham, Washington

I was born in Argentina and I came to this country when I was 12. I went to a yeshiva in Argentina where I spoke Hebrew perfectly. When we came to this country, we moved to Boston and I went to a yeshiva there. I didn't know much English, but I knew Hebrew well.

I was so upset to be in this country! I did not want to be here. I had one teacher in Argentina whom I kept in touch with through the mail. I wrote her that I was really upset and that I wanted to come back home. I told her that I really didn't like it in America, that the kids were so different, the school was different and I didn't understand the way they did certain things. She wrote a letter back to me telling me I would get used to it, that once I knew English better, I would be able to talk to the kids. And then she went on to explain whatever questions I had about grammar or whatever. It made me feel so good that she not only had enough interest to write back to me and tell me that things were going to be okay, but to also then explain something that I had trouble understanding. It was a very sweet thing that I always remembered about her.

She was so caring and she took an interest in me. She didn't have to write back to me. The fact that I even wrote to her must have meant that I really felt I could be open with her. She didn't act like my needs were frivolous, that my fears were irrational. She was so much more calming than other people. This teacher was able to tell a great deal from the letter I wrote to her. She really gave me exactly what I needed, reassuring me that, "Yes, it's hard, it's difficult. Things will get better." She helped me with a difficult transition. In a way, she was the good parent I didn't have.

Marcela Kogan, 37, Writer, Chevy Chase, Maryland

I had an economics teacher in high school who was able to stress the relationship between economics and real life. He taught consumer economics, which was really very practical. He got across the importance of being a good consumer and how a consumer has certain rights, and that really made a difference in my approach to being a consumer throughout life, knowing to complain at times and not just accept things.

He just got me interested in economics as a discipline, which led me to major in that subject in college. I just got back from an interview where I'm going to start writing a monthly column for a business magazine, and that, too, is related to the fact that I got interested early on in economics-related issues.

This teacher took a more positive-reinforcement approach in telling me that my work was good and creative. He told me, "You're on the right track doing what you're doing. Now try to push yourself beyond that," rather than using the more critical approach of an English teacher I had who was more likely to have said, "The work's no good. You're not doing very good work and you could be doing good work."

I liked my economics teacher. I thought he was a nice guy. He came across as someone who knew what he was talking about. He was not condescending to the students. I had a lot of respect for him. He was one of only a few teachers I had who earned my respect, and teachers who managed to earn my respect tended to be the ones who influenced me. They were basically nice people who could be a student's friend but not the kind that palled around with the students all the time. They were still in charge.

The teachers that stand out most clearly knew what they were talking about and were able to communicate it to me in a way that I not only understood but found interesting as well. The best teachers had an interest in helping us learn. The difficulty in teaching is that you're working with people short-term and the impact is usually long-term. You may see day-to-day progress, but the bigger impact is usually over someone's lifetime.

Mitchell Bard, 35, Executive Director, American-Israeli Cooperative Enterprise, Chevy Chase, Maryland

The teachers who have made a difference in my life have all been music teachers.

There was Mrs. Kirschner in the sixth grade. She took just a few of us to concerts and museums every Sunday, and regularly put me on stage in such roles as the Sugar Plum Fairy in the Nutcracker Suite.

There was Mr. Russ (my violin teacher at Music and Art High School), who made me aware of the fact that I was doing too many things—dancing lessons after school each day, playing in the violin section of one of the school's orchestras, etc. What he didn't expect was that I would give up the violin, but he took it in good graces!

But most of all, there was Eda Morris at Herman Ridder Junior High School in the Bronx. My mother had been my piano teacher all my life, and Mrs. Morris realized that: (a) I should go to Music and Art High School; and (b) I didn't play well enough to get in.

So she said, "You bring a bag lunch each day and I will work with you for an hour at lunch and prepare you for the audition." Twelve hundred children auditioned. One hundred got in. I was one of those lucky kids, and Music and Art High school changed my life.

Shari Lewis, Entertainer, President, Shari Lewis Enterprises, Inc., Beverly Hills, California

The person who most influenced my career was my mentor during my endocrinology fellowship in Boston. He was one of the most wonderful men I've ever met. He was an incredibly humble guy and seemed very reticent and very quiet because, unless he had something significant to say, he didn't say anything. He was also very shy. I was with him for four years and for the first three years, he called me "Isaacs." By the time he finally got to know me, it was the last year of our association. At that point I became "Gil."

He was one of the most rigorously honest and careful scientists that I had run across. I remember numerous experiences with this man teaching me the importance of rigorous intellectual honesty. I can remember endless, endless sessions where we'd sit down to write an abstract together for a paper we were doing. He always, of course, waited until the end of the day because he never wanted to interrupt me in my valuable research efforts during the working day. At 5:00 or 5:30 in the afternoon he'd say, "Gil, let's sit down and go over this abstract."

He would do things like take a sentence that said, "Such and such a finding indicates," and then he would wonder whether "indicates" was really an honest connotation. So we would try "suggests," and he would say, "Well, 'suggests' may be too weak, but 'indicates' might be too strong." And we'd end up considering five, six, seven or eight synonyms for a word and then pick the one that most honestly reflected what we had come up with. He was just so wonderful, with this ability to keep a young doctor who was doing research on track. He was a very sincere, very dedicated man.

I can remember once we went to a wonderful research symposium in Rochester, Minnesota. At that point in time, Rochester was this wonderfully exciting place that consisted of five hotels connected by tunnels to the Mayo Clinic, and maybe one movie theater. I can remember walking along together one evening, because that's about all there was to do there, and he began stroking his moustache. Whenever he began stroking his moustache, I knew I was about to hear a deep and profound statement. After a while he commented to me, "Isaacs, I bet you they never heard of a bagel here." It was a clear indication that we had reached the end of civilization in Rochester, Minnesota.

He was just wonderful. There was not a mean or malicious bone in his body, and he was completely dedicated to not only doing important research, but to being completely honest in terms of a research endeavor. Nowadays, when you hear so much about cheating and so much about the efforts to be the big guy in research and be ahead of everyone else, I think back on what a humble man he was and how hard he worked at really revealing truth. An absolutely fantastic individual!

I'm sure he influenced my research endeavors and my teaching efforts more than anyone else I've run across. He is why I'm in endocrinology today. He ultimately introduced me to the man who was, at the time, Chief of Medicine at Montefiore Hospital. That's how I wound up in Pittsburgh. He finally told me, "You've been a fellow long enough. It's time. I understand they're looking for people in Pittsburgh." That is how I wound up here. Well, maybe I should *blame* him for that!

Gil Isaacs, 60, Associate Professor of Radiologic Sciences, Allegheny Campus of the Medical College of Pennsylvania and Allegheny General Hospital in Nuclear Medicine, Pittsburgh, Pennsylvania

When I first started out in the Air Force as a brand new second lieutenant, I was assigned to the specialty of aircraft maintenance. The squadron was made up of over 500 aircraft mechanics and technical people, and the commander of this squadron is the person who made a real difference in my life. This commander had a very good intuitive sense about working with people, especially in this situation, which involved a wide variety of people from many diverse backgrounds. While working for him, I had the opportunity to observe a few of his personal leadership qualities. He was very approachable and supportive, he had a "tough love" philosophy and he had an excellent sense of humor.

Just as it can be a challenge at times in the business world for labor and management to interface well, it can be a challenge in the Air Force for enlisted personnel and officers to interface well. Because my commander didn't let his "management ego" (or officer ego) get in the way, he was very approachable. This allowed the officers and enlisted to communicate openly and thus work together well as a team. The commander's "street sense" helped him recognize the particular needs of both groups and then allowed him to develop trust and establish an excellent rapport with his people, both officers and enlisted. Closely related to his approachable style was this commander's ability to support you as one of his workers. He made it "safe" for you to express your ideas, and there was no hesitation to go up to him and ask for what you needed. Most important, he would not judge or criticize you. In all cases, you could count on him to keep his word—and his daily actions proved this. With this kind of support, you'd be motivated to challenge yourself, to learn from your successes and mistakes and to grow as an individual, rather than spending your time being worried about making mistakes or overly focusing on past errors.

Today, much of my work with fourth- through sixth-grade children is tied to the supportiveness that I experienced and learned from my commander. He was the first person to teach me at a deep level how important support is, although I wasn't aware of this until years later. Whenever someone approached my commander, he would say, "Well, let's take a look at this," or "Sure, let's make it happen." His positive, non-shaming responses created an environment that made it possible to gain the courage and confidence to pursue our most heartfelt dreams and goals. This clearly worked for my commander, for his squadron thrived. And this is the type of support I now offer to kids, to help keep them on their path of personal development.

This man also understood how to be fair, and would not shame nor condemn. He knew that while it was important to be approachable, supportive, and to give people chances to learn from their mistakes, it was also very important to know where and when to draw the line and hold people personally accountable for their actions. Everyone knew that the commander would not hesitate to use tough love with those who would not pull their fair share of the workload or perform their job well. This kept morale high in the squadron because it showed respect for everyone who did their job well, which was the majority of people. In more common management terms, he spent 80 percent of his time taking good care of the 80 percent of his people who did their job well. (How often is the situation reversed, with management spending 80 percent of its time working with the 20 percent of the people who don't carry their fair share of the work load?)

Lastly, this commander had a super sense of humor. He knew how to handle sensitive subjects with just the right amount of humor, as well as how to have fun. Because the officers and enlisted both respected and felt comfortable with him, they played good-natured jokes on him—and he did the same with them. This kept a wonderful balance between the serious nature of our work repairing airplanes and being able to laugh and have fun.

I'm very grateful for the opportunity to have had my commander as a role model. His ease at interacting with everyone, and his ability to be genuinely supportive, use tough love, and be able to laugh and have fun are lasting lessons that continue to have a positive impact on my life today. My challenge is to learn to display his same qualities at least half as well as he did.

Richard "Rico" Racosky, 41, F-16 Fighter Pilot,
Commercial Airline Pilot, Author of Children's Books on
Goal-Setting and Self-Esteem, Boulder, Colorado

When we were in sixth grade, we were in a split class with 16 sixth-graders and 10 fifth-graders in Bloomington, Minnesota. Our teacher's name was Mrs. Berland. Every Friday in the spring, we brought a sack lunch. Mrs. Berland would take us on a nature walk into the woods behind our school. We'd go to a huge tree that was easy to climb and could hold many children. As we sat in the tree and ate our lunches, Mrs. Berland read wonderful stories to us. The first and most memorable was *A Wrinkle in Time* by Madelyn L'Engle. It was terrific!

Throughout the year, Mrs. Berland used unusual techniques to make learning fun and interesting. She had a unique
tradition of inviting the entire class to an end-of-the-year hot
dog party at her home. We never had another teacher invite us
to her house, and that just made us all feel so special.

*Lorie Stelzig Laczny, 40, Administrative Assistant, Texas
Licensed Child Care Association, Colleyville, Texas, and
Janet L. Brunner, 40, Office Manager, Little Tyke Creative
Child Care, Hurst, Texas*

72

I had Bob Kaelin for Latin in the seventh and eighth grade.
I used to go to school early because I lived nearby. Mr. Kaelin
always used to come in early, too. I'd go to the library to study,
which is where he always was. Most of the kids hated him
because he was real strict, and he intimidated them by being
sort of withdrawn and stern. When I would see him early in the
morning, I realized he was a nice person, so I was never really
intimidated by him.

We just had a little bit of time together, maybe 15 minutes every morning in a non-classroom environment, and he
let his guard down. I guess this broke the barrier. He treated
me more as an equal, as opposed to someone that he was
supposed to be guiding. In class, he would allow me to get
away with a little teasing, whereas he would not tolerate that
behavior from anybody else.

I became real attached to him. He told me there was nothing that I couldn't do. He himself knew five or six different languages, and that made me aware that there really are no limits to what you could do. He made Latin very interesting for me. Because it's such an organized language, and I have a tendency to enjoy everything being in its proper place at the proper time, I fell in love with the language. I took Spanish, German and French, but I liked Latin best. I couldn't speak it fluently, but I liked it because I could figure it out. The course itself was interesting and that added to my learning as well, but there was a psychological bond, an emotional bond between the teacher and me, and that had a real personal impact. Mr. Kaelin taught me more as a friend, I think, and I respected him as a friend, as well as a teacher.

Eric Lundberg, 46, Self-Employed in the Swimming Pool Business, Phoenix, Arizona

I had an English teacher who later went on to become a counselor in east Los Angeles. Her name was Mrs. Maria Olson. She took a great interest in her students. She was always fascinated with the kind of writing that I did and she was always encouraging me to write. But I was one of those kids who was getting involved with gangs and hanging out with the wrong crowd and so I didn't pay any attention to my writing, plus I wanted to keep the attention focused on my peer group.

I was one of those very bright kids who had to force himself to get a C in order to be accepted by my friends. I was too much of a nerdy kind of guy. I was also one of those kids who never needed a hall pass: If I didn't like your lecture, I just got up and walked out, and more than likely you were happy to get rid of me. I was always acting up in class—I was a kid, right? I was never a major danger but always mischievous, and just bright enough to get by. I was on the periphery of gangs. I wasn't hard-core. I was bright enough to know that, whenever there was any violence goin' down in my community, I made sure that I was in charge of something non-violent, like the refreshments! You had to be in the gangs then, because that was your family, that was your neighborhood, that was where you lived, and that was where you were the happiest.

One day I was out in the hallway, and I was doing what I always did, just standing around talking to people. I was always talking, a very talkative kid. I always had something to say. She caught me in the hallway one day. I was dressed in my gang attire then, and trying to act "bad," you know, to the crowd. Mrs. Olson came up to me and she said, "You know, Lou, you're gonna wind up dead or in jail if you don't listen to me. I'm gonna give you one more chance. I want you to take these classes. I'm gonna drop you from your woodshop class and your auto-shop class."

Now I was one of those kids who used to take all the shop classes. I majored in every shop class imaginable—my counselors kept trying to put me in the college-bound courses, but I didn't want to do that, because it wasn't cool. She took me to this class by the scruff of the neck and said, "I want you to take this class. I just want you to sit in this class and I want you to tell me if you like it or you don't like it, but I want you to try it."

The class was called Speech and Debate. I couldn't believe that young people in this class were getting paid to do what I was doing for free out in the hallway, talking and acting out.

They were getting paid with A's, B's, C's and D's because grades are paychecks for kids. I could not believe it! I said, "Wow!" I remember sticking my hand in a hat, selecting a topic and defending it quite well. I said, "This is for me." And from that day on, I just soared like an eagle, went on ahead, went to college and did great.

And here I am, making speeches and debating and enjoying myself. But she's the one who turned me around. She was real special. It takes that one certain teacher to find out what it is that you're doing that's negative and turn it into a positive. She was able to identify this one kid who was standing out in the hallway acting like a fool, never going to class, and she harnessed the talents she saw there. She said, "You're a good thinker and a good talker. You're learning to negotiate your way through life. That's what people do, but you're doing it all wrong, and you are gonna wind up in a lotta trouble. Why don't you try this?"

Mrs. Olson, great teacher! I wrote a lot of good stuff for her in composition class and it turned out great for me. If it wasn't for her, I don't think I would have made it to where I am today.

When I look back, she was very, very instrumental in changing my attitudes. I often say that I would never have written my materials if it hadn't been for her. The lady that taught me how to diagram a sentence—she wouldn't accept anything less than perfect. She would ride us. She taught me how to write. Because of her, I got my doctorate.

Louis Gonzales, Ph.D., 52, Educational Consultant,
Director of Center for Safe Schools and Communities,
Minnetonka, Minnesota

In about sixth grade, I had a teacher named Mrs. Briggs. She was the first woman I knew who didn't really seem to care about her appearance. She was neat and she was clean but she was kind of out of style, and she didn't shave her legs, which was a shock to me. The kids teased her about it behind her back, but after they'd been in her class awhile, her appearance didn't seem to matter. She just had a presence about her, and she was an excellent teacher.

Getting to know Mrs. Briggs had a big impact on me, especially since back then we were all raised to really value somebody for how they looked. This was a really crucial time for a girl of 11 and 12, the age at which girls often begin to tone down their ability in favor of their appearance. And right at that time in my own development, I had a chance to look at a woman and noticed her accomplishments and her ability. Here was a woman whom I clearly had judged as being not attractive, but as I came to appreciate who she was and what she had achieved in her life, her appearance was no longer quite as important. This experience helped me as I grew. Although I had been rewarded a lot for how I looked and not for what I did, ultimately I wanted to be judged for my ability. I learned to stop judging people by how they look. I learned to judge people by their ability, instead.

*Diane Rosenker, 44, Student in a Master's Program,
Reading, Pennsylvania*

I was really struggling in school in a special ed course because they didn't think I was smart enough to be in mainstream. This was well before Student Assistance programs were around, so no one was prepared to deal with any of the variety of family issues that were going on at the time, and nobody really asked. At this time, my history teacher had the most significant impact. Many days, the only reason I went to school was to see him. I remember one thing in particular: he took an interest in something I was interested in, and he tried to apply that to his history lessons.

I had a brother-in-law who was collecting replica swords and spears from medieval times, and I started collecting the same things. Back then, this was the only thing that really fascinated me. This teacher designed some history lessons around this topic. At one point, he even came to my house to see the spears I had. We spent 15, 20 minutes looking at them. He said, "This is great," and then he left. That was probably the most significant experience of my entire school career—certainly the most positive. It made me want to go to school. It made me want to go to class.

When we were done with those lessons, I was ready and willing and wanting to listen to other things he had to say. He was the only one who actually paid attention to what was going on with me, what I was interested in, and how this applied to what I needed to learn in school. He just took a special interest. He really, truly listened.

David Rosenker, 38, Community Relations for a Drugs and Alcohol Foundation, Reading, Pennsylvania

A REALLY GREAT TEACHER IS SOMEONE WHO . . .

. . . understands your problems and helps you.
                    Stacie, 12, Farmington, New Mexico

. . . has patience with all of her students.
                    Jill, 12, Farmington, New Mexico

. . . loves her students.
. . . helps the students to reach their highest goals.
                    Nicole, 11, Farmington, New Mexico

. . . affects your life in and out of school.
. . . has a special liking for each child for a different
    reason.
. . . makes learning a fun adventure.
. . . never gives up on you, even if you get an F on a paper.
. . . spends all summer long buying things for their
    classes (like my mom)!
                    Sarah, 12, Farmington, New Mexico

. . . likes to comfort you when you're sad.
. . . lets your class have a party once a month.
. . . gives you lots of time on an assignment.
. . . tells you it's okay to make mistakes (and how to
    correct them).
. . . supports you in your good choices.
. . . tells you you're a really great student no matter what
    you do.
                    Karli, 11, Farmington, New Mexico

. . . explains what the assignment is before she assigns it.

> Sara, 11, Farmington, New Mexico

. . . is always there to answer a question about a math assignment or explain it better so you can understand it more.

> Holly, 11½, Farmington, New Mexico

. . . helps you when you have a hard time.

> Chris, 12, Farmington, New Mexico

. . . lets us get up and do stuff like go to the bathroom or get Kleenex or water, without raising our hands all the time.
. . . doesn't give us 100 pages of work a day.
. . . is really nice, basically.

> Candace, 11, Farmington, New Mexico

. . . wants you to learn.
. . . wants to be your friend.

> Alicia, 11, Farmington, New Mexico

. . . knows things about the children.

> Adriane, 12, Farmington, New Mexico

. . . is willing to help no matter how long it takes for understanding to occur.

> Tina, 11, Farmington, New Mexico

. . . makes sure the students know what to do.
. . . tries hard to teach the kids instead of just trying

to get money and let the kids do what they want.
... teaches responsibilities for work habits.
                    Rick, 11, Farmington, New Mexico

... has outside activities.
... has a sense of humor.
... cares about their students' lives.
... lets the slower kids work at their own pace.
... lets kids have free time to read, talk quietly, or
    play games quietly.
... can help kids learn with or without books.
                    Katy, 12, Atascadero, California

... lets you out to sport every day.
... does not judge you.
                    George, 12, Perth, Western Australia

... is considerate of people's feelings, race and culture.
... lets children go on excursions and camps for doing
    the right thing and finishing all their work.
                    Kristy, 12, Perth, Western Australia

... has an excellent humour, which makes him inter-
    esting.
... is kind to students.
... is a bit of a sport.
                    Jai, 12, Perth, Western Australia

... gives you rewards when you do good work or listen
    to instructions.

. . . lets you go out and play sport if you deserve or earn it.
. . . would help if you were stuck on work that you were
unfamiliar with.
>Robert, 12, Perth, Western Australia

. . . comes and sits next to me and helps me with
works that I cannot read or understand.
. . . tells me how to colour the picture the best way
when we do art.
>Thi Huyen, 12, Perth, Western
Australia

. . . understands other people's cultures.
. . . expresses her feelings.
. . . never tells you to buzz off.
>Adam, 12, Perth, Western Australia

. . . helps my knowledge flare.
>Chris, 12, Perth, Western Australia.

. . . is cheerful, caring and funny.
. . . always has time to listen to you.
. . . helps you sort things out if you need to talk.
>Samantha, 12, Perth, Western
Australia

. . . is hard to leave.
>Elizabeth, 11, Perth, Western Australia

. . . cares about all the people in his or her class.
>Jarney, 13, Perth, Western Australia

... relates to most students with respect.
... points out areas to be improved in a friendly manner.

Jared, 11, Perth, Western Australia

... gives students lots of privileges and never takes them away except for bad people.
... would help all students no matter what race or religion.

Chris, 12, Perth, Western Australia

... treats students how they would like to be treated.
... has at least a little bit of humour in their teaching.
... gets students to pay attention in a different way.
... treats the student in a reasonable and friendly manner if there is an argument.
... points out facts in an argument in a reasonable manner.

John, 13, Perth, Western Australia

My favorite teacher was Ms. Elizabeth Jordan, my tenth-grade English teacher in Lynchburg, Virginia. When I reflect on the teachers I had, and I had some really good teachers, Ms. Jordan stands out because she was very much a no-nonsense, you-meet-the-standards kind of person, but she was also a very caring person. I remember one incident in particular. I was a talker in school, always somewhere talking. Ms. Jordan did not like disruptions in her classrooms, even if you were just chatting quietly. One day, I remember someone trying to tell me that Ms. Jordan was waiting for me to be quiet, but I didn't understand what they were saying, so I just kept on talking. All of a sudden, I realized that the entire room was quiet and I was the only one talking. When I turned around in my seat, Ms. Jordan was standing at the front of the room with her arms folded. She had this steely look in her eyes, and they were aimed at me!

First, she asked if I had anything to contribute to the class, and I said, "No." Then she wanted to know if I wanted to share what I was talking about, and I said, "No." And then she said, "Well, perhaps you would like to share it with me after school." So I returned after school and we talked about my constantly chatting in her classroom and the fact that she had asked me on other occasions to stop talking and I had just persisted. And she said, "Well, since you have so much to discuss and to share, I'm going to let you share some of it in another way." She told me to write a paper on something about education and economy or something like that, because I was a vocational-education student. In those days, when the teacher told you to do something, you did it! It was unheard of for you to not do what the teacher told you to do.

I gave the report to Ms. Jordan, and she made me rewrite that paper five times, if I recall correctly. The first time she made me rewrite the paper it was because of the flow, the structure. Then she made me rewrite it because of some grammatical errors. Then she made me rewrite it because of some spelling errors. Then she made me rewrite it because it wasn't neat enough. And then she made me rewrite it just for good measure. I kept saying to myself, "Now why didn't you tell me to do all this in one time?" She seemed to read my mind, and she said, "You need to learn to always take pride in what you do, to always go back and double-check what you do, and you also need to learn that sometimes you have to do something more than once to get it right."

Well, I forgot all about the paper, and several months later I was sitting in her class and I was talking again. Again the class was deadly quiet. I turned around and looked and she was looking at me again, but this time she wasn't angry. Ms. Jordan's stare was friendly this time.

She indicated that she wanted to announce that a student in the school had won an essay-writing contest award. I was sitting there thinking, "Now why is she stopping the class to tell us this? She can just give it to whoever." She said, "I thought you might be pleased to know that one of the winners is in this class." And then she called my name. That was the first time I ever won anything. She had taken that essay that she made me rewrite five times and entered it in a citywide contest, and I won third prize.

Ms. Jordan was always very insistent that we meet very high standards, behaviorally and academically. She spent a lot of time with us, talking with us, and encouraging us and telling us that we could be whatever we wanted to be. She was a very strict teacher, but she used a lot of creativity in her classrooms. When I look back at all the teachers I had, I had many who were very good. But Ms. Jordan, I think, was a great teacher because she motivated us to always do and be the best that we could. She always taught us never to set or accept low standards, and to always do whatever you're going to do with a great deal of pride.

I didn't tell her while I was in high school that she was my favorite teacher. But when I was president of the NEA, someone asked who my favorite teacher was, and I told them that story. It ended up in the Lynchburg newspaper. By that time, Ms. Jordan had retired and moved to Appomattox. Someone shared that newspaper article with her, and I got a phone call at the NEA. I was just flabbergasted that she was on the phone! I had a chance to tell her that I really appreciated all that she had done for me, and I tried to emulate her when I taught. I also told Ms. Jordan that she had a tremendous impact on Mary Futrell the teacher.

Many of the things I learned from her I practiced in my classroom. I learned to hold students to high expectations, believing that every last one could meet those expectations. And I also viewed the students as human beings and cared about them. I was willing to meet them more than halfway: "If you put forth the effort, then I will make sure that I do everything to make sure you achieve your goals. You may have to go back and do it again. But there's a sense of pride, knowing that whatever you produce is well done and represents you." That was the way Ms. Jordan taught us.

Ms. Jordan didn't say that we had to sit in our seats rigid, without speaking every moment of the class. Her point was, when class is in session, you are to be respectful and you are to pay attention. She believed that everyone should have a chance to stand and express his or her opinion to build confidence and poise, but to also listen to others and respect them. She taught us that there's a difference between laughing at something that's funny and laughing at someone. She would not let the kids ridicule or make fun of one another, and when we disagreed, it was without being disagreeable or resorting to violence.

When I look back at my own teaching experience, there were lots of kids who were probably like me, who wanted to sit around and just talk and maybe not do a whole lot of anything. But because someone said, "You can do better, and you can do more," and insisted that those standards be met, they were willing to do that. I hope I have made a difference, just like I know Ms. Jordan made a difference with me.

Mary Futrell, 54, Director, Institute for Curriculum Standards and Technology, Washington, DC

77

Her name is Miss Galligan and she lives in Marysville, California. She was my first-grade teacher. After all these years I finally called her up to tell her what a difference she made in my life. I said there were three instances that I recall. First of all, I remember every day when I looked at Miss Galligan, it was as if she had a halo around her braided hair. I looked up into her eyes and I thought, "You know, someday I want to marry Miss Galligan."

The second thing I remember was the second day of school. I was so excited to get there in my new, pretty little dress, I forgot my underpants. I was terrified when I was playing out in the playground and realized they weren't there. I ran to Miss Galligan. She was compassionate and loving and helped me get a brand new pair of underpants.

The other thing I remember about Miss Galligan is that in first grade I met my first love. His name was Darryl Rice, and in first grade we became engaged. He even gave me an engagement ring. During recess I was playing in the sandbox, and I lost the engagement ring! I went crying in to Miss Galligan's room, and she had another teacher take over the class so she could escort me out to the playground. We looked together in the sandbox for that ring. We never found it, but I'll never forget how dedicated Miss Galligan was, not only to me, but to all of her students.

She's made such an impact on my life that today I want to emulate her and make a difference in the lives of the junior high students I teach. It's taken me over 40 years to make that phone call to tell her what a difference she made. I'm sure there are a lot of us that never get that call, but I'm truly glad I let her know.

Arlene Kaiser, 50, Middle School Teacher, Speaker, Milpitas, California

In my freshman year of college at Central Michigan University, I took a social psychology class that turned me on to the whole psychological field. The teacher was probably one of the first I had who really, really challenged me to think. In this class, we studied how groups form and how things happen in group interactions, sort of the psychology of society. It certainly challenged my own thinking. I learned that there's always more to a story than meets the eye. I remember projects that he made us do that were hard, really hard! I resented these assignments at first, but came to really appreciate how much I learned from doing them.

One of the things he had us do was to create a social change within some structure and observe what happened as a result. At the time I was working part-time in a high school. There was this pecking order in which the secretarial and support staff were called by their first names, and the professional staff, administrators in particular, were called Mr. or Mrs. So-and-So. As a challenge to this imbalance, I decided that I was going to start calling the professional staff by their first names and just see what happened.

They went nuts! They didn't know what to do. I got a lot of pressure from the other secretaries saying, "You can't do that." And I said, "Well, it just doesn't seem fair to me." The bottom line was that the administrators had kind of a big pow-wow and they changed their policy so that *all* grownups would be Mr. and Mrs. So-and-So. I really didn't care which way it went. I wasn't invested in any of their decisions, but it did go in the direction of calling the secretarial staff Mr. and Mrs. It was really fun and it was a great experiment. The whole class had similar things happen.

I have thought of this teacher often. In his class I learned that I am capable, and if someone has really high expectations of me, I will rise to the occasion.

Diane Rosenker, 44, Student in a Master's Program, Reading, Pennsylvania

Connie Claussen was my physical education instructor from the University of Nebraska at Omaha. After I graduated from high school, I intended to major in business. I was doing horribly in my business classes because my heart wasn't in it. One day in class Ms. Claussen said to me, "Have you ever thought about being a teacher?" It was just like somebody had given me this huge compliment, and my self-esteem was like, "Wow! You mean like I could really do that kind of job?" I thought about it, and I talked to her a little bit more, and decided I would take some education courses and see how I would do.

Because I had done so poorly in business classes, I was on academic probation and money was extremely tight. Ms. Claussen said to me, "How about if I find you a job?" So she hired me as a secretary for the P.E. department. I was a horrible secretary! It would take me about six times to type the same letter before getting it right. She'd say, "That's okay, no problem. You can just type it again." I believe in her heart, she wanted me to have the job because she wanted me to stay in school.

She went to bat for me a lot. She helped me to stay in school and encouraged me. During my sophomore year, when my mom became ill, Ms. Claussen would call to see how things were and she would ask what she could do. She really was a mentor for me. Without her, I would not have finished college. I'm not sure what else I would have done but I certainly would have dropped out. She kept saying, "Oh no, we'll find you a job, and find somebody who can tutor you." She gave lots and lots of encouragement and provided the opportunities I needed to stay and graduate.

I just completed my 25th year in the profession. I'm grateful to this woman today because without her, that never would have happened. And it all started with those simple words: "Have you ever thought about being a teacher?"

D. Moritz, 48, Counselor, Omaha, Nebraska

I am a physician and a psychiatrist. I'm the founder of the Center for Attitudinal Healing in Sausalito, California, and I've written a number of books. One teacher that I remember very clearly is a man named Dr. Fishburn, who was at the Brighton Marine Hospital when I interned there in Boston in 1949. I was a dyslexic kid who turned out to be a dyslexic adult. As a kid I was always clumsy, spilling the milk and bumping into things, and I continued that same kind of behavior as an adult. If I tried to carve a turkey, it would invariably end up on the floor! Dr. Fishburn didn't see this in my past and took a particular liking to me. He was able to instill in me a confidence in myself that I had never had before.

Usually when you're an intern, you hold retractors and help the surgeon. In my case, Dr. Fishburn was the guy who held retractors for me while I did the surgery. He wanted me to become a surgeon. That was the last thing in the world I would have imagined myself doing. I always wanted to be a psychiatrist and although I considered the idea, I declined the invitation to go onto residency and become a surgeon.

He was a wonderful teacher in that he saw me in terms of my full potential. As far as he was concerned, there were no limits. That was a wonderful gift.

Jerry Jampolsky, M.D., 70 (chronologically, otherwise ageless), Author, Founder, Center for Attitudinal Healing, Sausalito, California

When I became a teacher, I was assigned to the same building as my former eighth-grade teacher, Myrna Jensen. It was great to be in a different relationship with her than when I knew her as an eighth-grader, particularly because I spent much of eighth grade trying to be a juvenile delinquent. Back then, she just kept a firmness on me, which I needed. I would do things like advance the clock in the class, and somehow this woman would walk right in and she would know that I did it. I couldn't lie to her. She would say, "You changed the clock, didn't you?" And I'd say, "Yeah, I did."

Then I would go to art class, and I would be a real clown in there. One day the art teacher said, "Write your name on the board," because I was always talking. I proceeded to write my name in the largest letters I could, covering the entire board. As I was writing, Ms. Jensen was standing behind me, and I looked around and saw her and I just melted into the floor.

Nonetheless, she must have seen that there was some good in this person who was doing all these attention-getting kinds of things, because she made me the monitor for the principal's phone. When the phone rang, I got a chance to leave the class-room, go and answer the phone and take the message. It was wonderful for me! I didn't have to act out after that. I didn't have to be the clown. Today I would have probably been placed in a behavior-disorder class.

This teacher had this wonderful insight, along with a phi-losophy of win-win. By giving me this special privilege, I won and she won and I didn't feel like I had to go back in and chal-lenge her again. She even picked me for the eighth-grade com-mencement speaker. There were 14 kids in my graduating class, but I thought there were about 4,000 out there. She always said to me, "You'll do okay."

She never raised her voice. She never said anything cruel or in a shaming way. She didn't bully us or call us names. I would get into fights, I would change the clock, I would come in late just to see if she would get upset—I did everything to test her. She always caught me at everything I did, but I never felt less as a person in spite of all the stuff I was doing. I always had the sense that what I did was inappropriate, but *I* was still okay—I never felt that I was an awful person. She was one of those teachers who never smiled before winter break, but I always had the sense that she really did care about me.

D. Moritz, 48, Counselor, Omaha, Nebraska

I had a chemistry teacher in high school who inspired my interest in sciences. She had worked on top secret projects when she was in graduate school. We were told her name was on the patent for a method used to extract uranium from ore. She was a phenomenal woman to have as a high school chemistry teacher. In her chemistry class, we used to do calculations where, using scientific notation such as 6.023×10^{23}, you must perform many multiplications, divisions, cancellations and so on to solve a problem. These equations would sometimes take up several lines of a page. As she worked the problems on the blackboard, it always appeared that she could arrive at the answer in her head, without the use of calculator or notes. At first we thought she knew the answers because she had worked all the problems before.

One day, we challenged her to solve an equation after we changed all the numbers to create a new problem. With the problem written out on the board, we raced her with our calculators to see if we could beat her to the solution, punching the numbers in as fast as we could. She finished before the first of us with calculators, wrote the answer on the board, and said, "See if this is what you get." As we finished the calculations, we looked up to discover that she was indeed correct to the fourth decimal place.

Needless to say, we were quite amazed. I will always remember her. She let you know that anything was possible, that you could do anything if you put your mind to it.

Joseph Dye, 33, Pharmacist, Graduate Student, Laurens, South Carolina

His name is Walt H. and he was my sponsor in AA until his death. He was the first man in my life who seemed to understand the nature of my anger, my fear and my defiance. In the beginning of our relationship, he demanded that I put my trust in him completely if he was going to commit himself and his time to me. Never before had anyone really negotiated with me the terms of a healthy relationship, and certainly never at the core level of trust. He gave me the experience of tough love, the kind of loving direction that parents are often called upon to provide for their children so that in later years there is something to fall back on.

What I learned most clearly from him in these early years of recovery was that I did not know myself very well, and that I was a person who carried unrealistic expectations of himself and others. Because of these lackings inside, I was more than a little resistant toward people like Walt and their efforts to slow me down. After all, if I did what they instructed, I would have had to have been with myself. Fortunately, he was not the kind of person to be easily manipulated or put off. He stood firm with me on my issues and helped me to focus on myself. "No, Bob," he would say to me, "What you are doing will not work. You just have to try and find another option."

Walt was a man who taught me in an adult world that love needed to be unconditional but that relationships were not. This was one of the most important lessons he taught me. In his unique way, he was able to help me slow down, confront my own demons and recognize that what I was looking for had to come from within. He helped me to understand the childlike side of my nature and how to give it healthy direction. He was the first person who challenged me to build my identity from the inside out, instead of the other way around.

Through his mentorship, I began to discover and develop my own inner adult and parent directors who could help guide me through the ups and downs of life. Walt used to say, "The man who knows he is lost is a man who knows a lot." This pearl of wisdom, like so many others he gave me, continues to be a source of strength and hope in my life. "When the student is ready, the teacher will come." And I will be eternally grateful for the teacher I found in this man.

Robert Subby, 45, Licensed Psychologist, Author
Bloomington, Minnesota

When I was in high school, I was often very depressed. I knew I was gay but I thought I was the only one. One day during my sophomore year, I went into the counselor's office and I noticed a sign that read, "If you're gay, you're not alone" and I'm looking around like, "Okay, I misread the sign."

My next step was to tell her about myself and I was kind of scared and uneasy about coming out to somebody I didn't really know too well. I ended up telling her about a gay cousin of mine, and I thought that would break the ice because I do have a gay cousin. Eventually I told her about myself and she gave me a hug and was very supportive and understanding. She said, "You're not alone, and you're very gifted." She gave me a lot of encouragement and some literature, and she gave me the phone number of a youth support group. I went and it was quite interesting.

This woman is known throughout the community for her work, and throughout the years she's really inspired me, and she's taught me so much. I've learned that there's a lot we need to do to make a difference in the world. Since then, I've been a part of a lot of panel speeches, workshops and all kinds of different programs devoted to helping out with gay youth, for example. She's told me about what will happen as I get older—watch for this, watch for that. Basically, she was like a second mother to me. She was really supportive. We found a few of the gay teens in the school, and we just kind of met and sat around in her office, and if she could get her hands on some literature, she would give it to us so we could have something to read and educate ourselves with.

I wouldn't be the person I am today if it wasn't for her because I actually think I would probably still be lost somewhere. She's helped me a lot, and I've met a lot of wonderful people through her.

When I came out to my family, they had a chance to meet her. She's educated them on a lot of issues and she's broken down a lot of stereotypes. She's made it much easier for my family to understand, and some friends of mine as well. When I speak at some of the local colleges around here, I talk about how difficult it was until this counselor came along. The whole counseling department was really supportive because they had the signs up, and they were really, really gay-sensitive. We get a lot of older gay people at these panel speeches who say, "You're really lucky. When we were younger, we didn't have a counselor we could talk to." I feel very fortunate to have had this person in my life.

Ken Collins, 19, Sales Verifier, Omaha, Nebraska

I have had the opportunity to work and spend time with a young man that moved into our district at the beginning of the school year. His name is Jeff. Jeff moved to our community with nearly no credit hours from his last semester at his last school. Although he lives for basketball, he is ineligible for sports until Christmas.

My concern was, and still is, not his ability to play basketball, but the decisions he was making in his everyday life. So we've started going to the school building at 6:30 every morning. We work on a lot of basketball skills, but we spend more time talking about acceptable behavior in our society. Things like language, cooperation, schoolwork, Christian beliefs. Jeff presently is doing C to B work in school. He hasn't been in any school suspensions. The negative behaviors are decreasing. Although sometimes he still talks before he thinks, he is trying.

I have always loved working with young people like Jeff. There is no doubt in my mind that children like Jeff can succeed when given the opportunity to establish a positive relationship. Jeff is really a good young man. He just needs a male role model in his life.

Clark Coco, 39, Drug-Free School Coordinator, Concordia, Kansas

I was 16, a junior in high school, taking Mr. Wheeler's American history class. He was a big, round-faced, barrel-chested man with a bald head and peppery beard. His voice boomed through the classroom, but to me his heart always boomed louder.

I would watch him work really hard to light a spark in a kid who was turned off to school by the third grade. One of our projects had to be something we made with our hands, which allowed the kids who were less verbally skilled to excel. One day I was standing at the podium by his desk, waiting to give the synopsis of the week's current events. He said, "How are you today?" I said, "I feel pretty nondescript." He replied, "Miss Ogorzaly, you will never be nondescript." I could only grin in response, and I don't think I've ever doubted myself a day since.

Gina Therese Ogorzaly, Doctor of Chiropractic,
Albuquerque, New Mexico

There were a number of teachers in my life who had a tremendous impact on who I am today. For example, Mrs. Hart, my fourth-grade teacher, demonstrated that we can have fun while learning—that life shouldn't be so serious all the time.

She instilled the importance of respecting others no matter what their ages, differences of opinions or ability to learn quickly.

Mr. Billet, my tenth-grade history teacher, had us spend half the year studying China—the country, its people and its culture. He taught me to look at the bigger perspective, that my view of the world was a rather narrow one. I learned through his teachings that we can learn a great deal from others if we respect their differences.

Mr. Atkinson, in ninth-grade geometry, and Mr. Bickleman, in tenth-grade biology, gave me memorable, positive experiences by helping me to excel in math and science classes. They instilled a confidence in me that encouraged me to try the assignments. I was often surprised that I actually found their classes fun! I had assumed these classes were "boy" classes until this time.

Ms. Zarfos, or "Z," was my gym teacher several times throughout high school. She made me feel special simply by asking me about my thoughts on things, many unrelated to school activities. She emphasized that what's important is what I do with my life.

Lisa Cramer, 38, Quality Improvement Manager, Federal Way, Washington

Ray Fleming was my history teacher in both my junior and senior years of high school in Palo Alto, California. He was a retired army sergeant who was rather strict. He also happened to be African-American, although back then, in 1967 and 1968, he was "black."

I always had an interest in history, but he gave me a perspective on history that I had never heard before. He opened up a world of education, or lack of education, in the black community that I had not been aware of—the role that black people had played in American history, people like Crispus Attucks and Sojourner Truth. In 1967 and 1968, nobody really seemed to be learning about this facet of history except, perhaps, anthropologists.

Ray Fleming introduced me to the need for history to be taught not just to black students, but even more so to white students. When I went on to college, I decided my major was going to be in African-American history. I thought that I would not teach black history to black students, but to white students, in the hope that maybe I could have some effect on stemming the tide of racism. He was a tremendous influence in his love of education and in his love of humanity, all humanity. This was very, very powerful to me. Unfortunately, he died a very young and tragic death the year after I graduated.

How different this was from my experience in college. I went on to San Jose State, majoring in African-American history. My first professor was at the forefront of the militant black movement. I was the only Jewish, white student in an otherwise all-black class, and he introduced me to what it must feel like to experience discrimination. He mostly ignored me, but really taught me what hate was all about from another perspective. When I confronted him at the end of the semester, he said, "I just really wanted you to get a feel for what it was like for a black student in an all-white class. Maybe that will help you for whatever you do, but I think what you're doing is a waste of time." A different approach to education!

I later was involved in school administration and I have taught from time to time at the substitute level. I never really got back that passion to do what I wanted to do in the field of education, although it still exists in my personal life.

David Lapin, 44, Rabbinical Supervisor and Kosher Food Service Consultant, Pittsburgh, Pennsylvania

I had been a high school dropout at the age of 17, and finally I decided to go back to school to finish my high school diploma. The following September, I found out that community college was free. So I thought, "Oh well, what the hell? I'll try it," because college had always been a dream, and I didn't think I'd ever, ever get there.

The first teacher I bumped into was an English teacher by the name of Ralph Hansen. He was an extraordinary human being. I could tell that from the moment I walked into his classroom. He had the kind of rapport with people that automatically created an "I can" attitude that his students would adopt. There was no fear at all in the room. You had to study and work real hard, but he was rooting for people to succeed.

I was scared. I was a 26-year-old wife and mother who had returned to school, and I just knew that those youngsters would be much more intelligent and much more capable. In the middle of a class one day, as we were all preparing to study for a big exam, he said to the entire class, "Listen, if you really want to pass this test, I would suggest you form some study groups. If I were you, I would make sure that Mrs. Redenbach is one of the members of your group." I looked at him and said, "Why?"

In front of the entire class he said, "The reason I say that is that I'm sure that one of these days you will be a gifted teacher." I said to him, "Don't be ridiculous. I don't even like teachers." And he said, "Someday, you'll not only like teachers, but you'll be a great one."

And three years later, when I graduated from the university, they asked me what I wanted to do for graduate study. I thought about Ralph Hansen and I quietly said, "I want to be a teacher."

I think that for me the real crux of the issue is how clearly teachers touch the future. By their actions, their habits and their modus operandi, they have such an enormous impact on people with tiny things that they never, never know begin to make a difference.

Mr. Hansen is now deceased, but each time I stand up in front of my own classroom, I watch myself from afar and I see his habits of leaning close to students and looking into their eyes as he asks them questions. There's a sense of hopefulness and a sense of assurance that they'll have the answers, that they'll have taken responsibility for studying and that they can really be everything they can be. And just as sure as I'm alive, he's still alive, in the work that he has invested in me.

Sandi Redenbach, Educator, Author, Consultant, Davis, California

I guess there's one thing that connects all the different people who influenced my life. The common thread is that they encouraged me to search and to go beyond what I already knew.

For example, my math teacher, Mr. Conrad, sold me all of his photography equipment. He was always amazed when kids had interests outside of playing baseball or other sports. He wanted kids to go on with further education, so he was helpful in explaining all the things about photography and gave me many other photography items to get me started.

I had a history teacher, Mr. Hirsch, who didn't believe in the use of textbooks for the whole class. He thought you should go out and study the world and encouraged us to build things from what was around us.

My English teacher in ninth and tenth grade was just amazed that I was always reading books. He gave me extra free time to do some reading or to use the library to get things done because I had my classwork done before everyone else. I was also reading things above and beyond what everybody was reading at the time. That interest was inspired by my friends, Jerry and Butch. We used to read all the time.

Jerry's Uncle Walter was always building things or trying to do things of a positive nature, like volunteering to maintain a portion of the Appalachian Trail, and helping kids out who didn't have much. He would take us out to the trail and let us experience nature for a while. He had an enriching nature. He was always inquisitive.

All my uncles on my mother's side were very positive and very instructive. Whatever they were doing, they would always try to show me things. They taught me how to shoot and how to hunt, then they took me hunting with them. When we were coming back, I'd tell them all of the different ridges and hills that we were on, and they were surprised because I'd absorbed what I experienced with them. Evidently, I was more observant than the other people they showed the woods of Pennsylvania to.

The kids I hung out with were an influence on me, also, and always in positive ways. Their attitude was always, "Why not try it?" They were very encouraging.

A lot of the people I knew always talked about building their dreams. That's probably the key. It was up to me: I had the talent, and I could make it work. These were people I could talk to, not gurus to follow. I could go to these people and I could get intelligent advice or assistance. They didn't place themselves above me. We were all equal, no matter what our ages were. I now work with a number of plant breeders who are all in their 60s and 70s, but there is no age difference to them. They always go above and beyond in sharing and giving of their time.

The other thing I've noticed is that when you talked to any of these people, no matter how much time had elapsed since your last contact, it's as if the conversation had never stopped. You get together and it just connects, as if there was just a pause in a sentence, and everything flows after that. The teachers I had and the people that I knew that were gifted—you could see them after years, and continue on with the conversation wherever you had left off.

Ed Fitzgerald, 44, Graphic Artist, Hybridizer (Plant Breeder), McMurray, Pennsylvania

Her name is Coeleen Kiebert. She is a psychotherapist in her early 60s who does organizational development work. Most of all, she is a potter, a ceramicist, a sculptor and an edgewalker. She's definitely an evolved, actualizing human being, very much in her power, and a lovely, delightful, graceful woman. Many, many facets of her diamond are polished and continue to be polished. Coeleen is very much into music and she also sings and plays piano. She loves beauty and truth.

She came into my life right after my mother died. She was the one who struck chords in me in my longing for and missing my mother. They live in a similar place.

When I was married, I had a ceramics studio set up for about seven years. I put it down when I got divorced and became an acupuncturist. Three years ago I opened it up again. I was coming out of another long-term major, major relationship, and I knew I had to throw myself into something; something that was completely and totally me and so, so healing.

At that point, a friend told me, "You gotta go meet Coeleen." I saw some of her work, then I went down and met her. It was love at first sight for me, and I think for her, too. The creative process is in her being; it just is a part of her. She also has a tremendous capacity for spaciousness, simplicity and beauty. We've done Tai Chi before we start working, which is really nice. She lives on the coast, with a 180-degree view of the ocean in her studio. She also plays very beautiful music—anything from tribal African music to the most beautiful sonatas or jazz.

It's all inspirational and it all taps into different parts of ourselves. It's a vogue thing now for people to tap into their creative selves from a really deep place, and have it come out and to use the experience as a way to heal or to empower themselves. I've been working with her for these last three years and I've watched how my body of work has been paralleling my inner growth and my inner empowerment, really going into scary places sometimes. Here I find a safe place to express these feelings. There's actual healing of my soul and my creative self spontaneously. I think a lot of it has to do with Coeleen and the environment that she provides.

She doesn't say a whole lot. She'll come around and she'll say a one-liner that will in some way speak to my deeper self, and I'll go, "Ah-ha!" She's full of "Ah-ha's." She's refining herself so diligently all the time. She's become my friend. I think what has happened is that the process of her seeing me, having her as a person in my life, is filling out parts of myself. I would say it is putting colors in my mandala, so to speak—filling in the spaces.

There's also humor and laughter in there. It's making me a richer person because of who she is and where she's taken herself. She's an example and we learn from examples. I have a lot of trust in her and I have a lot of admiration and respect. A lot can happen when those ingredients occur.

Kathleen Marie Pouls, 41, Acupuncturist, Artist, Santa Cruz, California

I am a self-made man. It is necessary to start my story with this statement because that, for a good part, explains why Mr.

Teunissen, a teacher of mathematics, played such an important role in my life. I was born in 1923, as one of the youngest of my parents' eight children that survived their first years. Before I arrived, my father—a crane driver in the harbour of Rotterdam—had given up his job as a skipper. My parents wanted to be involved in the education of their children, but for so many of those there was not enough space on the Rhine barge that served as their home. That move also gave my father the opportunity to have a second job in the evenings, so he could provide his children with a decent living and education. Well, education . . .

The first part of this century certainly was not yet the time of equal chances for every child. And higher education—i.e., high school and further—was not something that "became" children from the working class, less so if they belonged to a big family like ours. So, when I finished elementary school at the age of 12, there were few opportunities available. Furthermore, as a child I had found an outlet for my creativity in woodwork: building boats that could sail in the bathtub and other toys like that. "Born to be a carpenter," my parents concluded. And that meant two years of technical school, after which, at the age of 14, I was legally permitted to have my first job.

Mr. Teunissen was one of the teachers at that technical school. His subject, as I already mentioned, was mathematics. Not that a carpenter in his day-to-day job needs math to figure out how to hit a nail with his hammer. But a first-class carpenter should be able to make a technical drawing of a staircase, for example, that he is going to make. And for that, some elementary knowledge of geometry comes in handy. That was Mr. Teunissen's job: teaching mathematics to some 30 boys that he would see for one hour or so once a week.

Funny teacher he was, Mr. Teunissen. A big sturdy man in his late 40s, who had traveled to and in many places, he was acquainted with different cultures and loved to talk about them. And mathematics seemed to give him a lot of possibilities to do just that. Hardly had he written something on the blackboard, and off he went. Say he wrote, "A squared + B squared = C squared." That was a good reason to start telling about the Greek mathematician Pythagoras. From there to Athens was just one step, and then on to how important ancient Greece was as the cradle of our European culture. Till after half an hour or so, he would say: "Oh, good grace, boys, get your books; we have to do math." The rest of the hour would then be used to do some exercises with that formula.

The next week he would take us to London, and talk about the peculiar attitudes of the English people regarding Britons, animals and foreigners (in that order); or to Paris, walking the Champs Elysées or admiring la Cité Universitaire. And in doing this, he opened new and exciting worlds for us, or at least for me, for whom his stories were a kind of "water on a thirsty field." Was it Mr. Teunissen who awoke in me the longing to go and see the world like he did, once I grew up? He certainly was a stimulus.

Many years later when, at long last, I got the chance to fulfill that dream, I often thought of him, wherever I went all over Europe. These years of traveling started in 1963 with a fortnight in Paris. And of course I did not forget to visit la Cité Universitaire, as a tribute to Mr. Teunissen, who nearly 30 years before had brought me there—during "mathematics" class.

Long before that, I had understood what motivated Mr. Teunissen to this method of teaching: He knew for sure that only a few of the boys in that classroom would ever need mathematics, once they had finished the two years of technical school. I believe that his train of thought was something like this: "The few that will get so far as to really need this stuff in their career will easily pick up what I have to teach them in half the available time. But all of them can do with some cultural education, and this may be their only chance to get some. So, why not give it to them?" And to me, for sure, he has given a lot by doing so.

And now I come to think of it: He really must have been good at teaching math, after all. Not long ago, while clearing away some old stuff, I ran across my school reports from that period. Well, let me tell you that I don't have to be ashamed of my marks for mathematics. I think Mr. Teunissen earns high marks for that. As his pupil, I acquired sufficient affinity with the subject to become, many years later, a "homemade" actuarian and consultant. And for that, too, I give him high marks.

Aadt Jonker, Business Consultant, Earthsteward (Dutch), Lagoa, Portugal

When my son was a junior in high school, we were practicing for college interviews. We came to a question that asked: Which teacher most inspired you in your years of schooling? He thought for a minute and then he said, "Mrs. Gardner, my eighth-grade math teacher." I asked him to explain.

When Jamie was in seventh grade at his private school, that's the point when they made distinctions about which kids would go on to honors track and which would not. Jamie is one of these surfer kids who always gets super test scores but doesn't come across as the most motivated, academic sort of kid in the world. He scored high enough to go into the honors track, but a seventh-grade math teacher said, "You know, Jamie, you don't really act like an honors kid, and I really would not encourage you to go on in that direction." Jamie just kind of said, "Well, yeah, okay," and he just went on to the regular track into eighth grade.

His eighth-grade math teacher worked with him, saw the test scores and talked to Jamie and got to know him. She said, "Jamie, you can really go for the moon on this math stuff. You're really talented!" So she worked with him and helped him make up what he had missed in the honors class so far that year, and got him back on the honors track.

He went on to take advanced math courses, and he scored 780 out of 800 on his SAT math test. He's now majoring in mathematics in college. All it took to make a difference was that willingness to see beyond the blond "surfer kid" image to the real ability and motivation deep within him. Mrs. Gardner just took him on as her own little project! She was going to boost this kid up, and she really did it. That faith that she had in him made a real difference and turned him around in that particular area of his life.

Kathleen Kukea, 46, Coordinator of Curriculum and Instruction, Educator, Kamehameha Schools, Honolulu, Hawaii

It was through the 4-H youth program that I met two individuals who have made a tremendous impact on my life. In 1967 I was awarded a trip to the National 4-H Congress in Chicago. As one of six national winners in home economics, I was fortunate to be seated next to Mr. Edward S. Donnell, president of Montgomery Ward, the sponsor for my trip. I was amazed at how friendly and "ordinary" he was. He said the people in his office would fight over who attended the annual 4-H award banquets. We, the 4-Hers, were the ones treated like royalty!

In 1968 I attended the National 4-H conference in Washington, D.C. At that time the Wyoming delegation also took a side trip to New York City. While in Washington, I was thrilled to have been selected hostess for Mr. J.C. Penney for one of the banquets. During the meal he invited the Wyoming delegation to visit his office while in New York. He appeared to be just like any grandfatherly-type gentleman. Extremely private concerning his family, it was obvious that he was a devoted husband, father and grandfather. His most prized possession was a cane that had belonged to Benjamin Franklin.

Meeting these two powerful and influential men has truly made a difference in my life. Since those encounters, I have not felt intimidated by people with more money or impressive titles because I realized that neither money nor titles makes any one person better than another.

Barb Pearson, 44, Teacher of Two-Year-Olds, Western Nebraska Child Development Center, Scottsbluff, Nebraska

I came to Hardin, Montana, in 1965 and I knew no one in the community. When I started teaching, I had probably 189 students. I was a typing teacher. One of the reasons I was hired was that they had a lot of vandalism on the type-writers the year before, more vandalism than what my $4,000-a-year salary would have covered. I was told that I was to cut down on the vandalism of the typewriters, that I was responsible for them, period.

So one of the rules of the class was that if you destroyed a typewriter, you also destroyed your grade. If there was something wrong with the typewriter from the previous person, you were to let me know so that you wouldn't get charged for it. Well, I had this one student, a troubled kid who I thought was an orphan and was living with his grand-parents. One day he was in class, getting ready to sit down to the typewriter. The typing tables were old and not real sturdy and the typewriters were big, heavy Olympias. Someone either poked him or tickled him and when he reached out to them, the typing table went over with the typewriter hitting the floor.

After all of these years, I can remember thinking, "Oh Lord, why did it have to be him?" And as I started back to the typewriter, my prayer was, "Please let the typewriter be okay." I picked up the typewriter and put it on the table and when I typed on it, it typed beautifully. It didn't even seem like any-thing was bent.

I didn't remember much about the incident other than feel-ing relieved and saying that it was okay. I didn't think much about it. Well, this person was in and out of trouble through-out his youth. He eventually transferred to another school and went and lived with someone else. He ended up dropping out of high school and for whatever reasons, didn't feel like he could come back to school here. Years passed and I was work-ing part-time teaching adult education. One evening this per-son came in to the class and he said, "Do you remember me?" It was the student from that typing class!

And I said, "Yes, I certainly do."

There wasn't anyone but the two of us in the classroom. He said, "Do you remember the incident about the typewriter falling in class?" I said, "Oh, yes. How could we ever forget that?"

He said, "Yeah. You came charging back there like a mad bull." He said, "Do you remember what you said to me?" and I said, "No, I don't have a clue." And he said, "Well, you told me I was born under a lucky star when the typewriter worked."

And I said, "Oh, that's interesting. Were you born under a lucky star?" And he said, "Yes, I was."

He said, "After my grandfather died and I didn't have my high school education or anything and times were really bad, I decided that I was going to end my life. It just wasn't worth it. I started thinking about how I was going to go about ending my life and I decided that I was going to drive and wreck my car." He figured that the best place to do it would be somewhere in Colorado. He said, "I was going to drive off one of these overpasses on the highway. So I got in my car and I was going fast, but when I got to the first overpass there was suddenly a lot of traffic."

He said, "I never wanted to hurt anyone else. I just wanted to end my life. And so I thought this wasn't the place to do it. But I knew that there were two or three more of these overpasses down the road, so I really floored it and I hurried to the next place. The traffic thinned out but all of a sudden, there was a lot of traffic when I got to the next overpass. I couldn't do it there because I'd hurt other people and I didn't want to hurt other people. So I hurried to the third one, and at the third overpass, it was the same way. At that point, I remembered what you had told me, that I was born under a lucky star, and I realized that someone up there didn't want me to die."

And he said, "I just wanted to thank you."

He came back to me and has since earned his G.E.D. We have a real bond, as much as a teacher and student can have. I haven't seen him for over a year, but I know that if he wanted to talk, he'd still give me a call.

Barbara Bennett, 59, Certified High School Business Teacher, Adult Basic Education Teacher, Hardin, Montana

Kalgoorlie is a town on the edge of the desert in Western Australia. It is a gold mining town with deep red dirt and rich orange sunsets. It is the town where my dad worked on the North Kalgoorlie mine, the town where my mum gave birth to my brother, sister and me, and it is the town where I had my first knowing that when I grew up I would be a teacher. I'm not exactly sure when this first teacher thought occurred, but it was early enough for me to think that I was born to teach.

Certainly the desire to teach went hand in hand with the desire to learn. Even then I knew that the best way to really learn anything was to teach it. My first pupils were my pretend friends, friends I made up with my imagination, friends who loved to play football with me, play Tarzan with me and play "school" with me.

I taught them all kinds of things and I taught myself at the same time. What my mum read to Garry and me (my sister came a little later), I would later pretend to read to my pretend friends, and we would all display that learning was fun.

The year I turned six I gained the rites of passage of walking to school ten feet behind my big brother and his friends. Day one was not too successful for me, as I spent the day crying in a corner and was used as the example to other students of what not to be like. Day two was a lot better, when I was moved to Miss Sawyer's class and found Miss Sawyer to be wonderful.

In fact, each of my teachers at Kalgoorlie Central Primary School gave me some special memory that reinforced my early knowledge that I would be a teacher. Miss Sawyer smiled and taught us using colored blocks, and I loved colored blocks. In year two, Miss Carter had us make mangers as we got near Christmas, and I loved making things. In year three, Mrs. Pain read us *The Wizard of Oz,* and books started to live for me. In year four, Miss Mulder introduced the class to Enid Blyton's *Famous Five* and *Secret Seven*, and a desire to write started to live for me as well.

One day in July in year seven, we were all pretty excited because a man named Armstrong was going to walk upon the moon. We didn't have televisions at school, but our principal, Mr. Hopkins, invited our whole class to walk down the street to his house and sit in his lounge room to watch the walk. To this day, I still don't know what left a bigger impact on me, that "one small step for man" or sitting on the floor of my principal's lounge room. In one giant historical event, Neil Armstrong taught me what could happen when teams of people had immense vision and drive; and with one simple act, Mr. Hopkins taught me what impression you could make with a simple act of kindness.

By 1970, and through until 1974, I was a student at Churchlands Senior High School, where some excellent teachers continued to teach me the wonder of learning and the beauty of being a teacher. Mr. Playle was my English teacher in 1971, and he was extremely creative. One day he walked into class and stood on his table and started making chicken noises. After a minute of this he simply looked at us and said "eccentric." This was an introduction to a theme on eccentricity, which led us into heaps of reading and writing and new vocab words. Unfortunately, Mr. Playle was dismissed from the school because his methods were not appreciated by the administration at the time.

In 1973 my English teacher was Gary Hodge, and it was from that moment that I knew I would not just be a teacher, I would be an English teacher, and that in my teaching of English I would be teaching life. Gary Hodge was the first person to ever see one of my poems and the first to praise them. Now, as a songwriter, I often wonder what might have happened if he hadn't looked at my writing and seen something special (as he wrote in my workbook).

Wandering back through my primary and secondary schooling, I feel blessed that my parents and my teachers all combined to plant seeds of learning with creativity and dedication. It obviously worked because so many of the students of Doubleview and Churchlands went on to become teachers themselves. (Many went on to become athletes as well. Eight Churchlands students represented Australia in the 1984 Los Angeles Olympics!)

My influence by wonderful teachers did not stop when I left school. In fact, it took on a whole new era of wonder when I returned to school as a teacher myself in 1979. My first appointment was the opportunity to teach at Wanneroo Senior High School. The staff was hand-picked by the principal, Glynn Watkins, and his deputies, Betty Cockman and Tony Simpson. I was a first year out and was learning my craft from the best of them.

In 1981 I started my many years of traveling, and everywhere I went, teachers appeared. In Israel it was my kibbutz roommate Genia Landa, who taught me not to fear mistakes. His very words were "The first pancake is always lumpy," and since then I have continued to make the pancakes, knowing that practice makes progress. In 1982 I worked as a counselor for Blue Star Camps in North Carolina. Everywhere I turned were lessons for the learning and teachers galore. I was learning from the camp directors, my staff colleagues, the campers themselves, and what I wasn't learning from them all I was learning from moments of wonder in simply soaking in the mountains and lakes of the Blue Ridge.

Each year, each day, each moment teachers appeared, and all because somewhere along the road of life I had been helped to discover that learning is an attitude. It is the vehicle to helping us honor the talents we were born with.

Now, many years down the track, I have the joy and honor of running workshops and seminars for all kinds of educators—principals, trainers, managers, parents, students, teachers, coaches—all over the world. Every time I stand up to tell a story of the art, science and ethics of being a learner and a teacher, I do so as a proud educator paying respect to a host of magical people who helped me to love learning and life. And each day, wherever I may be, I look for the wonder of learning and teaching in every event on this journey through life. We are all learners and we are all teachers, and each of us sets the example for each other.

Glenn Capelli, Educator, East Perth, Australia

Two years ago, I was part of a group of adults studying Hebrew for the first adult Bat Mitzvah class at our synagogue. Normally, this ritual is performed by 12- or 13-year-olds, although when I was 13, only boys were accorded that honor. I worried about doing it properly and about how embarrassed I would be if I made a mistake, since we performed the ceremony in front of the entire congregation. I decided to drop out and told Rabbi Kenneth Cohen, our teacher, how I felt.

He was sure that I could complete my studies and assured me that I would do well. I accepted his confidence and validation and completed what I set out to do. My certificate of Bat Mitzvah is a source of pride and accomplishment for me. It exists, in large part, because my teacher had faith in me and my ability.

Evelyn Mercur, 70, Homemaker, York, Pennsylvania

When I started band at Seymour Junior High, the two band directors there were Kermit Mann and Mr. McGrew. Mr. Mann was always the fun, happy one and I try to teach a lot like him, but Mr. McGrew was the one who changed my life.

I wasn't very good in school. In all honesty, I didn't come to think of myself as being capable of doing anything academically until I was in college. But I remember that music was just fun, it was always fun. I played football and I was real good at football. And I wrestled and I was okay at wrestling. And I ran track to stay in shape for football. But band was great. I was first chair in the best band as a freshman and I stayed there all through high school.

I would do anything to get out of my other classes. Mr. Mann and Mr. McGrew would give me permanent passes for four years to come in during my study hall and work in the band room. Sometimes a couple of my friends would come down and we'd practice or we'd work up songs by ear or play rock songs or whatever we liked.

Mr. McGrew was a runner, stocky and well-built, a teacher through and through. He was professional looking and well organized. The man never cracked a smile with me. He was always the mean one. I remember we were talking in class one day, another tuba player and I, and this kid wouldn't shut up. Mr. McGrew yelled and yelled and yelled, but Bill wouldn't quit talking, so Mr. McGrew threw the baton and it stuck in the bulletin board in between us. I'll never forget that day. Bill never talked again after that.

One day I was in the band room, practicing by myself, when Mr. McGrew came in. Now, Mr. McGrew only stands about 5'6" (if that—he might even be 5'2"). He is a small guy, a very little man and here I am 6'4"—I've been 6'4" since I was in sixth grade. Anyhow, I was sitting in this room and here's the man who never cracked a smile. He walked up to me and I had this big tuba sitting on my lap. He pulled on the bell and made me set it down. He kicked my legs together and he jumped up on my lap! He pointed to me right between my eyes and he said, "I want you to listen to me and this is the only way I can see you eye to eye." Well, I started laughing, you know, 'cause here's this little bitty man sitting on my lap, and he told me that the tuba could make money for me. He told me that it could pay my way through school, that I needed to forget about athletics and go audition. He even offered to drive me. And we went. It still shakes me up to talk about it.

He gave me my first teaching job as a private instructor with his band. He hired me to play in his band. I still play there.

He called me any time he heard of a job that was opening and told me which jobs I wanted and which ones I didn't. He was the first person to tell me I needed to be a teacher. It was kind of funny after being such a poor student. And here I am. . . .

But you know, he's always there. If I'm short a part, he'll send me music. I can say, "Hey, I don't know how to do this." He'll say, "Try this." If I need a horn, he'll lend me a horn. I don't think there are too many people around who can say that they've had a teacher who has supported them from seventh grade through college and, you know, I'm 30 years old and he's still teaching me. He's still in my life, real strong. He played in my wedding. I just wish that everybody could see how much so many of the teachers care. It's important. He not only changed my life, he gave me one.

Richard Branaman, 30, Band Director, Elementary Music Teacher, Medora, Indiana

At Cherry Hill High School West, Phyllis Omenson was my Spanish teacher for three years. I always did well in her class, but I never thought I was fluent enough in conversation. Mrs. Omenson would sit out in the hall with me during lunch or free periods and speak Spanish with me. We corresponded while I was in college, always in Spanish. Although I gave up Spanish as a major, I wound up teaching for a while in a bilingual preschool as the only non-Puerto Rican staff member, and later tutored many of my high school students in Spanish. I still love the language, and I thank Phyllis Omenson for her friendship and inspiration for those many years.

Berna Levine, 46, Special Education Program Coordinator, Marietta, Georgia

Mrs. Margarite Keeling of Louisville, Kentucky was both my master teacher during my student teaching and my little sister's sixth-grade teacher. Mrs. Keeling inspired me to be understanding and appreciative of student differences and to be creative in meeting their individual needs. She was open-minded, caring and interesting, and she made learning fun. She was an excellent model for doing what she asked of her students, including me—her student teacher. Mrs. Keeling made a difference because she looked for the best in her students and helped them succeed. She taught both my sister and me very well.

Fifteen years after I completed my teaching credential courses and student teaching, I was honored by the University of Louisville as the 1991 Alumni Fellow for my teaching and research efforts. Mrs. Keeling and her daughter were on hand to congratulate me and share in the special event. I consider her a major contributor to my own teaching successes. I now train student teachers at San Francisco State University to become effective and caring teachers, using many of the same techniques, approaches and strategies introduced and modeled for me by Margarite Keeling.

C. Lynn Fox, Ph.D., 40+, Education Professor, Tiburon, California

A REALLY GREAT TEACHER IS SOMEONE WHO . . .

. . . believes that children have the right to enjoy their
childhood.
. . . points out areas to their pupils where they can
improve.

> Ahmed, 12, Perth, Western Australia

. . . helps students when they are having problems and
doesn't put them down.

> J.S., 12, Perth, Western Australia

. . . gets along with his or her students.
. . . comes out and plays sport with the students.

> Jamie, 12, Perth, Western Australia

. . . understands and cares.

> Jason, 11½, Perth, Western
> Australia

. . . knows the children well.
. . . knows what the children need and want.

> Kandy, 12, Perth, Western Australia

. . . allows the children to joke around by having a few
minutes of telling jokes but doesn't let the class
get out of control.

> Rebecca, 12, Perth, Western Australia

. . . can actually talk to the most disturbed student— the most closed student.
. . . listens.

. . . just has to be him/herself.
                    Trinity, 12, Perth, Western Australia

. . . helps other people in different schools and on
    other people's carnival days.
. . . doesn't put the students down.
                    James, 12, Perth, Western Australia

. . . knows what kids think is fun.
. . . takes a break from learning to tell us stories.
. . . lets kids participate in everything.
. . . lets kids share their feelings.
. . . tries to incorporate the lesson with things that
    are fun, like skits, artwork or different projects.
                    Lily, 13, Rye, New York

. . . remembers what it's like to be a child.
. . . understands how kids think and knows what kids
    like.
. . . divides homework up over a period of days, so you
    don't have to do it all in one night.
                    Jena, 13, Mequon, Wisconsin

. . . plays with us and brings Miss Piggy to watch us
    clean up.
                    Kara, 4½, Mahtomedi, Minnesota

. . . cares for his students as much as he cares for his own
    kids.
                    Richard, 10, Oakdale, Minnesota

. . . lets you play outside every day.
> Ryan, 7, White Bear Lake, Minnesota

. . . is enthusiastic and has energy that is contagious.
. . . is unpredictable and has a bright smile, which
helps to make learning fun and exciting.
> Katie, 17, White Bear Lake, Minnesota

. . . never stops teaching.
. . . is always sharing the knowledge she has and
learning new things to share.
. . . can think, act and be like a child.
> Heather, 14, Mahtomedi, Minnesota

. . . can tell a dumb joke every day of school.
> Zach, 17, Mahtomedi, Minnesota

. . . is someone you can trust all the time.
> Sverre, 8, Anchorage, Alaska

. . . does art projects.
> Aislinn, 8, Anchorage, Alaska

. . . not only helps you to spell, but to understand how
to spell, too.
> Alice, 10, Callington, Cornwall,
> England

. . . comes over to cheer you up when you're upset so
you can get it out of your system.

. . . gives you a lot of confidence in your work and reading.

. . . is delighted to come over to your seat and tell you more details about your work.

Thomas, Callington, Cornwall, England

. . . helps you realise your talents and abilities.

. . . gives your life a boost.

. . . helps you back on the right track when you go wrong.

. . . pushes you to be better at everything you do.

Luke, 10, Callington, Cornwall, England

. . . is not afraid to teach what is right and wrong, because some parents won't do it.

Renee, 18, Mays Landing, New Jersey

. . . has the patience and understanding to get inside a student's head.

Jennifer, 17, Mays Landing, New Jersey

. . . takes time to regard the students as individuals.

. . . is able to use different methods of teaching.

Rachel, 17, Mays Landing, New Jersey

. . . can find a happy medium between being too strict or too lenient.

. . . can talk to and reach students who are having problems inside or outside of school.

Mark, 18, Mays Landing, New Jersey

. . . relentlessly gives of herself to further not only the
    education but the growth of her students.
. . . shapes the way students become responsible,
    aware, individualistic and independent.
. . . never gives up.
                    Amy, 17, Mays Landing, New Jersey

. . . ignores all precedents and designs her own curriculum.
. . . designs a system that helps each student individ-
    ually to reach their potential without feeling that
    they are competing.
. . . conceives each student as her responsibility for
    almost a year of growth and maturity, as if they
    were her own children.
                    Joshua, 17, Mays Landing, New
                    Jersey

. . . knows that a student can teach and a teacher
    can learn.
. . . integrates him or herself into the learning environ-
    ment, literally taking a seat among the conglomerate
    of desks, proving that he or she enjoys associating
    with the minds made of sponges, ready to absorb.
. . . appreciates that what one thinks and says is
    more important than what one uses to fill in the
    blanks.
                    Krista, 17, Mays Landing, New Jersey

I met Roy Pierson, a management consultant, in Chicago on a peer review of a Head Start program. On the same trip was another professional, a woman named Mattye Nelson. Both of these people are African-Americans. We were all on a team evaluating the program.

In the evening, most of us would get together and have great and lengthy discussions about the problems of the world. One night I was listening to these two people talking about political strategy. Hey, Chicago is a very political place, where children grow up with political savvy. It's a major subject of discussion. But while I was sitting and listening to them, I started to feel very, very young and very small. I was like the Incredible Shrinking Woman. I kept feeling smaller and younger and very naïve. I didn't even know what they were talking about. But more important, at the same time I felt surprised! I had accepted the fact that Chicago's white residents grow up with political savvy, but it had never occurred to me that Chicago's African-Americans could be politically astute. Hence my surprise.

As I look back, I feel very lucky that I identified the feeling of surprise, because with that came a tremendous, blinding light saying, "Why are you surprised?" And then I was overcome with shame. I asked myself, "Oh my God. Why am I surprised that these people, who are African-American, know more than I know?"

It was like an encounter kind of experience. I thought, "Well, if I've been perceiving this wrong, maybe I've been perceiving other things wrong."

In the next few months, I did a lot of reading of African-American literature, and I did a lot of crying. Finally I thought, "It's time to get on with my life. I can't do anything about how unaware I was in the past, but now I can do more, and I can do it better, because now I am more aware. Now I can plan more appropriate action whenever I encounter bias and stereotyping." I've learned that with awareness and understanding, appropriate action evolves naturally. The right words come out of my mouth if I am emotionally aware. My understanding changes and becomes more complete. I can see opportunities for teaching anti-bias everywhere that I might have missed before.

You know, I've been writing two columns a week for the *Detroit Free Press* for over ten years. I'm in about 100 papers on the Knight-Ridder Tribune wire. People say, "How did you get that job?" Well, I'll tell you, I went and bothered the *Detroit Free Press* for seven years, from 1977 to 1984, until they said "Yes." And you know, I think it was good that they didn't let me start the column until 1984, because I wasn't really ready. I wasn't aware enough in 1977. I wouldn't have been able to write good answers to the kinds of questions we get from today's parents. I'd had very stifled, narrow, middle-class attitudes. I hadn't been out there in the real world. So I'm glad that God didn't let me do it, because I couldn't have done it right.

Roy Pierson, who became a longtime friend, put this concept into words for me. He would say that when you're dealing with racism and most other human issues, awareness has to be first, then understanding, then action. That whole thing of letting go and letting God is a part of that. You have to be aware and understand, but you must let people make their own choices whenever you are consulting or advising them.

Roy's mother, who is named Evelyn Pierson (this used to be a little joke between us), was also helpful to my growth. When I would get really frustrated and impatient with things in my life that were not happening as I wanted them to happen, I would call her up and we would talk. She would sing me this song about God being there for you. And she'd sing in her soprano voice about, "He's not there when you want him, but He's always right on time."

Evelyn Petersen, 58, Early Childhood Education Author, Consultant, Head Start Trainer, Parenting Columnist, Traverse City, Michigan

Many people have contributed toward helping me to become the person I am. First of all, my parents, Mr. and Mrs. Albert Fujii, were very positive people who encouraged me to do what I wanted to do as long it was not detrimental to my growth. Although I was brought up as a Buddhist, I was allowed to attend churches of other faiths. I was not forced to attend the university, but somehow it was an expectation.

I remember Mrs. Eleanor Kukea, my third-grade teacher, who gave us extra responsibilities in class. There were three Franceses in class and we were often asked to help write assignments on the chalkboard. That made us feel pretty important.

In the seventh grade I had Mrs. Katherine Fong for homeroom. She told me that I had done well in my standardized test. Although she did not tell me that she was going to recommend me for a higher group, I know she must have been responsible for my being recommended for the college-bound track.

Mr. Minoru Ezaki encouraged me into a leadership role. He was my principal in 1961 when I was teaching kindergarten. He counseled me to apply for the Administrative Internship Program, which would lead one to become a principal or an education officer. I declined at that time, since my third child was only one year old and I was not ready to take the challenge. Eight years later, I applied for the program and became an education officer.

As I was registering for a summer class in 1964, Dr. Roseamonde Porter at the University of Hawaii noticed that I had only one year left to complete my master's degree. She offered me a graduate assistantship for the next school year, to give me a chance to pursue my graduate degree. I was grateful for the opportunity. Thanks to Dr. Porter, to my husband, Albert, as breadwinner, and to the Department of Education, which allowed me to take a professional leave without pay, I was able to obtain an M.Ed. in elementary curriculum.

The graduate degree led me to become a member of Pi Lambda Theta, a professional organization. My friend, Janet Shimogawa Ingils, encouraged me to join. Here was the beginning of a chance to take on some leadership responsibilities. In 1967 I was elected president of Beta Zeta Chapter, a type of position that I was not used to performing, as I had always been a good follower.

In 1982 I met the national president of Pi Lambda Theta, Dr. Helen Diamond. She appointed me to my first national position as a member of the Credentials Committee during the 1983 Biennial Council. Later, she appointed me a member of various committees, such as the Creative Finance Committee, and as chair of the 1985 Hawaii Study Tour. In 1986, her nomination led me to serve as national vice-president. I have continued to serve in this capacity and am now ending my fourth year as international vice-president.

These and many more people too numerous to mention have helped build my self-esteem. I am thankful to all who have been in contact with me to have helped me grow.

Frances F. Shimotsu, Retired Educator, Honolulu, Hawaii

Harriett Edwards was known as a tough sixth-grade teacher. She was not too different from many teachers of that era. She wore long dresses, cotton stockings and low-heeled shoes. Her gray hair, which was almost all white at age 60, was always formed in a neat bun at the nape of her neck. She presented a serious countenance, but frequently her eyes would twinkle at something humorous and her face would break into a big grin. She challenged those of us in her class well beyond what we felt we could do. But most important of all, she believed in us and made each of us feel special. A common expression of hers was, "I'm sure you can do this or I wouldn't have assigned it to you!" She expected neat papers, correctly done, or she wouldn't accept them.

She assigned the memorization of extensive material each week, including Shakespeare and most well-known poets. She challenged us with problems in science and math because she believed we could think for ourselves. She never professed to have the answers, but instead expressed wonderment and curiosity in ways that made us seek information. She would ask, "Did you ever wonder why . . . ? Why don't you look into this and report back to the class."

She was a great listener and was always available after school or at home to answer questions about anything. It was not uncommon for six to eight of her students to sit around her desk until 4:00 in the afternoon talking about a variety of topics. I can recall a favorite pastime on Saturday mornings was to visit her home and discuss her fond memories or her favorite characters from literature. Even after we left sixth grade, she was always interested in what we were doing and kept in touch with most of her former students. The outcome: 18 of the 27 students in that class became teachers or school administrators because of our love for education and because of Harriett Edwards.

Bob Reasoner, President, International Council for Self-Esteem, Port Ludlow, Washington

The day after 323 students graduated from our local high school, I learned one reason why my friend, Janet, received the newly-established, student-determined Teacher of the Year Award. My friend and I had decided to celebrate the end of the school year with a shopping and lunch outing. As we walked along the mall, she suddenly said, "Wait a minute, I just want to pop in this store to see if one of my students is still working here." As I entered the store, I saw my friend and a young girl deep in conversation. They stopped long enough for introductions. Then teasingly, I asked the student, "Oh, were you one of the seniors corrupted by Mrs. Cutler?" The girl became very serious, tears surfaced to her eyes, and she looked right at me and said, "Actually, Mrs. Cutler saved my life."

Janet replied, "You were worth it," and then continued catching up with the student's news. As we left the store I asked, "What was that all about?" Janet replied, "Kim was having some huge family problems: Mother an alcoholic, Dad gone, boyfriend giving her a hard time. She had been absent the total number of days allowed by the school district. If she was absent one more day she would not graduate. So Kim and I made an agreement. I would call her every morning for the remaining eleven mornings and harass her, and she would come to school. I just had to tell her to get her rear in gear and hit the road to school. One day it took four phone calls. But she made it and graduated."

When I remarked how wonderful I thought this was, that a teacher invested the time and interest to help a student in this way, my friend remarked, "Someone had to," and changed the subject.

Peggy Bielen, Executive Director of Enhancing Education, Newport Beach, California

I went to school in Pigeon, Michigan, which is a small farm community in the Saginaw area. I had been a product of a one-room country school for my first nine years, kindergarten through eighth-grade. There was one teacher for eight grades, a coal-burning, potbellied stove, outdoor toilets and no running water. That was my first nine years of school.

The first teacher that comes to mind is my high school math teacher, Reva Leipprandt. I had her for all four years of high school math because it was in a small high school, where we only had one math teacher. She also taught my father, who I believe graduated in the 1920s. She taught all nine of the children in my family, and even had a few of my oldest sister's children, so she taught three generations.

If she taught my father, she was old when she taught me, but every teacher is old to the children. I assumed she was probably in her fifties when she taught me, which meant she wasn't very old, especially as I'm talking now and I'm in my fifties. I would guess the main reason that I appreciated her and thought she was such an excellent teacher is that she was very, very strict in class but never mean or cross. She was strict in a very kind way. We also all knew that she had eyes in the back of her head, which, having been a teacher myself, I know is a prerequisite for being a good teacher. We never got away with anything when she was up at the board, even when she had her back to us. She always saw what we were doing. We never could figure out how, although I know now it's because teachers have that sixth sense, those eyes in the backs of their heads.

She expected us to do our best but didn't expect all of us to get A's. She never made those students in her class who got C's feel as though they were less important than those of us who got A's. She made everybody in the class feel important as long as they were doing their best, and to be very honest, you did your best in her class, because she expected it and you knew that. Interestingly enough, I ended up being a math teacher. That's usually the way it works.

Some time in the early 1980s, I was an usher in People's Church in East Lansing, Michigan. One Sunday when I went back to get my boutonniere before the service started, I saw this little, frail lady standing there and I recognized her right away. I said, "Mrs. Leipprandt, what are you doing here?" She was close to 90 years old then. She had been retired for years and was living in a rest home in East Lansing. She said, "I saw your name in the bulletin. I was here at the first service and I saw in the bulletin that Keith Geiger was an usher in the second service. I had to make sure that I stayed around to say hello to you and wish you the very best." This was 25 years after I had her as a teacher.

Another teacher, Carl Emerson, was special. He went to the same church I did, and not only was he my social studies teacher in high school, but he was also my Sunday School teacher. But I think the thing that made him special was that he always went out of his way to come up to you and talk to you in the hall, and ask you how you were doing and how you were doing in your other classes. It didn't matter whether he was my social studies teacher or whether I was in somebody else's class. He always came up to me in the hall and talked to me about my other classes. He cared about everybody.

And finally, there was Bob Waterworth. I think I probably had him in his first or second year of teaching, and I also had him for social studies. He was an excellent social studies teacher, and the thing I remember best about him was, where I went to school, if you were a Democrat with a capital D, you were in the vast, vast, vast minority, like maybe one or two in a class. Bob was a Democrat with a capital D, and it was obvious to everybody in the class. But he was able to engage students in debates on political topics without it becoming an "us versus them" situation. It would have been easy for him to do that if he were in a community that was overwhelmingly Republican and he was a Republican. But he was a Democrat, and everybody in the class knew it, but it was never a problem.

Keith Geiger, 51, President, National Education Association, Washington, DC

Let me set just a little bit of background about my own life during the time that this particular teacher was significant. I had never been a very good student, from very early in school. It wasn't that I wasn't bright. I probably was very bright, but I was kind of a behavior-disordered child, always in lots of trouble. Ordinarily, when teachers found my name on the roster for that year, they would either retire or select some other student to take my place.

My eighth-grade English teacher, Miss Connors, was very special to me—not because of anything she did with me or for me or to me, but just by virtue of the way she conducted herself in the classroom. The thing I noticed about her right away was that she never raised her voice. She was a lovely, controlled person. In my life, most of the people I had been around seemed to me to be a bit out of control, which, interestingly enough, was what I was considered to be.

Miss Connors always smelled wonderful. She dressed in business suits and looked extremely clean, tidy and neat. She wore her blond hair pulled straight back in a wonderful chignon, a bun at the nape of her neck, and never had a hair out of place. So for me, she was perfection. She looked like perfection, she smelled like perfection and she acted like perfection. She behaved like my idea of what it meant to be at peace, and having come from an extremely dysfunctional home, that was something I didn't know much about, being at peace.

But the interesting thing about Miss Connors, and how she connected with me, is that she didn't seem to know who I was. She wasn't one of these people who looked at my name with fear struck in her heart. She treated me the way she treated every other child in the room. That was so significant to me, that I'm sure she is the person who has shaped the kind of teacher I have been for the past 20 years. It would never occur to me to treat any child differently from any other child because of his behavior, appearance or ethnic background.

She taught us Shakespeare that year, a play called *The Merchant of Venice*. I was in a school system where I was sort of an oddity, if you're looking back on it from a current-day, multicultural perspective. I'm Jewish; most of the students in that class were Protestant and didn't really have a sense of what being Jewish was all about. So when I heard that she was teaching *The Merchant of Venice* and I discovered, through her synopsis, that it was about a Jewish moneylender who lent money to a Christian, I immediately got very, very nervous. But in the hands of this gifted teacher, this play became a very clear vehicle by which to show how closely connected and how human all people are, how everybody experiences the same hopes and fears and feelings and desires. She showed all the class that both Antonio and Shylock were victims of circumstances. Their greedy and selfish motives became more human and understandable in the way she instructed the class.

I don't know just what it was that created this solid bond of love that I feel for Miss Connors even to this day, and it's many, many years since I was an eighth-grader. But she was a magic sort of teacher, who really let all of the class know that human beings are simply people who have feelings that are necessary to understand in order to begin to understand the human condition. She made an incredible impact on my life by virtue of the fact that she treated everyone equally, and that she didn't put any boundaries on the possibilities of any of us in class. She didn't operate on reputation as sometimes teachers do. She allowed everybody to be exactly who they were. She was open to everyone's ideas and everyone's contributions. I don't know if any other students in the class had the same kind of experience from her, or if she had that kind of effect on anyone else, but I can tell you that years and years later, when I became a teacher myself and started working with students at risk, Miss Connors was the ultimate role model for me, the ultimate way in which I knew instinctively how to treat students in order to get the very best out of them.

Sandi Redenbach, Educator, Author, Consultant, Davis, California

I barely got out of high school with a C average. In those days you could get into the University of California with those kinds of grades, although that's no longer true today.

I had to take an entrance exam in English and I flunked it, so I had to take a dumbbell English course in grammar and spelling. That was always difficult for me and it still is. I believe I got a D- in the course, and the last day of the course the professor came up to me and said, "Jampolsky, I don't know what you're going to do in life, but for God's sake, don't ever try to write a book." I must admit I thought that he was right, and I gave him the power to decide my limitations. It wasn't until after I was 50 years of age that I decided that I did have the potential to write a book and have written several since. I realize that he was a great teacher because he taught me about not giving my power away.

Jerry Jampolsky, M.D., 70 (chronologically, otherwise ageless), Author, Founder, Center for Attitudinal Healing, Sausalito, California

When I was 11, I was 4 feet 9¾ inches tall and weighed 89 pounds; by the time I was 18 I was exactly a foot taller and 59 pounds heavier. How do I know that? It is all part of the information recorded in the report book issued by the school I attended at the time.

I treasure that book. It is now a faded green and has the school name, crest and motto on the front. I can remember virtually no Latin after six years of study, but shall never forget that "Tentando Superabimus" means "By striving we shall succeed."

The whole book is a storehouse of memories. As I look through it and see the names of the teachers and the comments they wrote about my work, people and events come flooding back. I can see those faces as if it were yesterday and not 40 years ago. How appropriate that the school song, sung at the final assembly each year, should begin, "Forty years on, when afar and asunder parted are those who are gathered today. . . ."

The vigour, the energy, the competent, conscientious approach those teachers took to their work I did not realise, or even really appreciate at the time, but I do know now what a sound education I received because of their efforts. They were working in the most appalling conditions because the war was on, and it was nothing to stop in mid-sentence so that everyone could dive under desks while German planes droned overhead, or to evacuate and run like hell across the field to get in the bushes before the expected air raid. It was rather fun for us, the pupils, having lessons interrupted in this way, but the responsibilities for the staff must have been tremendous. I have no recall about what they said when expected to take their class on a long monthly coach trip to some remote farm in order to contribute to the war effort by picking potatoes, but I can well imagine they were thinking that they were not trained for this! All this missed time had to be made up, and I sincerely believe the highest standards were maintained in spite of it all.

My happiest memories are of the sheer wit employed in their teaching styles, certainly enough to keep me well awake and concentrating on the work in hand, and often provoking a roomful of laughter. Each one had his own unique mannerisms, which, as you can imagine, were studied intently by all of us. The Head had a habit of checking his fly frequently when standing in front of assembly of 600 boys. Perhaps this indicated he was not as confident as he appeared, but who knows? Rather aloof and stern, my gut feeling about him now was that he was a kindly man, and I have no grudge against him for giving me one stroke of the cane after a harmless scuffle in the hall. He must have been having a bad day. I know that he brought Shakespeare alive for me when he spent a year teaching literature to the fourth form.

All the teachers had nicknames, of course. One was called "Tank" because he was built like one, and when he got on his moped to go home, moved like one. It was a wonder to behold because he completely covered the little machine and appeared to defy gravity as he went along the street. A crowd gathered to watch every day. He used to refer to his "relatives in the western Desert." He taught me Latin and Greek with the greatest patience.

The one I remember best, however, and the one I believe I have most cause to be grateful to, was a man called Bailey. I can see from the report book that his initials were T. L., but all the boys called him Ticker. I can't remember the reason.

He was over six foot, or at least seemed like that in comparison with me at the time. He was very thin on top and big built. He stood out from the rest, however, because of his age. He was much younger than the rest of the staff. Being wartime, all the fit and able had been called up for service, so we were in fact in the hands of the older generation.

Except for Ticker. He was with us because he was unfit. He had frequent severe upsets in class that used to scare the hell out of me. He would be talking normally, then begin to slow and slur his words and eventually stop. I seem to remember he put his handkerchief to his mouth. There would be an embarrassed silence and then he would resume as if nothing had happened. All except one time, when he made the mistake of sitting on a desk so that when it happened, he fell off and knocked himself out. Someone did run for help that time.

I suppose if there had not been a war on he would not have been teaching, and I would not have had the opportunity to have contact with such a gifted person. He was my form teacher when I entered the third form. Up till that time my report book indicates that my performance in school had been indifferent to say the least, and the teachers' comments mainly ran from "Fair" to "Very Fair." From the third form onwards the picture changed completely, with "Excellent" being the key word, although I notice the Head had to qualify his praise. He wrote, "I have rarely seen a better report, though some subjects need attention." (Some teachers cannot seem to resist the sting in the tail, can they?)

I attribute this change to Ticker. I'm sure it was not his physical condition that made me like and respect him so much, keen and willing to accept his advice and suggestions. I don't think it was his teaching of English that persuaded me either, although I'm sure he was good at his subject. I would even deny being influenced by his brave attempts to introduce sex education into form periods to a class of embarrassed, sniggering adolescents. No, it was just the way he had of making his relationship with the class special. He knew exactly how to create an easy, relaxed environment that gave people the motivation to learn. He gave me just the right balance of challenge and support that I needed at that time. I would describe it as a subtle confrontation; it was just right to get my motors running. Had it been too sharp, my habit was to withdraw and pull up the drawbridge; too soft, and I would ignore it. He got it just right; he certainly made a very significant contribution to the development of my self-esteem.

What he did for others only they can tell. What he did for me affected my life completely. I shall be eternally grateful.

Murray White, U.K. Representative, International Council for Self-Esteem, Cambridge, England

Her name is Helen Coverdale and I took French from her. She was the type of teacher who understood what it was like to be bashful. My folks came from Lebanon and I had a little bit of a complex being from foreign-born parents. I was very bashful and shy. I couldn't look anyone in the eye and talk. She understood how to handle somebody like me.

She'd say, "Now look here. You're just as good as the next person. Speak right up and look at me when you talk!"

She had a great sense of humor. There was a kid in our school who wanted to take French 3 and he hadn't even taken French 1. I tried getting him into our class. She told him, "You can't take French 3. You didn't even have French 1." He said, "Well, I already know a lot of French." She said, "Yes, but not the kind we use in French class." Even though this kid wasn't prepared for French, she turned that aside, to make a cute little joke about it. She was wonderful. She wasn't the kind of a teacher who worked best with only the brainy students. She liked somebody she could help develop and mature. She did that with me.

Back in those days, teachers were on the same plane as priests or doctors or lawyers. Everybody respected them. Helen was a strong believer in parent-teacher relationships, in keeping in touch with the children's families. We used to invite teachers into our homes back in those days. She'd come and she'd talk to our parents and say, "Oh, George is doing very well in school." And while my folks weren't sure whether I was doing well or not because they didn't understand English, it was very gratifying to them that she visited.

She worked with me nights after school. If I had a tough French assignment that I couldn't get, she'd stay after school with me and go over it. I had to have three years of a language to get a Regents Diploma. She stayed right with me. She said, "I'm gonna make sure you get all your requirements because sooner or later you're gonna go on to college and we want to do all we can to help you." My parents were proud of me, you know, because I stayed in school. Helen talked to my folks and encouraged them to let me go on to college.

My wife had her, too, and Helen interested us both in horticulture. She said, "You ought to go on to college and make that your life's work. You ought to get a degree." Without Helen's influence and guidance, I would never have finished high school and gone on to Cornell University. Without her encouragement, my wife and I would never have accomplished the things we did—together. We've been married 53 years, survived five-and-a-half years of World War II apart from each other. We collaborate on everything together. We've written 12 books and we do a radio and television program together.

I never have forgotten Helen Coverdale. We see her once a year. She still has a great sense of humor.

George "Doc" Abraham, Horticultural Journalist, Naples, New York

My high school English teacher, Bill Hogan, had the problem class at the high school, which was my class. We were the discipline problems. We were all real bright, hyperactive kids who got bored easily. We were known as a difficult class to teach.

Bill Hogan was absolutely extraordinary, and part of the reason was he just had tremendous energy. He would do unbelievable things to keep us going and focused. He used to walk into the class every day and he would do something at the beginning of class just to grab everyone's attention. It was almost like a vaudeville act! He would sometimes come into class in costume, sometimes he would come in reciting poetry at the top of his lungs. He had this really dramatic flair to him.

One of the things I remember most was an assignment that seemed very odd, but absolutely captivated the class. He walked into class in a very somber attitude, while everyone was sitting around and chatting. He reached his hand into his briefcase and he pulled out an empty beer can. He slammed it down on his desk and said, "What is this?"

Everyone thought, "Oh, God, who's been drinking on campus?" No one wanted to say anything!

He shouted, "What is it?"

Some smart-aleck kid said, "It's a beer can."

He said, "Ah! It only looks like a beer can! Do you realize how many of these are out there in the trash and on the side of the highway? For your assignment I want you to come up with things that you can do with this empty beer can that we can make money off of. Write up a proposal for it as if we were going to the Patent Office." That was the assignment.

I don't even remember half the things that people did, but they did these absolutely wild things with beer cans! One guy came in with a beer can painted black, with a fuse sticking out of the top. He walked up and put it on Mr. Hogan's desk. Hogan was looking at him like, "Oh, God, what have I done here?" The guy pulled out a lighter and he lit the fuse. Hogan sat there with a silly look on his face while the guy ran to the back of the room and cowered and everyone got up from their chairs and hid in the back of the room, also. Hogan was staring at this thing knowing full well that it was not really going to explode, and the fuse burned down right to the very top of the can. Meanwhile, there was a guy at the back of the room who had inflated a bag. And when the fuse burned down, there was a huge explosion! Hogan was practically crawling up the side of the wall, grabbing onto the blackboard! That was typical for that class. It was a totally free, wild, interactive class. But he managed to captivate people and get them excited about using their brains. I think about him a lot. He taught me that imagination in learning is really fun. There are no wrong answers when you are talking about creativity.

He was a very good English teacher, but he was not interested in being the perfect grammarian. He was much more interested in getting people to take risks in their writing, in terms of what they were writing about and how they wrote about it. I'm a writer today, and I think a lot of that really has to do with Bill Hogan letting me know how much fun it could be to just let your imagination go wild and then try and do something with it.

Will Glennon, 46, Publisher, Writer, Attorney, Berkeley, California

This summer I was attending a wedding and one of the bridesmaids was a former fifth-grade student of mine. She greeted me with the usual niceties that we receive from former students, then she said, "Mrs. Peterson, I remember one day when I was in your class and I talked you into postponing our spelling test to the next day because I wasn't ready for the test. You said that, yes, that would be okay if the rest of the class voted to do this, too."

Then I responded, "And now, Dawn, ten years later, it really didn't matter, did it?"

Wow! The things our students remember about us!

Yvonne Peterson, Elementary Teacher, Ceresco, Nebraska

My grandfather was six feet tall. He was big and I was a very little girl. Every time he saw me, when I visited my grandparents at their farmhouse, standing in the kitchen, he always smiled at me, and then he would take my arm and rub it up and down. I didn't know what that meant, but obviously it meant something. He would say to me, "Sora Yenta"—that was my Hebrew name—"some day you're going to be rich." And my mother would repeatedly say, "Don't tell her that! That's not something you should tell a little girl." But he always would.

And then my father used to do something else. My father used to say to me, "Turn your hand toward you and look at it, and what do you see?" And I'd say, "I see an M." He'd say, "That means money. Now turn your palm upside down the other way, and what do you see?" And I'd say, "I see a W." And he'd say, "That means you have to work for it."

What I'm trying to say is that these events had a definite effect on me. It gave me a mind-set for success. I remember when I was in seventh or eighth grade, we had a magazine sale. I don't remember even what the prize was. I have no idea. But I sold more magazines than anyone in H. L. Reber Junior High School. They asked me how I did it, and I said, "It was easy. I went out when it rained. I think people didn't want me out there in the rain, so they all bought magazines." Can you believe it?

I went into teaching because when I graduated high school, you had three choices. One was to get married, and that was horrible to me, like ending your life. I mean it. Get married and have someone boss you around? The second option was to be a nurse. Well, I had had my appendix out when I was 15, and I definitely didn't want that.

So I decided on the third choice, which was to be a teacher. I tried to be a good teacher but never really got into it. The other teachers I worked with didn't like teaching and all they talked about was their retirement. I decided I was too young to plan my retirement.

After my mother died, I decided that there had to be some major changes in my life. I decided that I wanted to be a money manager. I really loved anything and everything that had to do with business and money. In 1972, it was tough for a woman to get into this business, but I decided that the worst thing I could do was fail, and I didn't think I was going to fail. I remember walking out of Drexel feeling very bright. I had a good feeling about myself, that I was smarter than most. I think it was a combination of those predictions of my father and my grandfather that gave me that self-confidence.

I still feel today that I can do anything I want. This belief layers over into everything in my life. For example, here it is a few days after a terrible crash of a commercial airline, and I'm planning to fly that same airline out to help my daughter-in-law, who's about to give birth. My daughter called me last night, upset, and said, "Mom, I don't want you flying that airline. I want you taking the train." She said, "Aren't you scared?"

I said, "Not really."

She said, "But look what happened. It could happen again."

I said, "It won't happen again, honey." You want to know the truth? I'm not scared. I figured that was a freak accident and it's not going to happen to me, and I really believe that. I'm excited about going. I'm not fearful, and I feel that way about my life in general.

I think that the things that happen to you early in life either produce good feelings about yourself or bad feelings about yourself. And these feelings can come from the things that a parent, grandparent or teacher might say or do without realizing the effect they're going to have on you. It's always little, tiny, quiet, insignificant things that at the time seem like nothing, but in the end can have an impact on a person's life that is absolutely staggering.

Shirley Rich, 63, Vice President, Legg Mason Wood Walker, Philadelphia, Pennsylvania

It's so hard to pick a single mentor because there are so many people who influence your life as a professional. I think it's especially true when you work with children and families because you meet so many wonderful teachers and parents, and all of them have an impact on you. But I think that for me, one of my turning points came a long time ago, maybe 20 years or so, when I was teaching and directing a cooperative pre-school.

I was licensed by a Child Care Licensing Consultant by the name of Blythe Whalen. She was, oh, probably 10 or 15 years older than I, and she was a very positive person, very low-key. She would never tell you what to do. She would ask you questions and she would have great patience, waiting for you to mull them over and think about them, and maybe even weeks later tell her what you thought. But she made you come to your own conclusions, and she made you do your own growing by the questions she'd ask.

The stumbling block for me at that time was something I think many teachers have to get past. It's sort of an ego trip to teach, and especially to teach young children, because it's so much fun. But sometimes you get so "into it" that you think you have to do everything and you end up doing it all. So many people in the early childhood field are helpers—they want to fix things, they want to rescue, they want to control everything so that everything will be nice and smooth. I needed to involve my students' parents more fully; being in a co-op, this was especially important. But I was doing too much myself and not involving my parents enough. Blythe Whalen, by her questions, helped me to see that I really didn't have to do everything by myself. I didn't have to control every minute of the day. Some of the parents could do things far better than I, such as sing, play the guitar and tell stories.

The other part of this same problem is sort of a mind-set that many of us in the early childhood field have about our philosophy, and about things like hands-on learning and free-choice time for children. We sometimes start believing that our style of teaching is the best and only way, and that everybody should do it our way and why in the world can't they see it?

Blythe Whalen helped me learn to be patient with people, to accept them where they are now, and not where I want them to be. Her modeling of this kind of attitude and her patience and acceptance really helped me. When I began to see that I needed to be more aware, and I needed to be more accepting, I was able to be more patient with parents and teachers who had different philosophies and teaching methods.

This was extremely important, because in the next years, I became a Child Development Associate Representative. The CDA credential is a competency-based national credential given by the Council for Early Childhood Professional Recognition. As a Representative, I evaluated 450 teachers in nine states for their CDA credential. As a true professional, I could not go into an observation and assessment situation and be judgmental. I had to accept that teachers have their own style and their own philosophies. My job was to learn whether or not teachers were competent. That's really all that mattered. Their style of teaching didn't have to be like my style.

The same thing is true of program evaluation. I do a lot of peer reviews and evaluations of Head Start programs. I have to go into a program as a part of a team. Blythe Whalen's influence has made it possible for me to keep an open mind and an accepting attitude and say, "Why is it that they're doing it this way? There's a reason. Let's find out if that's a valid reason." I do not just jump in and say, "Hey! You must do it my way because my way is right."

Evelyn Petersen, 58, Early Childhood Education Author, Consultant, Head Start Trainer and Parenting Columnist, Traverse City, Michigan

I was a classroom teacher teaching fifth grade. Bob Reasoner was my district superintendent. I thought he did a really wonderful job. At one point, he wanted some feedback on the activities in a book he was working on. I was one of the teachers who tested some of his ideas. Later, when there was an opening at the middle school, Bob suggested that I go there and teach sixth grade. I thought that sounded interesting. I had taught sixth grade before in an elementary setting, so teaching in a middle school would be a new challenge. I was there three and one-half years, and toward the end of that time, he came back from a trip to India, or someplace like that, where he was a keynote speaker at a conference. He handed me a puppet that he had picked up on his trip, saying, "I got this for you when I was there." I thought, "What? He actually brought back a souvenir for me!" I didn't really feel that close to him and was absolutely shocked.

He asked me if I would be a creative art specialist, which would involve working with younger children. I was a little leery because I had never taught first, second or third grade. He wanted me to do puppets and to teach things like dance and singing. It was kind of scary. He said, "I'll tell you what. Take the position for the rest of the year, and if you don't like it, you can come back to your sixth-grade position at the middle school." It was the middle of the year, anyway. I couldn't lose! He gave me the basic framework that he wanted me to follow, then set me free to create the program. It was absolutely unreal that this would happen, that I would be able to plan a curriculum, that he trusted me enough to do this all on my own. I started working on the program and the ideas started flowing. He never even interfered. He would ask me, "What do you need?" At my request, he bought me a stereo and the kind of materials that I would need for the activities I wanted to do, but otherwise, he just left me alone.

Here I was, in charge of all these students. I had three schools. At the time there were 20 classes of 30 kids or so in each. I would see each of those classes once a week for about an hour. I kept thinking, "Bob really has faith in my ability." As a result, I saw tremendous growth in my abilities. I did things that I had previously thought would be fun to do, but seldom took the time to do. I was so excited about my job that I often worked all weekend, in addition to the regular week, on school projects. I would start researching ideas, picking a theme and doing all the songs, dances and activities around that theme. I wrote stories, chants and poetry for the children, composed songs, choreographed dances, wrote puppet dialogues and parodies and learned to tell many stories. I am a ventriloquist, too, so I would start the lesson with a puppet and then do the other stuff that went with it. It has become quite a different type of a job! When I walk in the room, the kids say, "Hello, Mrs. Greene!" like I'm Elvis Presley! I walk into the faculty room and the teachers say, "Oh, am I glad to see you today!" Imagine if every teacher could have this kind of freedom to do what he or she felt was right!

Bob's impact was so intangible. He is very low-key. He never said, "You have to do this." But by taking a special interest in me, believing in me and offering lots of positive feedback, it inspired me and gave me the confidence to try new things. It made me want to do my very best and more. I found that each week I tried to do better than the last. I wanted to live up to the image he had of me.

This experience has opened a lot of doors for me. Not only am I doing things like writing stories and poetry and composing songs, but I've also been published. I write a column in a magazine called *Laugh-Makers Variety Arts Magazine.* I have performed for other schools, for hospitals and at large events. I go to puppet festivals and take classes and workshops. I even present my own workshops to teachers, hoping to inspire them to do similar activities with their classes. This is a direct result of this job, of having a superintendent who came into my room and said, "You can do this!" He truly gave this teacher self-esteem!

Carol Greene, 53, District Creative Arts Specialist, San Jose, California

Probably the most significant and maturing event of my school life was when I got caught cheating on my Spanish final in 11th grade. There were so many of us taking this test that they had us all in the cafeteria. I was sitting in the back of the room but somehow my teacher, George Ziegler, saw my crib sheet. I remember him tapping me on the shoulder and marching me out of the room, all the way through the cafeteria. It was embarrassing from beginning to end.

George's mother had gone to school with my mother, and I thought that their lifelong friendship would have some influence on the outcome of this event. I was sure he'd let me off the hook. But he nailed me. He didn't give an inch. After school let out, I had to go back and spend the first week of summer vacation moving books from one end of the school to the other for several hours a day, cleaning up and getting the school ready for summer break and the following year. He eventually let me take the test over, but he made me work for the opportunity.

The amazing thing was that he managed to maintain a personal relationship with me. I even went to Spain with him for six weeks that summer and stayed friends with him throughout high school. He made me see that my cheating had not been a betrayal of our friendship, but a betrayal of myself. He held me responsible for my behavior but he never held it against me personally. (I did pass the test!)

Steve Blank, 43, Real Estate Salesperson, Denver, Colorado

The teacher I had in the third grade went up with the class to the fourth grade at Donaldson Elementary School in Greenville, South Carolina. Miss Bess Allen was a very strict disciplinarian. She had a little bell on her desk, and any time that anyone in the class was the least bit disruptive, she would hit that bell. When Miss Allen hit the bell, everybody really tuned in to behavior.

One event that made a strong impression on me was when we were sitting in the auditorium listening to one of the students who later became a concert pianist. At the time, I was struggling with piano lessons and Miss Allen leaned over to me and said, "Dick, if you work hard and practice, you, too, could play like that." That kind of overwhelmed me—I never had any idea that I could come anywhere close to that, but her comment alerted me to my potential.

I remember Mr. Bob McClain, a speech teacher I had in high school. He happened to have taught Joanne Woodward, and she gives him a lot of credit for her success. She was a year ahead of me in Greenville Senior High School. In addition to being a very good speech and drama teacher, Mr. McClain was head of the little theater. He taught me to communicate with audiences and with people, and I've used those skills throughout my career.

Another big influence on me was Miss Louise Austin, who taught advanced math and algebra in my junior and senior years of high school. I never felt that I was particularly good in math, but she had very high expectations of me and eventually convinced me that I was very capable in that area. I rose to her expectations. I really got interested in math and made very good grades all through college. Ever since, math has been one of my strongest areas of interest. That usually surprises people, since I went into law and government. She was a wonderful teacher who took a special interest in me. I remember that she would keep me in the afternoon sometimes—not as punishment, but to give me special help because she really thought I had potential in math. She was demanding and I tried to do well for her.

Another teacher who had an impact on me personally and professionally was Miss Mary Wilds. She taught English literature in my senior year in high school. We did Hamlet and Macbeth, and it was through her that I really became interested in Shakespeare. Through her teaching, I developed a real love of poetry and plays and literature. She is still living, and I have corresponded with her from time to time over the years.

I have always had a very warm spot for all of these teachers, especially Miss Austin and Miss Wilds. I was old enough then to begin to truly appreciate education. I was involved in a number of things during that time in my life. I was a student leader and a football player. I also worked at the drugstore in the evenings and carried a paper route. I had an awful lot going on! I really developed a relationship with these two teachers, who were appreciative of all I was doing and still pressed me to pay strong attention to my education. I knew that they were interested in me, and I really tried to produce for them. In the process, those teachers really did have an impact on my life.

Richard Riley, 61, Secretary of Education, Member of
President Clinton's Cabinet, Washington, DC

As a counselor educator I often serve as a consultant to public school systems. During these times I sometimes encounter teachers who seem defeated by their situation. They tell me that their buildings are old, their classes are too large, their students are unmotivated and the parents don't care. They say: "There's nothing I can do." When I hear this I think of Mrs. Field.

During my high school days I was a very unattentive, uninterested and underachieving student. At the beginning of my senior year I was assigned to an American history class taught by Mrs. Field. Although the building was old and the class was crowded, she clearly had great expectations for each student. If homework was not turned in, it was never a matter of if it would be turned in, but when. It could come in today or tomorrow, but it would come in. Mrs. Field thought we were better than we were, so we were.

One day she stopped me as I was leaving her class, waited until we were alone, looked deep in my eyes and said: "Bill Purkey, you can become a good student, I know you can." I made some sort of flip remark and went my way, but her words echoed again and again in my mind. Gradually, I began to risk some small effort in her class. Because of her belief in me, I began to put my mind in the path of learning. Perhaps she saw this as a small victory, but it was a major turning point in my life.

A dozen years later, when I received my doctorate from the University of Virginia, I made a special trip back to my old high school hoping to tell Mrs. Field what a difference she made in my life. When I arrived I learned that Mrs. Field had been killed in an automobile accident some months before. Today, when teachers tell me that there is little or nothing they can do, I tell them what I wanted to say to my most memorable teacher: "When you work with human beings, everything you do makes a difference, and every one of your accomplishments is major." There are no small victories, Mrs. Field.

William Watson Purkey, Ed.D., LPC, Professor of Counselor Education, University of North Carolina at Greensboro, Greensboro, North Carolina

I grew up and was educated in South Africa and attended a very traditional high school, where strict discipline was enforced. This school is run along the lines of an English public school and has a long and proud history and tradition, being almost 100 years old.

In this all-male school, students are required to wear school uniforms, and matters such as long hair are not tolerated. Teachers at the school are treated with great deference and respect, and students usually stand when addressing them. Each day starts with a short religious ceremony, followed by a morning assembly in the school hall conducted by the Headmaster, who wears an academic gown for these and other occasions.

Accordingly, when I attended Alexander Ramsey High School in Roseville, near St. Paul, Minnesota, during 1969 and 1970, as an American Field Service exchange student, I found a very different educational environment. First, there was an entirely different dress code, with students at liberty to wear their hair long and to wear all kinds of casual clothing. In addition, there was also a much more relaxed atmosphere in class. Students very rarely stood when speaking to their teachers, and they never called their male teachers "Sir," as was the case in South Africa. Sometimes the teacher was even referred to by his or her first name.

Another difference that I encountered between the two educational systems was that in South Africa, the student was presented with educational information and rarely invited to question it. It was rarely suggested that there might be different approaches to a matter.

With regard to the circumstances outlined above, I found my American literature and American history classes with Mr. James Warren particularly fascinating and, in fact, revealing. He taught the classes in a very stimulating way, further inviting and teaching all students to be critical of what he taught, not only as regards the information presented by him, but also his own personal interpretation and application of that information. This was certainly a very novel approach for me.

I found this brief exposure to him and to his methods helpful to me in later life, and particularly in my university education and my current vocation as a lawyer. I find that as years go by, I am able to deal with more and more information, much of it of a complex or technical nature, and a lot of it new information. I have to learn, more and more, to deal with new and changing legislation, often having to think on my feet and many times being required to advise clients under situations of urgency. Much of this ability I relate back to my experiences gained during my stay at Alexander Ramsey High School.

With me in Mr. Warren's class was another exchange student from Japan named Yoko Hayashi, who had also been subjected to a strict and traditional form of education in Japan.

One day in class, having heard a submission by the teacher, Yoko was terribly shocked to hear one of the students call out that they regarded the teacher's views as "a load of crap." Yoko frantically searched her ever-present Japanese-English dictionary to try and determine the meaning of the word "crap," which she automatically sensed to be derogatory. After failing to find this word listed in her dictionary, she raised her hand and called out to the teacher, "Please, I no understand this word crap." To the great amusement of the class and to her eternal embarrassment, the teacher called out to the student who used the word and said, "Okay, Marcie, you got me into this position; now please take Yoko out into the hall and explain the meaning of the word to her."

Yoko, however, quickly mastered English and went on to become very accomplished in the language. This so impressed me that when it came time for me to choose a university in South Africa, I in fact selected one that was not English-speaking, as she gave me the confidence to realise that I would soon be able to master another language and cope with the academic requirements.

Vaughn Harrison, Attorney, Johannesburg, South Africa

119

I didn't have Lee Nesbitt just one year in school, I had her several times. It seemed like every four years as I progressed up the ladder in the small-town school that I attended, she moved a few years ahead of me so that I'd catch up and have her again. I had her the equivalent of about six years for various subjects, four years in high school and two years in elementary. She was an inspiration because she set standards for herself that a great many of us felt we needed to live up to. She set standards not only in what she asked of us in her teaching, but also in the way she behaved. Just walking down the hall in the school, you knew that you were supposed to have a certain type of behavior. You were not supposed to be running and screaming up and down the halls, for example, and if you did, she didn't have to say a word to you! She was one of those people who could just look at you, and she didn't look at you with a mean look or anything. She just looked, with kind of a quizzical look, like, "Why are you doing something so foolish?" It always put young people on their mettle to try to live up to her expectations.

She set high standards in the classroom. You did not pass her courses without doing the work that was expected of you. You didn't try to shirk because you knew that she would see through it in no time at all. For me, she was the epitome of what a teacher ought to be.

She wound up having to teach us a foreign language. And I'm quite sure she didn't know that foreign language any better than we did. She had to study at night to keep ahead of us in order to do it, because teachers were in short supply in this small town and none were qualified in that particular subject. She managed to stay ahead of us and to give us the sense that she knew exactly what she was talking about and exactly what we needed to do. To me, that was no mean accomplishment right there. I think that high school kids, then and today, are just as sharp as they can be, and we would have immediately sensed if she were insecure in her teaching with that foreign language. She was not.

She taught for many, many years. She made an impact on the whole community. She donated money to start the first public library in the town, and the library is named for her because she also endowed it in her will. She really was a very exceptional lady.

Kathryn Whitfill, President, National PTA, Chicago, Illinois

My parents were killed in an automobile accident when I was a year and a half old. I lived in an orphanage and in foster homes until I was six, when I was adopted by a French family. I'm of Irish heritage and I'm five-foot seven and the adults in my French family were five-foot two. I looked like I never belonged. As a result, I never felt very positive about myself. When I went to school, my mother told me that I had to get good grades except in art and in music, because you had to be talented to get good grades in those.

A lot of bad things happened to me in the adopted family that I lived with, some of those things that you hear about on TV these days. As a result, I had this very negative orientation toward life. I didn't have a relationship with my adopted mother at all. She was a very melancholy person. She cried all the time and she kept me in the house with her but didn't talk to me. I felt that I was not worth much of anything in life. I had always been told that I was this big, stupid kid.

My father was after me sexually, and I didn't know how to jump out of my life. I was like a tree growing crooked; I didn't understand that I needed nourishment and sunlight. I was getting food, but my other needs as a child weren't being met. I was growing pretty crooked and I didn't understand why. I did not even know that I wanted to be a very beautiful and straight tree. I was full of bitterness and full of self-pity. I had these emotional problems as a child and wasn't able to do well in school. I got lost in thoughts about what had hurt me that morning before I came to school, how many times I got hit before I came and how much I hated my parents. My mind would fade off from the dull things that the teachers were talking about to the things that hurt me, and I would indulge myself in thoughts like, "Poor me. I've got it bad."

I thought that I could never really do anything with my life because my family was poor and I couldn't get out of this cycle. I imagined that maybe, if I made a lot of money and brought a lot of money to my parents, they would be happy and they would love me. As a kid, I worked on strawberry patches and in tobacco fields. I made a lot of money. I had a lot of energy, I was very industrious, but even though I brought home tons of money, my mother never paid more attention to me.

The turning point came when I was in Catholic high school. One day, Sister Innocenta said to me, "I can see by the way you walk that you're very bitter." She told me, "Life is like an ocean. Whatever bad things have happened to you, just throw them out, just dump them. Don't carry that baggage around with you."

I didn't know what that meant, and I still was bitter. It sounded like a good statement: "Well, throw it all away," but I said, "I don't have much of a chance in life. I've been adopted, I've had a horrible life."

She said, "You can be whatever you want to be in life—you can be a bum or a king. It's all up to you."

Inside of myself I said, "You're a liar. I can't ever be anything because I got all the cards stacked against me." At 17, I believed that everything was against me. I couldn't be successful because I'd been dealt a bad hand. But Sister Innocenta kept trying to get me to believe that I had the power within to be successful in life. I decided at that very moment in life that I would prove that she was a liar, I would prove that she was wrong. I would show her that I could do everything that she told me to do and I would still not be successful. Of course as time passed, I began to realize that I had the power to change my life.

Carl Jung says, "Good teachers we remember, but those who touch our humanity we will never forget." When Sister Innocenta looked at me and saw this bitterness, she told me, "Whatever it is that you need in life, whatever it is—if it's love, if it's friendship, if it's understanding, I want to give it to you. I want to give you whatever it is that you're so lacking." I think that it was at that particular moment that she reached out and touched my humanity. She believed in me! She thought that I was really smart and I really could do things. She began giving me extra time and attention, telling me that I was worthwhile. She kept reinforcing me and telling me all these wonderful things. She had a very positive attitude toward me. I thought that I wasn't any of those things she thought I was, but I wanted to do better. I tried to do better in everything I did because I wanted her to be proud of me. I wanted to be this person that she thought I was.

All of these things came from one person reaching out, just one person who cared enough to touch me and say, "I see you're hurting. Whatever kind of bandage you need, I'm going to patch you up." What a great thing to offer a child!

I became a schoolteacher and even though I never finished high school, today I have a doctorate degree. I've spent the last 40 years as an educator and I learned from that one teacher that if I reached out and touched one person as she touched me when I so needed her in life, then I would have done a great thing. It wasn't about the factual information I teach kids, like the day Lincoln was born. I wanted to teach people how to cope with themselves and with their lives, even if I couldn't change their lives or get them better parents.

I remember my first year teaching, when I was19 years old and had 45 kids in Grand Rapids, Michigan. I had written a little poem that I read every morning before those kids walked in. I don't remember the poem entirely, but it goes something like: "God, help me to leave all adversities outside of any door that I enter. And help me so that together with the children, we can indulge in the magic of life. And that I can help them to forget all the things that hurt them, and to just be happy for today."

I spent ten years as a schoolteacher, ten years as a university professor, and I'm 17 years into owning my own pre-schools. All I ever wanted to do was make children happy because I realized that despite all the unhappiness in life I had the power, and every teacher has the power, to make this day the best day of anyone's life.

Trudy Comba, Ph.D., Teacher Trainer, Pre-School
Owner/Director, Boise, Idaho

My parents were survivors of the Holocaust, and they pretty much stayed in that survivor mentality, filled with depression and fearfulness in regard to life. At home I lived with chaos, despair and dysfunction, so school was a shining light. I looked forward to going to school! It was a haven for me. It was a safe place for me to learn that there was something more than the pain and suffering that I saw in my family growing up.

I feel incredibly grateful to a pantheon of teachers who made an unbelievable difference in my life. I remember Mrs. Daitch and Mrs. Kemp at the Yeshiva Rabbi Moses Soloveichik, a Jewish school that I went to for my first eight grades. What I got from them was the love of learning, the absolute desire to learn about anything and everything. I'm very grateful because I picked up that enthusiasm, learning for the pure joy of it. I remember Mrs. Kemp reading to us every day from a book that took the entire year to complete. It was a 500- or 600-page book, and just listening to her read for about 15 minutes at the end of every day, following that story throughout the year, was an amazing experience. She believed that we could learn anything we wanted to. Anything! And she daily helped fuel my imaginative powers.

Later, in eighth grade, there was Mrs. Frasier, who had faith that I could learn anything, too. I remember that she expected us to learn our favorite poem and recite it by heart. Mine was "The Day Is Done" by Henry Wadsworth Longfellow. It was about two pages long and I thought, "My God, I could never memorize this!" But I did because I loved it and I loved pleasing her, and I still remember the poem to this day!

I had the great pleasure to go to Stuyvesant High School in New York City—the greatest high school in the world! Here I had Mr. Schwartz for math, a man who could almost taste the joy of geometry and trigonometry and calculus. After a while I experienced these subjects in the same way. There was also Mr. Penzer, who taught biology. Through him I was able, for the first time, to experience the pleasure of studying life.

All along, since I remember my first thought, I think I wanted to be a doctor. I am grateful to the people who wrote the books that wound up inspiring me, who made an incredible difference in my life and were important teachers to me. I remember reading *The Doctors Mayo* and *The Scalpel*, and I later read the works of Sigmund Freud. These books inspired me to continue on my own personal quest.

I was always taught to look up to teachers and to really respect them as I would my own parents. In return, I was blessed to have teachers who may have demanded a lot at times from me, but it was a gift to learn from them and to be in a classroom where everybody to varying degrees enjoyed our time together. School was a pleasure. Without the teachers that I've mentioned, I would not even remotely be the person that I am today. I wouldn't be able to enjoy my life and earn my living doing what I love doing. I carry my teachers inside my heart. Whenever I'm at my best, I attribute it to them. They have made all the difference in the quality of my life.

Harold H. Bloomfield, M.D., 50, Psychiatrist, Author, Del Mar, California

I was so disappointed when Dr. Beatty walked into my classroom. He was going to teach me English literature and poetry, and I was expecting this most romantic figure, someone along the lines of Lawrence Olivier or Richard Burton. Instead, this skinny little guy with a crew cut, a square jaw, dead eyes and no smile walked into the classroom. I thought, "God! I'm in the wrong room." He said, "My name is Dr. Beatty," and I thought, "I've been had!"

But before the semester was out, I was madly in love with him and never noticed any of the physical characteristics in which I was originally so disappointed. I'm even surprised to see him in my yearbook 50 years later and realize that he did look like that!

I, who had such a love of poetry, had never known a man who had ever admitted to even reading poetry, let alone who could read it aloud and make it seem like a love story. When we studied Shakespeare, he played all the different parts. I think I count from that day on my love of English poetry and literature. The stern face and the sad look and the eyes that had no personality to me just became so unusually wonderful when he would take a role other than the role of Dr. Beatty.

What did it for me was the fact that this was a man! There were plenty of English teachers who were women, but I chose my whole schedule around the fact that I could take his class because I wanted a male perspective. I was very young and immature in so many ways, and the male figure was one that I really never fooled around with. If I had a male teacher, I was much different than when I had a female teacher. There was a certain sense of not just respect, but almost fear of his authority. When the principal walked down the hall, I became two feet tall and I was scared to death, even though I had never done anything wrong. Dr. Beatty was the first and only man who opened up, who had a heart and wasn't ashamed to show it, who had a romantic side and wasn't afraid to show it. The boys in the class, when they had to recite the poetry or play the Shakespearean parts that he asked us to play, lost their shyness because he was a man and he had done it first.

I got a lot out of that class. I never wanted to go to a girls' school after that. I was very pleased that we had male and female roles; we even interchanged them. That was a first, that he had some of the men playing some of the women's roles and the women playing the male roles, and we giggled and laughed at first, but you know, it became like a job after a while.

This was the first time I realized that physical stature is so unimportant after you get to know the person, because looks meant a lot when I was in school and he did not look like someone who would appeal to me at all. By the end of this class, I could have married him. I fell in love with him and I think of him even right this moment with the softness that I reserve for people that I love. That's how I felt about Foster Beatty. I was in awe of him by the end of the year and I hated to have the year pass because I couldn't have him again. I felt cheated and I felt blessed that I had known him at all. He is probably with the cherubs somewhere, reciting poetry and playing a lyre.

It only took one year and this one class for me to become an English major and an English teacher in the vein of Dr. Beatty, I hope. If I've inspired even one person, then it's as though I've carried the torch he handed down to me.

Lynn Cramer, 62, Housewife, York, Pennsylvania

I'd like to think that we've all had teachers who were dedicated and spent much effort on their "craft." Perhaps we've known teachers whose enthusiasm for their subject awakened us to the joys of that area where none had existed previously. (I still remember my 11th grade history teacher and his colorful description of those wonderful British uniforms the

English wore in the American Revolution with their helpful X-marks-the-spot, bull's-eye-on-the-chests, colorful red-with-white-cross uniforms.) Or maybe we've had teachers whose general excitement for life inspired us to look at things in a new way. However, I will always be most grateful to Miss Peplow, my eighth-grade teacher, for more than just helping me to be enthused about a particular subject. I'm grateful that she got me enthused about me.

It was in the late 1950s, in the solid Midwest, I was a "bright girl who didn't work as hard as she could." Mom was told that at every conference, so it must be true, right? But if I was so bright, how come I didn't feel bright? How come I couldn't breeze through with all A's if I was such a brain? Note that the second part of the message, the part about "working harder," hadn't sunk in yet. I was still pondering the smart part!

I really felt the whole world was smarter. In October of eighth grade, we had several days of testing—the Iowa Test of Basic Skills, I believe. I'd never liked testing. I'd felt confused about math all my life and I was never confident about my ability to figure out all those "bird is to tree as fish is to ?" kinds of questions. Besides, I was certain that the tests would give written proof I wasn't as smart as everyone thought.

So it was with much trepidation that I completed those exhaustive tests, and quickly put the thought of them out of my mind upon completion. Several months later, the results were in. I was horrified when I learned Miss Peplow was going to go through the lists and tell us about our highest subject and our "needs work" subject. Out loud, in front of the whole class! I was sure I'd be humiliated as she got to my name and proved that I was the class moron in front of all my friends.

A million deaths later, she came to my name, looked at my results and in a clear voice said, "Marilyn, there are no low scores on your test. They're all well above grade level. Some are off the chart into college level. These are terrific results. Let's all give her a round of applause."

I was stunned! I was also validated in a big, public way. Miss Peplow later called me to her desk and said, "I'm going to do something I've never done before. I'm going to show a student her scores." Wow! Even I could see how high they were. Grade level was a straight blue line on the graph—my scores were a spiky little zig-zag line way above that little blue line. After letting me look at my scores, she took my hand and looked me right in the eyes and said, "Marilyn, do you realize what these scores mean? The whole world is open to you. With effort, there's nothing stopping you! You can do anything, be anything." Then she looked serious: "Please don't waste it. Not everyone is so lucky."

To say I wandered in a fog for a while is an understatement. It took awhile for me to process all this information. That year, however, my grades were the highest I'd ever received. Every so often from then on, if I saw myself slipping I'd remember Miss Peplow's words that validated my "smarts" and, more to the point, gave me a sense of responsibility regarding them.

Years later, when I had in excess of a 4.0 GPA (thanks to a couple of A+ grades) in my master's program, I smiled to myself and said, "You were right, Miss Peplow, I guess I am smart after all."

Teachers can give their students many gifts: a love of life, a love of learning, a love of a special subject—all important gifts. The greatest gift I received, however, was from a compact, talcum powder-scented Midwestern school teacher, Miss Peplow. That gift was a real recognition of my true abilities and a sense of responsibility to use them well in whatever I did.

Marilyn Giovanetti, M. Ed., Alexandria, Virginia

Milt Kessler is a professor of English and poetry—and a poet—at State University of New York at Binghamton, which we used to call Harpur College. I took a few courses with him as a lit major between 1965 and 1968. Until his classes, I had experienced college as being a place where the intellect was valued and where the body and feelings were not. At that point in my life, I was deeply, passionately dedicated to staying in touch with my rooted, personal, human self, and I was kind of upset with the mental emphasis on everything. Although I had a lot of wonderful, innovative teachers, he was the only one who was in touch with feelings, sensations and body experience.

In one of his poetry courses, we were discussing e. e. cummings. Now you can interpret e. e. cummings very mentally, but his poetry really reaches me deep down inside. I started to describe this physical sensation I experienced reading cummings that went right across my chest and into my being, and Milt Kessler was thrilled to pieces. He started to bring in information where we could all witness the direct experience of the poem and not just talk about it in a cerebral way. He was someone who was almost desperate to bring the living experience, not only of poetry but of everything, into the classroom.

Every class, every session, he agonized over trying to find a way to make it real and alive and relevant and moving, and I knew that if I were to be a college professor, which, in fact, I thought I might want to be, I would do it that way, too. He evoked enthusiasm, passion, the power of the poem. He was very strong at reading a poem out loud. I remember him reading Walt Whitman's "Out of the Cradle Endlessly Rocking." He would read the poem in such a way that you got the rhythm, got the feeling, you got inside of it and you were absolutely there in that poem.

In one of the courses I took with him, he branched out and introduced me to Marshall McLuhan, the French philosopher Gaston Bachelard, and a lot of other amazing people. He had a way of always introducing people who became crucial influences in my life, poets and others. I also took a creative-writing course with him, which featured some of the most remarkable students in the whole college, which was saying a lot. And in that course, he was perhaps the most impressive because he drew out of each student his or her own unique writing skills, and he did it in such a way that everybody else was interested in what they were doing, and he wove together a group of the most eccentric individualists into a coherent group organism in a sort of simple, subtle, interesting way.

The other thing that stands out to me is that he invited students to his home. He cared about his students tremendously and he kept up with them for years and years. He just feels connected with anyone he has taught. He's just a remarkable man.

He taught me that what really counted in life was showing up, putting as much of myself into my work as I possibly could, and what was not going to count nearly as much were the standard college values, which basically were how to impress other people and how to seem like you knew what you were talking about. What really mattered was my depth of involvement and my commitment to my experience, which absolutely became my entire existence thereafter.

Ellias/William Lonsdale, 47, Astrologer, Santa Cruz, California

When I was little, I had a lisp. At that time my name was Stephanie Small, so you know how it must have felt any time I had to say my name! I was always in the really slow reading group and I just had a terrible, terrible time. My parents had started me in school early because I was supposed to be so smart, but I just felt a tremendous amount of pressure. Finally, after getting a D in reading, my parents found this woman named Dorothy Kraft who lived nearby and agreed to tutor me after school.

Three or four days a week I went to her house for remedial reading. But it turned out to be much more than remedial reading. I always looked forward to that time. She had these orange carpets on the floor, and it was just like this house had a warm glow to it, kind of an embrace as I walked in the door. Dorothy had something the matter with her hip and walked in a funny way. When I came to her house, she'd take me under her arm and walk me into her study, which was wood-paneled and with books everywhere. And there she'd sit with me and kind of hold me and we'd read together. There was something about the way she cared for me and the fact that she didn't belittle me because I was having so much trouble that made me feel accepted and like I wasn't an outcast. She fed me milk and cookies or some fruit every time I came over. On a very essential level I felt like she had seen me in a way that no one else had before.

She said she knew I was going to be a writer when I was a kid because most kids start every sentence with "I," and she said that I always started my sentences differently and wrote in a very distinctive, creative way. She always held that vision for me about what I was going to do, even before I knew what I was going to do.

She's a neat, neat woman. She has this incredible, positive perspective. And I think just having that time with somebody, that special one-on-one time with somebody who really believed in me, was like being fed on a very basic, essential level that you don't get very often.

We still write back and forth and I visit her. She's like a cheerleader. She'll call me up and tell me she read my book or saw me on TV. She just really always believed in me in a way that other people never did.

Stephanie Marston, 45, Writer, Santa Fe, New Mexico

A REALLY GREAT TEACHER IS SOMEONE WHO . . .

. . . is contemporary in thinking.
. . . gives challenging, fun work.
. . . understands personal problems, like when your dog dies.
. . . doesn't scrape her nails on the chalkboard.
              Alison, 11, Houston, Texas

. . . is not greedy.
. . . is not mean.
. . . is not too old.
              Tommy, 7, Houston, Texas

. . . reads books.
. . . is my teacher.
              Ann, 4, Houston, Texas

. . . won't criticize children's ideas.
. . . explains all the problems.
              Lauren, 11, Houston, Texas

. . . explains and doesn't tell.
. . . doesn't scream when you make mistakes.
. . . doesn't pack you with homework.
              Sammy, 11, Houston, Texas

. . . doesn't get mad at you when you explain.
              Patrina, 11, Houston, Texas

. . . lets us listen to music when we're finished with work.

... gives fun projects.
                Alyssa, 11, Houston, Texas

... is sweet and cuddly.
... treats you with respect.
                Jenny, 10, Visalia, California

... can assist you without getting frustrated.
... makes sure that you do not leave the room with
    questions.
... knows that you are having a bad week and maybe
    that is why your homework is not done.
... you thank for making you the person that you are,
    for without him or her, you may have ended up
    somewhere else.
                Dina, 24, Cleveland, Ohio

... knows what he is doing or saying.
... knows how to discipline.
                Chris, 12, Medora, Indiana

... doesn't treat us like little kids.
... doesn't watch and wait for us to do something
    wrong and then make a big federal case about
    it.
                Holly, 15, Medora, Indiana

... gives you work but not too much work.
                Josh, 13, Medora, Indiana

... pays attention to her students.
                Jessica, 13, Medora, Indiana

. . . will listen and talk to you and will help you no matter what.

> Christina, 12, Medora, Indiana

. . . explains stuff really good.

> Leslie, 12, Medora, Indiana

. . . teaches useful things.

> Brandon, 12, Medora, Indiana

. . . takes time for each student.

> Tiffini, 16, Medora, Indiana

. . . is forgiving.

> Jeremiah, 16, Medora, Indiana

. . . has a good personality.

> Ian, 16, Medora, Indiana

. . . doesn't think that he's always right.

> Holly, 16, Medora, Indiana

. . . brings herself down to the students' level.
. . . doesn't always try to be your superior.

> Dusti, 16, Medora, Indiana

. . . can relate to the students.
. . . can deal with students who have learning disabilities.

> Nikki, 15, Medora, Indiana

. . . will work with a student until she understands how or what she is supposed to do.

> Jessica, 12, Medora, Indiana

... tries to make each student a better person.
Chris, 16, Medora, Indiana

... doesn't just try to get through the book without really teaching the kids.
Tamica, 16, Medora, Indiana

... is easy to get along with.
Brent, 15, Medora, Indiana

... gives you time to work on your homework in class.
Trapper, 17, Medora, Indiana

... will take time out of his schedule if a student really needs it.
Ronnie, 17, Medora, Indiana

... gives us a break once in a while.
Michelle, 12, Medora, Indiana

... respects your privacy and lets you sit next to anyone you want.
... lets the children talk about what they had done during the holidays, weekend or after school.
Chandra, 12, Lockridge, Western Australia

... lets you talk to your friends, but not real loud.
Stanley, 12, Medora, Indiana

... has pride for his students.
... encourages us.

. . . is generous.
>   Luke, 12, Lockridge, Western Australia

. . . gives lessons that are fun and happy.
. . . is not too mean.
>   Amanda, 10, Perth, Western Australia

What I remember about school are the feelings, the emotional events that left me a different person. Certain people left imprints on my mind and heart that can never be erased or forgotten. I don't recall much about facts, dates, research, memorization or other mundane things that comprise much of school. Maybe that's what Charles Hummel was warning about in *Tyranny of the Urgent* when he said, "Don't let the urgent take the place of the important in your life." The facts felt urgent, but it was the feelings and interactions that were important.

For example, I had a second-grade teacher, Mrs. Alexander, whom to this day I absolutely love! I didn't tell her that back then. In fact, I didn't even realize it then. I knew she was kind and that being in her class was a joy, but I didn't realize at the time what an impact she was going to have on my life.

One cold December day, the following year, I was running to the bus for the last time at that school because our family was going to move over the Christmas vacation. Mrs. Alexander really surprised me when she ran out the door and hollered for me to wait. She rushed over and gave me a hug and handed me a gift. I thought how sweet it was for her to remember me, especially since I wasn't even in her room anymore. I rushed onto the bus and opened the gift and the card. The gift was a pink plastic box of powder—delightful to a third-grade girl! But the card—oh, the card! The card had such an impact on my life that it still remains a valuable possession many years later. The card made me feel so warm inside, sitting on a crowded bus of noisy, screaming kids just out for Christmas vacation, feeling as though no one else was around.

The card was about 3" x 4" with green and red Christmas flowers on the front. Simple. Simple in design, profound in its effect. She said how she had enjoyed having me in class and how she hoped my move would be nice. Then she opened her heart and said no matter what happened, that wherever I was in the years to come, that if ever I needed anything, to get in touch with her and she'd be there. She even signed it "Love." Love! Teachers don't sign "Love" on a note. Or do they? She did. Love . . .

Mrs. Alexander always made me feel like a winner—not just one of her students, but someone really special! And she kept making me feel special because I would take out that card and savor every word again and again. If she had just told me that day to call her, I would probably have forgotten it or even thought that she really didn't mean it—that those had just been some parting words to say.

But she wrote it down so that I could take a part of her with me. She took time for the important.

Years later, when I was a teacher, I had a student named Jeff, whom I also came to love. When he came to my sixth-grade class, his tough, macho image challenged me. He nearly drove me crazy. He yelled in class. He wanted to know why we teachers wouldn't let him fight it out at recess. He didn't turn in assignments. He was boisterous and demanding, hardly a candidate for a model "student of the year" award.

I remember him bouncing into my class after a breakfast of Sugar-Frosted Flakes with Coke poured over them. I suggested he try a slice of cheese on whole wheat toast in the future: "No Sugar-Frosted Flakes. No Coke. Nutritious breakfasts are important."

He must have taken it to heart, because the next morning he came up and told me how he had had a cheese toast for breakfast. The rest of the year our conversations would sometimes go to nutritious breakfasts. One morning Jeff caught my husband at the local convenience store buying chocolate milk and powdered sugar doughnuts for breakfast. He came to see me after school, appalled that I would tell him that he should eat a nutritious breakfast, but that I didn't send my husband off with one!

Then there was the night I took him and a friend home from a dinner at our school. Jeff had carted around my two-year-old daughter all night and even pinned a friendship pin on her tennis shoe. When he got in my little blue Celica, he asked, "Where did you get this sardine can?" By this time, I knew him better—the facade was wearing thin—and coming from him, that wasn't an insult. It was just Jeff. Then, when Neil Diamond came on the radio and I went crazy because I love Neil Diamond, Jeff said, "Well, that ain't half-bad music for a teacher." Coming from Jeff, that was a compliment—even with the "ain't." (We weren't doing so hot on grammar.) As he was getting out of the "sardine can," he leaned over to my daughter and said, "Hey, kid, how about a kiss?" Jeff, the tough, macho kid giving a kiss to a two-year-old. The facade had worn thinner still.

He looked shocked—as did the other kids—the day I decided to make him a team leader in the classroom. His academic endeavors hadn't changed that much. Assignments were still left undone. He still got in trouble at recess. But now I was seeing the real Jeff—not just a tough image. I wanted him to know that I believed in him. He did a great job as a leader!

I think Jeff knew how I felt about him. His visits the next couple of years told me that he knew I thought he was special, a real winner!

I am thankful that I didn't let Jeff's facade blind me to his sweet spirit. And I am so glad we had interactions that didn't have anything to do with school. I'm thankful for making him a team leader when others thought I was a little "off" for doing it. Looking back, I don't think I did an exceptional job teaching him math or spelling. That never really came together for him, which was probably just as frustrating for him as it was for me. I tried my best to teach, but I am so thankful it didn't stop there. For in the scheme of life, math and spelling will work themselves out, but self-esteem and believing in yourself won't. They need some help along the way.

On the day I learned that Jeff had been killed, it didn't matter that he wasn't a good speller. What mattered was that Jeff knew that I thought he was special. At one time, I almost let the urgency of teaching academics color my whole relationship with him. I am so thankful I took some time for the important.

Mrs. Alexander and Jeff. Worlds apart in time, space and circumstances and yet, both had taught me the same valuable lesson. The tyranny of the urgent must not replace the important. For all that really matters in life are the feelings. Thanks, Mrs. Alexander and thanks, Jeff. I love you both.

Nancy Krivokapich, 41, Sixth Grade Teacher, Farmington, New Mexico

Before I started school, I was always inspired by my mom. I thought she was very pretty and I wanted to dress the way she did. I used to love to see her in her heels. (She's 72 and is still such a sharp dresser!) I always wanted to be like her when I grew up. I just couldn't wait until I got old enough to wear makeup and purses and the shoes and that kind of thing. I thought that she was very, very attractive. She was what I wanted to be like.

My parents were achievers and they always strove for success. This was evident in the way they kept the house. There was consistency in my doing my homework, consistency in the kind of affection that I received. After that I had a teacher in my English class that I used to emulate. It wasn't just her appearance, it was the total person. I admired the way she dressed, the way she walked, her grammar and the way she spoke, which was not the typical Southern lingo. I thought she was very bright and very professional.

This teacher provided the total role model for me in the way she behaved, the way she dressed, the way she carried herself and the way she taught. She was the epitome of a lady. I wanted to hear what she said because I respected her so much. This has had an effect on the way I teach. Certainly a lot of what I do comes from my English teacher, who taught me to love Shakespeare and taught me to love the great plays and great literary works.

I suppose I'm a "total person" individual. I look at my daughter, who teaches with me, and I see how professionally she always dresses and keeps her hair and how much the kids love her. When I taught in the public school, the kids used to always say, "Our teacher is so pretty. Our teacher smells good. Our teacher looks good." When they see you in that light, they really fall in love with you and they want to please you.

All three of my children work with me. My daughter teaches with me, my middle son runs the school on the South Side, my daughter-in-law runs the one in the housing project for me and my youngest child works with me. Everybody that walks into that school can say, "That's your daughter, isn't it?" My three children are what I was, not what I said to them.

In our school, the children wear a uniform every day. The girls wear red and navy blue sailor dresses, a white blouse and navy jumpers. The boys wear white shirts, red and navy cardigans and navy slacks, black shoes. I just find when people look good, they behave well.

You just don't find kids who look great who come in and create disorder. My daughter took her three- and four-year-olds to a farm the other day, and they picked pumpkins and that kind of thing, and she said that everybody there said how well-behaved the children were. If we look bad, we tend to behave that way. If we're talking about success and the American dream, we can't come in doing our own thing. I see teachers today who come into the classroom in sweat pants or see-through blouses. If you want excellence from the children, you must be excellent in everything that you do; otherwise they don't know whom to emulate.

We tell the children we don't allow them to throw paper and garbage on the floor and that kind of thing because we think every seat in that classroom represents a family. We have a school in a housing project that the whole nation is talking about. We have to recognize the excellence that those children have pursued right in that same housing development for four years. I mean, the respect we have from the parents, from the children! We don't have the kind of violence that you hear about. This type of excellence, excellence for the children, begins with us. I have to first change me before I can ever change a child. I don't think it's fair to want children to be excellent if we don't bother being excellent for them.

This might seem trite to other people, but we are obviously doing something right when for 20 years we've never had a discipline problem in any of the four schools that I run. That's attributable to our own excellence, to the excellence of the teachers who work for me. I think our children have so few role models that they don't know whom to emulate. I see it all over the country and it's not just with black kids—it's very affluent white children who shave their heads, who dye their hair yellow, green, purple. They're seeking something to hold onto.

Marva Collins, Consultant, Director of West Side Preparatory School, Chicago, Illinois

My number-one teacher only went as far as the second grade, but she was the highlight of my life and she was my grandmother. She planted the seeds of success within me as far back as I can remember, from my pre-school years right on through. She always said that I could do anything that I wanted to do as long as I obeyed the Ten Commandments and didn't stab anyone in the back. She was the kind of person who nurtured me.

Whenever I had playmates come visit me, she would always say, "Virgie, why don't you play school and you be the teacher?" She let me know, then, from my early childhood that I was a teacher. By hearing it over and over, I believed it. I didn't know how I was going to do it, but I always knew that that was going to be my career.

Every time I came home from school, she would say, "Tell me what you learned today." She'd always put on a clean starched apron, because to her education was sacred, and to her it meant cleanliness. She ironed with the kind of starch you'd have to cook when you did your laundry to make your ironing real stiff. She would always get a clean apron when I came home from school and she would sit in her chair and I would have to tell her what I'd learned. Then she would say, "Get your book and read it."

At that time she couldn't read, so she would say, "Is that what the book says?" She had a way of evaluating what I was really doing whenever we had company. She would say, "Go get your book and read what you read to me today." I think maybe the company really got tired of me reading, but she'd say, "Go over and stand next to the person." She wanted to be sure that I was reading correctly, so that there was no mistake.

When I was in fourth grade she said, "Now that you can read so well, you can teach me." And I taught my grandmother to read by using the Bible, and that was how we spent many hours together.

Whenever I came home from school and complained, "My teacher doesn't like me," she'd say, "Well, then you have a job to do. You have to make her like you. She doesn't know that you are my grandchild!" She never talked down about teachers. She always put the ball in my court, so that it was up to me to sell myself to the teacher.

There were times when I didn't understand a lesson, and she would always find someone who could help me. She would use the bartering system because she didn't have money. She would say to the person, "If you would help my grandchild with the lesson, I'll iron for you, I'll wash for you, I'll clean your house," whatever was necessary. She was very proud and she didn't want someone to do something for her for nothing. She gave back something in return. She would tell me, "In this world in order to get a favor, you have to do a favor." That has lived with me through the years.

Any time that I doubt myself, I always remember that little record in the back of my head with my grandmother saying, "You can do it if you try, so try harder." I think that anything that I have ever accomplished in my life was because of this first teacher who made a positive impact on my life and gave me what I didn't know then was self-esteem, but that's exactly what it was.

Virgie Binford, 70, Educational Consultant, Part-Time Faculty Member of J. Sargeant Reynolds Community College, Richmond, Virginia

Quite frankly, I was not the greatest student at all. There was a bit of insecurity on my part, thinking that I was not a good student. The funny thing is that if you believe you're not a good student, you certainly tend to act the part. Debra Tupper, who taught world geography when I was in high school, evidently saw something within me beyond what I was demonstrating in class. She kept working with me throughout the year. She was a gentle person, and she talked to me. She never embarrassed me by asking me questions that I just couldn't answer in front of the class because that would have put me down further.

She made it fun! World geography was a subject that, before her class, I would say to myself, "Oh, gee, I gotta go through this again—another period of world geography!" But after being in her class, I couldn't wait until it was time for world geography again. It became my favorite class.

She asked questions like, "Why is coffee grown in South America?" She made me think about things like the climate, the soil and all of the factors related to that question. As a result of her working with me and giving me the opportunity to think things through for myself, and of not making me feel horrible if I couldn't figure something out, I went from being the worst student in world geography that year to being the best. In fact, I came out with an A+ that year. So my hat's off to this lady.

The long-term effect was the belief that I could do things on my own, that I didn't need someone to think for me. What I needed was what I got from Debra Tupper—somebody to give me the tools to help me work through a problem. I may not always have the answers, but I have the equipment now that's necessary to start thinking about the problem. But I needed somebody to guide me through, to help me learn how to think.

John Moultrie, 50, Television and Radio Personality,
Middletown, New York

Dear Mr. Ab:

I never met you, but your youngest daughter has told me a great deal about you. It wasn't until recently that I really came to appreciate the kind of man you were and the impact you had and are still having. Your life confirms the old saying, "Bread cast upon the waters will come back buttered." Here are the circumstances. While doing a film on my life, we invited a former teacher who had considerable impact on me, Coach Joby Harris of Hinds Junior College in Raymond, Mississippi, to participate. You undoubtedly will remember him, Mr. Ab, because as his scoutmaster you spent a great deal of time with him. As a 12-year-old, Joby Harris was in your troop. Coach Harris told me that you were like a second father to him and that you had a great deal of influence in helping him to mold and shape his life.

Twenty-five years later, Joby Harris was Coach Harris at Hinds Junior College, and I was a student in his class. Never will I forget that first session. I was taking American history, not because I wanted to, but because it was required for me to graduate. I honestly felt that history was a waste of time. At the end of that class, however, I was a history major. Coach Harris had thoroughly sold me on knowing my history, on waving our flag, and on the free-enterprise system. He was tremendously influential in "selling" me on taking an active part in doing something about making America an even better place in which to live.

Actually, much of my interest in people today and my philosophy of life was influenced enormously by Coach Harris. I honestly feel that Coach Harris helped to make me a better man and, hence, a better husband—for your daughter. I know, Mr. Ab, that since you went to be with the Lord many years ago, you knew all of this before I did. I just wanted to put it in the record that the good each individual can do today will live on and on and on. That's the reason many of us believe that our Lord does not judge us upon the day of our death, but waits that one thousand years. I don't know you yet, Mr. Ab, but I sure do love you.

Your son-in-law, Zig Ziglar

Zig Ziglar, Author, Motivational Speaker, Carrollton, Texas (Excerpted from **Dear Family,** *Pelican Publishing Company, 1984, Gretna, Louisiana)*

My third-grade teacher taught a really comprehensive program. She was a good model. She looked good, she smelled good. She was so human. She loved us and it was a genuine love. She was a marvelous teacher. She brought in home economics, she read stories, she did all kinds of things that made you know that you could do anything in the world.

I can remember hearing about New York City from her reading a book, and I got the idea back then: "One of these days, I'm going to go to New York City."

She talked about the high-rise apartments and the elevators, and I could just feel myself going up the elevators and coming down, and I'd never seen an elevator before, growing up in rural Mississippi!

She was the kind who always gave you incentives for doing something. She would take two people from the class, either weekly or monthly, to go to her house for a meal. She had all kinds of ways you could earn that privilege—maybe by coming to school every day, by doing your work every day, or by being a good citizen; all kinds of things. It was possible for everybody to earn that nice gift. You didn't have to be an A student, you could always do other things. I am sure that she had it set up so that every student got a chance to go to her house during the school year. The way she had it fixed, everybody was a winner; nobody would lose. When we went to her house, we would help her to prepare the meal. She would teach us how to set the table because we didn't have the silver at home to do it. She taught us that you put the fork on the left and the knife and the spoon on the right.

Then we would sit, and it would always be a party, just for us. She would say that we have to be thankful for what we have. She taught us to say grace, which we had to memorize. I can still remember one was, "Be present at our table, Lord. Be here and everywhere adored. Thy mercies bless, and grant that we may feast in paradise with thee. Amen." And then she would say another one that I still remember: "Lord, be our holy guest, our morning joy and our evening rest. Thy daily bread impart, bring peace and love to every heart. Bless this food to our use and us to Thy service, and may we ever be mindful of the needs of others."

You know what? That was in elementary school and I still remember them! That was one of the requirements, you had to remember things like this. In addition to the curriculum, she taught the social graces. She put humanism into education. It was not enough just to study what the curriculum said that she had to teach us; she taught us about life. In all of the books that she would bring to enrich the curriculum, she gave me dreams to pursue.

Virgie Binford, 70, Educational Consultant, Part-Time
Faculty Member of J. Sargeant Reynolds Community
College, Richmond, Virginia

I had a lot of really good teachers in high school partly because I went to a private school. I had a science teacher named George Dorsey who was very focused, thorough and supportive. He stimulated my interest about things like nature and biology. I studied about two years with him.

My geometry teacher was named Mr. McNaull. He was superb in the way he taught us. He would give an explanation of the geometric principle or solution, and then he would show us on the blackboard how to do it. All that would take about 20 minutes. Each class was about 50 minutes long, and he would then give us two or three problems to work out right there in the class. If we got those right, we could leave the class. That meant in five or ten minutes, we could be gone, so we could be in class for 30 minutes and have 20 minutes free. That was a great motivation, because every day before we came in, we knew he was going to teach us in this way. It was tremendous motivation for us to pay attention to him and to focus and to not miss a trick of what he was teaching us. The only rules were that when we left his classroom, we couldn't make noise, slam doors or be disruptive to any of the other classes.

I took an advanced algebra class from Richard Yankee. He was the headmaster of the school. He was like a father figure to me throughout the high school experience. He was a firm but fair guidance-counselor type. He was what I didn't have in a father. I had a father who didn't know how to be a father. I had this empty spot in my life because I had no healthy guidance from a masculine energy perspective coming into my life. This man fulfilled a lot of that. He set limits with me but not too strictly. He was there if I needed somebody to talk to. If I made a mistake in one way or another he would call me in and we would have a talk. Usually you think of a principal, like a headmaster, as not being a person you want to see. Generally, I didn't want to see him either, but after every encounter he was so fair and so concerned and compassionate that I came out feeling okay about it. He had treated me the way I would want a father to treat me, or somebody who really cared about me.

Another influence for me was Tinsley Harrison, a teacher in medical school who wrote a famous textbook on internal medicine. He had a special technique that I remember. Teaching rounds in a medical school is when the students, interns or residents present the patient's findings to the attending physician. The attending physician gives advice, suggestions, guidelines and recommendations on what to do that the young physicians may not already be doing. If they're doing everything right, they'll say, "You're doing fine. I don't have anything to add." What Harrison did was different and it was impactful for everybody. He would tell us at the beginning, "I don't want to hear any laboratory results. I don't want to hear anything that would tell me what the diagnosis is. All I want to hear is the patient's history, and I want to hear what you found on your physical examination. I want to go see the patient, ask them questions and do a brief exam." And nearly every time his diagnosis would be right. He would get the diagnosis right, and then he would talk more about aspects of what the person's medical needs were. But it was important for all of us to learn that you don't need all this extraneous stuff. All you need to do is get an accurate history and do a good physical examination. That's really strong, basic medical training there.

I've also learned a lot from non-human teachers, including nature, animals and adversity. Meditation has also been a great teacher for me. I still meditate daily and have been doing so for over 20 years. I continue to learn from these kinds of teachers.

Charles L. Whitfield, M.D., 56, Psychotherapist/Physician, Author and Teacher

Ten years ago at a very, very low point in my life, I'd gone through a divorce, changed careers and had just moved from a large city of several million people to a very remote area of California, where there are 6,000 people and only three stop lights in 6,000 square miles. I'd lost a lot of finances due to the divorce and at 34 years of age, I was out of work, out of a marriage and at the lowest point of my life.

I had just gotten a satellite dish and I was flipping through the 115 channels one night, depressed and bored and not really knowing what to do with my life or where I was going. I happened to come to a PBS broadcast with Joseph Campbell and Bill Moyers. Joseph Campbell is a world-renowned mythologist; the show was called "The Power of Myth." I just caught the last 10 minutes of the show, but it touched my soul so deeply that I knew that was what I needed and what I wanted. From that little 10-minute segment, I called PBS and found out when the show was airing again.

I started watching the whole series of six shows. Joseph Campbell had just passed on, but I met his wife and went to a memorial for him. I began to read his books and study his work. I bought his tapes and videos, and listened to them. Eventually I ended up going to Pacifica Graduate School, where I am now getting my master's and my Ph.D. in mythological studies. Joseph Campbell left a giant library of mythology from all over the world to the Pacifica Graduate Institute. He lives on through his books and the 15,000 hours of his tapes and lectures in this library.

When I go to school every fifth weekend, I do my research in his library. I am surrounded by Joseph Campbell's pictures and images. I'm now becoming a depth psychologist and a Jungian analyst, using mythology to describe the different psychological aspects of one's soul life. So Joseph Campbell, in those ten minutes, changed my whole life.

I read Joseph Campbell's book, *Hero With a Thousand Faces,* and it had a similar impact. I'm now writing a book based upon the path that the hero takes. This path is found in all cultures throughout the world; this is a universal theme.

When I first encountered Joseph Campbell that night on television, my soul was starving. I had been in the television industry, a money machine, a business machine. My life was in a materialistic world of making money and buying things in the fast lane of Los Angeles. My average work week was 70 hours and oftentimes I'd put in 80- or 100-hour work weeks. I was a workaholic who had hit bottom at 34 years old. When I unplugged from all of that and moved to Mt. Shasta, I found myself very soul-weary and soul-starved. What Joseph Campbell did was touch me at my deepest level of my soul. His work is what gives meaning and purpose to my life. It is what touches me at the deepest level and makes me want to get up the next day and go on with life. The note that he struck gave me the will and incentive to go on. It was a very personal, very powerful experience.

LeRoy Foster, 44, Depth Psychologist, Author, Speaker, Mt. Shasta, California

I have been fortunate in my life to have had a number of exemplary teachers—unforgettable individuals who were honorable people and colorful characters with a great deal of vim and vigor! All have deeply influenced my life. But perhaps the greatest teacher was the youngest: my daughter, Jennifer.

Of the many experiences in my life, raising my daughter was the most intense and taught me some of the most profound lessons. It was a joyous yet arduous exercise in perfecting my own nature, an impassioned experience that left an indelible mark. Jennifer motivated me to move beyond my own concerns and care deeply about the needs of another. The awesome task of parenting helped me focus on the meaning of my own journey through time and kept me from sleepwalking through life. The responsibility of caretaking changed my feelings of aloneness and forced me to reconcile my past experiences with a new reality. I learned to live more fully than I might have otherwise and discovered much about myself in the process.

Living with my daughter, loving her and being her soulmate and helpmate has taught me:

Love. By loving her, I tapped into a reservoir of love and found it bottomless. I didn't know I could love so much. Nor was I aware just how much this emotion would forever bond me to her and motivate me to provide for her.

Joy. As a result of my efforts, I have seen my daughter prosper as a healthy, intelligent and compassionate person.

Happiness. By giving and sharing myself with her, I've experienced the deepest level of happiness. I've learned that giving is more rewarding than receiving.

Empathy. In seeking to understand my child, I have had to put myself in her place and have learned the meaning of unconditional caring. Sometimes my heart aches as I watch her struggle with a difficult lesson or learn from a harsh consequence.

Patience. In meeting her needs, I have had to care for her when I myself was sick or had other impending responsibilities. I learned that I could. I discovered an unsuspected strength within myself.

To listen. I learned to decipher not only the various tones of Jennifer's voice but also her feelings and subtle behaviors, to hear what she was really saying rather than what I wanted to hear.

To grow. I have become a better, wiser and more loving person. And, of course, I have also learned what I am *not* but would like to become.

To be assertive. When you're in charge, you learn quickly from your mistakes and readily feel your accomplishments. I learned self-control and self-discipline. These practices resulted in positive self-regard and high self-esteem, which helped me become more assertive.

To be responsible. Because she is so precious to me, I learned to accept the duties and obligations of being a parent and to accept being depended upon to fulfill them—even at times when I might have preferred doing something else.

To be spiritual. The miracle of life and my daughter's birth became the catalyst for renewing and deepening my own faith. Daily challenges taught me to continually search out my heart and turn my eyes heavenward.

To be efficient and effective. Before I had my daughter, setbacks disappointed me, confrontations made my heart race. Energy I used to spend on tension and anxiety I now channel into getting things done. Other people appreciate it, too. They want to be around those who are performing their work efficiently and effectively.

To communicate clearly. Communicating in a clear and concise way is necessary when dealing with children. When other people depend on you at home or at work, communicating clearly is essential.

To live consciously. Because I am constantly observed by my daughter, I must be aware of what my actions and words convey. Setting a good example is an ever-present challenge. Confronting my own values is sometimes rewarding, and at other times unsettling.

To set priorities. Once I realized days were not going to get longer simply to accommodate me, I accepted the fact that my desire for perfection had to go. I learned that there is a difference between doing things right and doing the right things. I also learned that while some things must be done, other things are a matter of choice. People who stimulate and motivate, inspire or encourage me are important; people who drain me and are not supportive, are not.

The fragility of human life. Though this feeling began with my pregnancy, as soon as Jennifer was born I knew her life was mine to protect and that I was committed to doing so at all costs. As I began to understand and value the fragility of human life, I began to take better care of my own health. I also began to care more about others whose lives are in jeopardy anywhere in the world—from oppression, starvation or war.

The nature of adults. Basically, adults have the same needs and desires as children, though sometimes we express ourselves more subtly. Like children, adults behave in ways that show their needs.

Empathy for other parents. Parenthood connects mothers and fathers everywhere. At one time, I sympathized with the parents of sick, crying, injured or missing children; now I *feel* with them. Parenthood has made me realize that other parents have the same joys and sorrows.

That parenting is forever. When my daughter was an

infant, I looked forward to a time when she would be able to play independently. Once she could, she still looked around to see if I was there. When she was in grade school her curiosity was insatiable, and instilling rules for operating safely in the world was a must. In junior high, her many activities necessitated frequent bandagings and a daily carpool.

Her questions about her feelings and her need to understand them sometimes made me feel like a clinical psychologist with her as my entire caseload. Now that she is a young adult, her need to understand her place in the world and in her relationships through first-hand experience occupies much of her time.

Just as I worried when she was little that she might stick a finger in a light socket or be treated badly by another child, I'm still concerned that she might leave a burner (or an iron or hot rollers) on in the house, or that she or someone else will exercise poor judgment while driving a two-ton car. I still want to protect her from being emotionally devastated in relationships, even though she must learn such lessons on her own. Perhaps my concerns will remain for some time—possibly forever. Just yesterday my own mother called and expressed her concern for my safety on an upcoming trip abroad, though I have made the same journey nearly 20 times.

It was no small task to show my daughter that I both love and respect her, that I accept her for who she is and that my actions were designed to prepare her to live interdependently. My daily goal has been to build a foundation of self-esteem for her, set appropriate expectations and encourage her to live purposefully. It has taken much examining and refining of *my own* values to enable me to provide her the skills needed for living a healthy and functional life.

This daughter of mine—this teacher of mine—is always on my mind. She has inspired me to care enough, to grow enough to meet the challenge of shaping another human life. It was she who taught me to do this in a way that would make her *feel* my loving actions and therefore *assimilate* them.

Being a parent, nurturing a human being, has taught me the greatest lessons I've ever had to learn. Thank you, Jennie, for choosing me to help you find your way in this world—and for teaching me how to do it. Though I was the parent, it was you who were my teacher. You are the greatest teacher of all.

Bettie B. Youngs, Ph.D., Ed.D., Author, Counselor, Consultant, Del Mar, California

The teacher that had the greatest impact on me was Mr. Carl Weaver, my science teacher in tenth grade in Indiana. He was very motivated and very excited about what he was doing, which obviously rubbed off on me. That's the first major trait in being a good teacher, as far as I'm concerned. The thing that really stood out about him among all the teachers I've had is that he was very acutely aware of each student in his class, of their feelings and everything else. You could watch him watch the class. It was unbelievable. He was an amazing, unique individual.

At the beginning of the class, he'd do a little bit of a lecture and you could see him looking at every person in the room. If there was a problem, and there usually was, whether it was somebody just having a bad day or if there was something seriously wrong, he noticed. We always had a portion of the class, like the last ten minutes or so, to do some assignment. That was when he took the time to go pull somebody aside. He would say, "Well, I'm going to go just work with this person."

It never really occurred to a lot of us what was going on until he took you aside and said, "So, what's wrong?" He would sit and talk and work you through it, and he'd watch you throughout the course of the day. Even as you were going from class to class, he'd pull you aside and say, "You doing okay? How's it going?" His ability to pick out even those people whose look could conceal a lot of their emotions was unbelievable. It made that portion of the high school experience a lot easier, especially at that age, with sexuality and all the different things that you're faced with, to have an adult in your school that you could go to who genuinely was concerned about how you felt. He also genuinely wanted you to achieve what you desired to achieve, and he was willing to help you do that.

He had that fatherly feeling about him so that he seemed like he could handle the weight of the world. You got to the point where it was almost like having another parent. You would do something, and the first thing you would do was tell him about what had happened. He'd be enthusiastic and encouraging, and you'd leave all motivated.

There's a time in life where you think, "Who am I? What am I going to be? Where am I going to go?" He let us know that we didn't have to worry about that right now: "You don't need to figure out what you're going to be and where you're going to go at this point in your life, so relax. And you are who you are, so just be it and don't worry about it." It's very obvious now as an adult, but back then this was a revelation. He made it okay. That was a tremendous help and it relieved a lot of the anxiety and the pressures that are put on you by your peers.

After awhile, you didn't need him in quite the same way. The rest of my high school career, I was fine and I rolled right along. Ninth and tenth grades were the hump that he got us through. He was a shining star through all the difficulties of adolescence. If you have one experience in your schooling with the kind of self-esteem that he helped build, it can make the rest of your life a lot easier.

Brett Mello, 30, Manager of Information Services, Kentwood, Michigan

My kindergarten teacher, Miss Mary Mason, is my oldest and dearest friend. There's not a moment in my life when the helping behavior that's at the core of her instruction doesn't inform my thinking.

I think the influences in my life come from the individual characteristics of certain special people. I remember my sixth-grade teacher in Salt Lake City. He was the first person I ever met who could run like the wind. He represented a sense of achievement in a way I'd never seen before.

A year later I had a math professor, Mr. Black, who took this notion of achievement and taught me the same thing in mathematical terms. He gave me a sense about direction and about relative distance and speed and momentum. It was kind of basic physics but it was all taught in a math class. Mr. Black offered me this sense of an ordered world that gave me hope that there was a way of organizing both my thoughts and the world that was rational—not cold and dry, but rational and manageable.

I think the next person who had an impact on my life was

my eighth-grade history professor, Mr. Bill Purdy. He took that rational world and discussed it and represented it by teaching history in a way that gave me an appreciation of the progression of things, the evolution of things and the process of the world at work. He was the first teacher for me who was able to paint pictures of the world in verbal terms in a way that was totally inspiring. I felt like I was living with the people and the places that he was describing. That was the first time I had a real sense of a world of humanity, a world with spirituality at work, with a human face on it.

Geography was a fascinating subject to me. I think perhaps in that case the nature of the material was as powerful as the teacher. The content is so important and it was so important to me to have the content reinforced. When I reached a place where the content was really rich for me, it was absolutely critical that at those key moments there was someone there to draw out that interest, to work with it and to feed it, actually taking a little extra time at the moment when I expressed interest. I did extra work in this class because it was very clear that the standard material they were giving in the classroom was not going to challenge me. My teacher worked with me. He provided extra homework, which I just devoured, and presented concepts beyond those that were being taught in the classroom. I had a chance to then go and work with him one-on-one after class or in other sections. I went because it was just sheer curiosity, just joy of learning, and he was not just available, but encouraging.

Kenneth Miller, 46, Chairman, National Design Museum, Publisher of Computer Software, New Canaan, Connecticut

Teaching had become a daily struggle for me, beginning in 1988 with my transfer to the new middle school. Nothing seemed to work with these kids. It was a constant battle between them and me, and they seemed to be winning. I was seriously considering leaving the teaching profession to do any other job, until I attended a workshop introducing Fred Jones's Positive Classroom Discipline. I was amazed by, and curious about, how the junior high teachers in this workshop reported they no longer had discipline problems in their classrooms after attending Fred's week-long seminar. One of my fellow teachers let me borrow Fred's book for a week, and I sat at home reading and crying because I knew I needed this information.

I decided at the end of that school year to take Fred's seminar, even though it was miles away in New Mexico. It was either that or quit my job. My husband was very supportive and encouraged me to go.

That week in New Mexico with Fred and his wife, Jo Lynne, made such a wonderful difference in my career. They shared with me specific classroom management and discipline techniques that I had never learned before in any college class or teacher education workshop. I came back the following September equipped with new classroom management, discipline and instruction skills and a whole new attitude toward my students.

I was so much happier as a teacher and felt more confident in the classroom. At parent conference time in November, the parents would come in and say, "This is the first year my child has ever liked math," and "Oh, you're my child's favorite teacher and I just had to come and meet you because she talks about you all the time." This was really amazing to me! So every year right after parent conferences, I always send Fred a thank-you because I'm always so grateful for Fred Jones turning it all around for me.

Cathy Riley, 44, Seventh-Grade Math Teacher

I have an ongoing thanks for my physical education teacher at Robertson Academy in Nashville, Tennessee. His name was Coach Ledgerwood. He had a shoe-brush flat-top, a gap between his teeth and a vitality that showed beyond his years. He was an ex-military type. He was the man that we feared the most because he was "Coach" and because he was the only male authority figure at our small public school. As such, everyone kind of looked towards him as the substitute for their own father in the school and for his own approval in the gymnasium and on the schoolyard.

One Fall day, Mr. Ledgerwood had sent us out on a stop-watched 100-yard dash from the school playground through the tall sawgrass that was behind the First Presbyterian Church next door, then around a telephone pole and back again as fast as our little third-grade legs would allow. On the return course, we were huffing and puffing. The first cluster of runners must have been shocked to find Mr. Ledgerwood with his transistor radio seated on the jungle gym, which was generally reserved for the younger students. As they ran towards him to announce their completion and ask for their precise time, they were greeted with a "Ssh! Ssh! Shut up! Shut up!" and that was not his nature to say anything as abrasive as "shut up." So we knew something very serious had happened.

President Kennedy had been shot and killed. For many of us this would be our first encounter with death. Even at this tender age, we realized that the world was suddenly going to be a much different place than we might have believed an hour earlier. I looked at coach and saw tears in his eyes, and realized the magnitude by which our President was respected beyond the image we saw every night on the television with Walter Cronkite. But the fact that it touched Coach Ledgerwood in such a way made us realize that this must really be a truly horrible experience. This must really be a dark moment for all Americans.

After this experience with Coach, we felt as though we had all shared a bit of a nightmare as a collective group. When he would routinely tell us, "Okay, now quiet up, people. Make a line and let me see some jumping jacks," we discovered that we were motivated to follow his commands because we had shared this prior moment. Here it is 30 years later and that afternoon stays forever etched in my mind.

One of the lessons that I am the most grateful for came at an occasion after this when Coach Ledgerwood was not supervising us in the gym. You know, when the cat's away, the mice will play—and that day, the mice were frolicking! We were cutting up as most third-graders do, and he came in and he said, "Okay, I'm going to tell you, one more time, you guys, quiet down." Of course we maintained the attention span of about 30 seconds and then we started getting very loud again.

Now we would delight in the sense of structure and faux military thoroughness from Coach telling us, "Okay, make a line here. Put your arms down. Stand exactly there, and when

I tell you to come forward, you come forward." It was a world of being an adult, only we were still within the confines of a nine-year-old's post-Dr. Seuss world. When he returned this time, I knew that he was quite angry. Rather than finding one conspirator, it was easier for him just to take the three or four of us that were generating the ruckus and to summarily dispense justice to all. He announced that we would have to "drop out" and follow him to the wall, which of course we did with no idea of what kind of humiliation lay in store. He then told us, "I am going to punish you more severely than anyone else in this world can. Because you people have been goofing off when I trusted you to do your exercises as you're supposed to, you have caused us all to lose time. By wasting time, you have made others lose also. Now I'm going to teach you a lesson that I don't want you to ever forget."

We were all starting to shake wondering what kind of corporal punishment to our little bodies this could mean (as this incident predated the reluctance of the school districts to use paddles on the students). We felt that getting spanked might be part of what was going to come our way. Either that or being sent home to the same fate, as a note from Mr. Ledgerwood would warrant that form of parental discipline.

Instead, he said, "Okay, now you're going to stand there, and for the next 25 minutes, you are going to do nothing! You are not going to move. I do not want you to set one foot beyond that. You're not going to rock back and forth on your feet. I want you to just stand and look at the clock on the wall for 25 minutes. Realize that for your punishment, you will have 25 minutes of your life taken away because of your lack of consideration for others. That is the most severe penalty anyone can ever impose on you, to waste your time. I'm going to take 25 minutes out of your life and I'm not going to give it back."

We sat there in utter, complete dismay, thinking, "Wow, did we ever get out of that!" No one got spanked. No one got yanked up by their hair. Nobody was forced to do 25 pushups *right now!* We were just startled at this rather liberal approach and felt like a bunch of kids who were getting away with something. However, after about seven or eight minutes, the novelty of not being punished began to wear off and we began to watch the clock.

It was an indeterminately slow process, and we truly watched the physics of a phenomenon: The clock stopped! During that period of time, probably four civilizations of Mesopotamia occurred. Perhaps generations of kings were born and raised in Peru and built temples in the mountains that they later discarded when they found some form of corn that could be grown at a lower altitude. I figured man had probably already walked on the moon, forgotten about the moon as being significant, and went home to be able to see the oceans. And finally the very lack of air, the lack of movement within the entire universe for this period of time was enough to shudder the clock back to working. As we stood there motionless, a sudden numbing sound pierced the silence—the blast of the school buzzer. Recess was over. At that moment, the co-conspirators and myself looked up to the clock and realized that indeed God had intervened. He had turned the buzzer on because we had not witnessed the clock's long hand actually make its lethargic movement up to the 12.

When I left Coach Ledgerwood that day I realized, like any other prisoner of war, that I'd been forced to endure the punishment of my enemy. But in reality, he had trained me to be able to endure similar punishments dished out by other authority figures later in my life. I slowly began to recognize that time was a commodity that was precious, that was singular, that was narrative, and that I must protect the usage of my time for all consequences.

About six years later, while riding from Overton Park over to Franklin Circle to go to junior high school on Mr.

Holtz's # 69 school bus, one of the student passengers said that the fog-embanked area that we were passing was the same place where Coach had driven his car off the interstate. He had been in his royal blue 1955 Chevrolet. They said that they found the skin from his fingers still attached to the steering wheel after his car had plunged almost 160 feet over the unfinished I-60 bridge to this cavernous area below where the railroad ran from Franklin to Nashville. Another student sitting next to me said, "You know, the sad thing is that Coach's wife left him, and that's problee why he done it." The closest thing to a suicide note were Coach's words, "I just can't take the fact that I've wasted this much of my time with her."

The lesson that I learned from Coach Ledgerwood is that time is the only place we both live and work, dream and create. It is essential that we appreciate and value the passing moment in the same way that we appreciate the passing of our own life, and that our own abilities to create our life direction depend on how we use the time that we are given.

AWest, 40, Illustrator, Performer, Art Director, West Hollywood, California

Any discussion of important and influential teachers in my life must, of necessity, I believe, begin with my parents. My parents had a philosophy of teaching me to trust myself, even when I disagreed with them. Many times in my life I would differ from them, and sometimes even tearfully for them, but they would always encourage me to trust my own perceptions and my own process. That has been a key lesson throughout my life.

My mother and my great-grandmother were very active in my life when I was a young child. They taught me to respect nature, to live off the land and to recognize healing plants and plants that are good to eat. I always feel very at home in nature and very grounded with the earth, which has been very important to me all my life.

No matter where I go, I immediately feel a connection with the earth and feel at home there. I really appreciate their teaching me to think for myself, to trust my own perceptions, to challenge authority when I didn't agree with what they were saying, and to be just and fair.

I can remember in first grade when a little girl sitting ahead of me wet her pants. She was too afraid to ask to go to the bathroom. I helped clean up the mess and turned to my classmates and said, "If any of you teases her or picks on her, you'll have me to answer to." That feeling of justice has pervaded my life, creating a tendency to respect each individual regardless of his or her background and to always stand up for the underdog. That respect for justice came very, very early in my life and I can hardly tolerate something that seems to me to be unjust.

In our family, it was very important to tell the truth. Telling the truth was always rewarded, regardless of what I did or how bad it was. If I admitted to some thing I had done, told the truth about it and was ready to take the consequences, I didn't get in much trouble. And it was very clear that if I ever lied about anything and they found out, I would get in big trouble. This training has put me in good stead for my whole life, about being a truth-speaker and really valuing the truth. I realize as an adult that in some ways I didn't have much skill with lying because I had not been around it a lot as a child. As an adult, I had to develop an awareness of when people were lying and learn to trust my gut on that.

In the school setting, one of the most important teachers in my life was a man named Bill Lewis. I went to a three-room school in Indiana. He was my teacher for three years, for sixth, seventh and eighth grade. He was also the principal of the school. He was a farmer who really made his living by farming, and he taught because he loved to teach. How horrible it could have been if I'd had a really bad teacher for three years!

He was the kind of teacher who took us on a lot of field trips in nature. We learned about trees and leaves and bark, spending days and days out gathering leaves and observing bark samples and observing nature firsthand. He had a natural curiosity and, I believe, so did I. My curiosity was fanned and fueled and fed; it was not thwarted in any way by him, which I hear so many people have experienced in school.

I was really good in math. In my eighth-grade year, Mr. Lewis set up really simple problems that were based on trigonometry. My dad, an engineer, and I took a more advanced trigonometric approach to these problems as we worked on them at home. I came in with the right answers, and Mr. Lewis had no idea how I had achieved those answers because I was using trig at the time. He said, "Well, you're obviously on the right track. This is a math that's beyond me, but you go ahead and use it because it's working for you." That's the way he was. He was very, very flexible.

It rarely snowed in Indiana. If we had a good snow, Mr. Lewis would call off school for at least a part of the day and we'd go sleigh riding for the whole afternoon. We could explore anything we were interested in. He gave us the support for going to the library and getting material for reports or following up on an idea. I really felt that I could fly in terms of my own thinking, my own curiosity and my own interests with him.

When I went to high school I found that I had basically done everything that they were doing for the first year. I coasted that year because of the work that I had done with Mr. Lewis. We stayed friends over the years and I occasionally see him and his wife when I go to Indiana.

In high school, I had two teachers who were really amazing. One was my math teacher, Bill Hermans, and the other was my science teacher, Loren Studer. They said to me, "In a teacher's career, if we get one student like you, it makes the whole thing worthwhile." I'm a divergent learner and they supported me and my kind of thinking. In both these classes, they just turned me loose. I always did the required assignments and they always encouraged me to explore more. As a consequence, I was really way up there in terms of my base in both science and math, which was really great.

In college I was taught by this wonderful woman who was the head of the German department, even though she didn't have a doctorate. In the university world, a department head without a doctorate was unheard of, especially for a woman in the 1950s. Frau Deickman also taught classics and literature and she was such a magnificent teacher. She opened up the world for you to walk in. She was a great role model in that way and a great teacher for me.

The other person that I would mention continues to be a teacher for me, even though he's now dead. He was a spiritual leader of the Lakota Sioux—their ceremonial and spiritual chief, Frank Fools Crow. He taught me about what's important, about living with this planet and living with people, about my own spirituality. Frank gave me my Indian name and he made me a pipe carrier, which I haven't really respected because for many years, I didn't know how. I have such a disdain for people who go out and buy a pipe and suddenly become a pipe carrier, for people who abuse Native American spirituality because it's in vogue, that I would wouldn't even touch my pipe for years.

A Native American sister of mine said to me, "How could you shame that old man and be so disrespectful?"

I burst into tears and said, "I never would be disrespectful!"

She said, "You are because you're not valuing his decision and his choice, and you are assuming that you know more than he does about choosing you for this important work." I thought, "Whoa! I gotta get busy on this one!"

I felt really inadequate to be a pipe carrier, but what I finally realized was that being a pipe carrier isn't an honor; it's a responsibility. I now know how important it is that I pass on his teachings. What he really taught me was to return to my own spiritual base. Again, it's a full circle that takes me back to my parents and my great-grandmother.

Much of what he said to me I wasn't ready to hear, and I couldn't remember at the time. He's been dead now for several years and I'm aware that his teachings keep coming up for me. I keep remembering more and more of what he said, just as if he's walking beside me. I know his teachings aren't meaningful until I'm ready for them. When I'm ready, they just pop right into my right brain and zip over to my left brain and become available to me. Even though I was not at his side as much as I would have liked to have been—and probably as much as would have been good for me—he's had a tremendous impact on my life.

They say if you have one really good teacher in your school career, you're lucky. I have been fortunate all through my life. I always made good grades and I was a very different kind of thinker than your usual academic. I feel like I've been very, very lucky throughout my entire school career. I've had some bad teachers, but they were so insignificant compared with the good support that I've had from those teachers who helped me to come into my own, which is what I believe teaching is all about. That's the kind of teacher I am. I try to support people to live their own lives and come into their own knowing. You can get some information along the way, but in the long run, the information is not going to be nearly as important as knowing how to think for yourself and how to live your own life. That's what I've been taught, and that's what I teach.

Anne Wilson-Schaef, 60, Author and President, Wilson-Schaef Associates, Inc., Boulder, Colorado

My daughter, Jena, had a fifth-grade teacher named Mrs. Grube-Thur. At the beginning of the year, she gave all the students check ledger books that one of the local banks had donated. In the front of the room, she had printed a list of how the kids could get points—or "dollars"—for their checkbook. Most of the points would come from turning in your assignments on time, helping your classmates or helping your teacher—many different positive behaviors. They could also have points taken away for not turning in assignments on time or for certain inappropriate behaviors.

The points were visible to everyone and everyone had the same chances to earn these points. The children who had more aptitude than others did not necessarily get all the points. It was equally available to the whole class. The kids had a good time with this program. It offered positive reinforcement when they did something good, when they turned in their assignments on time, or when they completed something. It was great. It taught the students good behaviors, it gave them reinforcement and it taught them the life skill of how to use a checkbook, where they had to add and subtract.

About three or four times a year, Mrs. Grube-Thur would have auctions. She would have the parents and people in the community donate various kinds of foods and toys, like a soda pop or a candy bar, educational games, pads of paper in different shapes and colors, stickers or posters. The kids would bid on the various items with the points that they had in their checkbooks. The more points you had, the more you could bid for something. They had a ball with it.

This same teacher really went out of her way for kids. One day, she went to see Jena in a horse show. I couldn't believe it. For a horse show, you can stand around for hours waiting for your equitation class to be called. She was willing to do that for Jena. It was that kind of involvement inside and outside of the classroom that made the kids realize how much she cared. I think that's the key. You know that your teacher wants you to learn, but knowing that your teacher also cares about you personally is what sets the exceptional teacher apart from the rest. This made a big difference in her life.

Last year, in seventh grade, Jena had a really rough year with depression and a lot of other stresses resulting from the separation of her parents. What helped her through was the fact that she had a wonderful teacher. Her name was Mae Holup. There were times when this teacher would simply not expect Jena to do everything that all the other teachers were demanding. She expected Jena to do up to what her capabilities were at that emotional point of her life. She could not deal with additional stress. If she turned in her paper a day late, her teacher would compliment her for turning her paper in, because she knew that for Jena to get it in even a day late was the same as other kids getting it in a day early. That was really something! I think that as hard as it is for a teacher to have different motivational levels for each child, that's what sets the exceptional teacher apart.

As a result, Jena is right in there this year with the rest of the kids. She has no problem doing homework or classwork, no problem with the other kids, but it took that kind of a caring teacher for that one year. It also took me, as a parent, going in and talking to that teacher ahead of time and saying, "Please watch for these behaviors. She is having some problems." I think it was the combination of our efforts that helped. I went in and let her know what was going on and she would stay in touch, saying, "I am observing something. Maybe you might want to keep an eye on this." She really worked with me.

While Mrs. Grube-Thur was a very young teacher, Mrs. Holup has been teaching for more years than she'd probably be willing to tell you. So it obviously doesn't matter if you're a seasoned veteran or if you're a new teacher. What does matter is how you show you care.

Beth Bauer, 46, Owner of a Chain of Educational Toy and Teaching Material Stores, President of Middle School PTA, Mequon, Wisconsin

In my youth I was fortunate enough to attract the attention of two particular teachers who, by nothing more than taking a personal interest in me, did me a great deal of good.

One was a Catholic nun, Sister Mary Seraphia, who discovered, when I was in seventh and eighth grade, that I had the ability to write. Sister Seraphia made me the editor of a little school paper and encouraged my writing in other ways. Because I was born with a fairly high I.Q., I had never had much difficulty in at least passing tests and getting good marks. But this kindly teacher's personal interest was extremely helpful.

Much the same thing happened a few years later when I was attending Hyde Park High School in Chicago. An English teacher, Marguerite Byrne, discovered that I was missing classes and not taking advantage of some of those I was attending. She encouraged me to write, to submit my poetry to the *Chicago Tribune,* to enter an essay contest; she made me the editor of a school magazine, and in other simple ways helped to guide me in the right direction.

Even after having had the benefit of her wise counsel, I still occasionally missed classes—but did not spend the time in neighborhood pool halls, theaters or beaches. Instead, I went to the nearby Museum of Science and Industry, or to either the school or neighborhood libraries, where I read everything I could get my hands on.

From that day to this I have been passionately concerned about the large process of education, not only for myself but for the American people. A number of my books—for example, one called *Dumbth: And 81 Ways to Make Americans Smarter*— have provided a means to express my views on this issue.

Steve Allen, Comedian, Author, Musician, Van Nuys, California

My husband, Doc, had her first. Actually, we didn't know each other in high school because his class was four years ahead of mine, but we both had Helen Coverdale for English 1 and for French. In both classes, she was marvelous. She had a terrific sense of humor, but never directed it at any of the kids in any kind of way that would make them feel self-conscious, as though she were making fun of them. She would make fun of herself, too, and she was a wonderful role model for not taking yourself too seriously.

I remember going to her apartment with classmates when I was probably 15 or 16. We had a simple meal together, but we had a lot of fun. She was just so bubbly and felt that kids were very important, even though she never married and never had children of her own.

My mother thought that teachers should be invited to your home. The first time Helen came to our home, we happened to have a pony that was given to us by a cousin. It wasn't a big pony, but it could carry a lot of weight. Helen was a tall gal and she said, "Oh, sure. I can ride the pony," even though her feet almost touched the ground. And the pony enjoyed it as much as she did.

She was very gracious, very outgoing, and my folks really loved her, too. I feel most fortunate to have her as both friend and teacher. We kept in touch even during the war (WWII) and then, after she moved, we visited her several times after our children were old enough to travel. We're great-grandparents now but we've kept in touch with her. She corresponds with many of her students from years before, just as she does with Doc and me. She's still a very good-looking lady, in her 80s. She can't drive anymore because of an eye impediment, but her former students take wonderful care of her. They see that she gets wherever she needs to go. That tells you something.

Katy Abraham, Horticultural Journalist, Naples, New York

I started at Drexel University unsure about what I wanted to do. I knew that I wanted to be an architect but not exactly which career path to take. The first class I took was an architectural history class. The teacher was Professor Bob Ennis.

His style of teaching was very culture-oriented. He gave us the thoughts and feelings behind the architecture, behind what was actually built, and in doing that he raised our own consciousness about what's being built today. He made us look for societal and cultural reasons for why things are being built the way they are. I think in that respect, he forced us to change our way of thinking, which for some of us was life-changing, as well. I could take that whole idea of looking at society and cultural ideas and how they manifest in buildings and turn them inward, doing the same thing about myself: "Why am I doing what I'm doing? Why do I design the way I do? Why do I like a certain style of building? Why do I like a certain music?"

He fostered soul-searching in a way that most people aren't exposed to until the university level. He was there, not only to initiate and nurture that kind of thinking, but also to guide, and he was always open to questions. It was refreshing to see somebody who not only surprised us by starting us thinking in that way, but who was also there to answer all the questions that undoubtedly come up when you start looking inside and thinking in that way.

He was also very down-to-earth. The student organizations put on trips to various architectural sites and he was always on them, as an ad hoc tour guide. He was very involved with students in and out of the classroom. I think that's a very good aspect of teaching that not all professors value or even think is that important. When a student can look at a teacher and say, "Maybe we'll go out for drinks after," it's really refreshing. It broke down that barrier of unapproachability, which helped build confidence in my ability to conduct my professional life as well. For example, when I work with respected architects, I'm not put off and I'm not intimidated. I look at them as a peer, as somebody that I can go out and have dinner with.

Because of my contact with Bob Ennis, I am more aware of the reasons behind my decisions and I tend to think a lot more about the repercussions of things I do. That's a direct result of him making me think about architecture that way. I've come to look at life that way.

Dan Wright, 27, CAD Manager, Erial, New Jersey

The teacher who had the most impact on my life was my science teacher in the seventh grade. Her name was Mrs. Foster. She did her job and taught me about the world and how it worked. We had a few disabled people in our class and she helped me realize that everyone is a good person as long as we all try our best. Although I am still young, I am grateful she helped me in the education of not only school, but of life.

Chad Dexter, 17, Student, Phoenix, Arizona

The teacher that had the most impact on my life would have to be Mr. Thomas Marr, my visual arts teacher in my junior and senior years. Mr. Marr singled me out after class during the first week of school. He recognized the talents that I had and wanted to make sure that I knew that he knew. He prodded me to enter the student art contest in my junior year, even though I felt that the competition was fierce and that my entry would never match up to the other entries. With his encouragement and guidance on my project, my confidence increased and I entered, coming away with an honorable mention.

He continued to guide me in the coming year and the following year, and he made himself available after school for special sessions with those who wanted to work on their projects but never seemed to have enough time during class to make any headway. He spoke to me as an adult and did not treat me as a teenager or a child, as some of the teachers did in high school. We were able to discuss things during our class period that did not have to do necessarily with art or art history, but led into discussions about current trends, attitudes and general philosophies.

I have had occasion to follow up with him once or twice since graduation. I met him at school and discussed the path that my future has taken and the part that he had played in helping to formulate my goals and future. I could see by the looks of his classroom, and the projects that were scattered around the room, that he was still devoted to helping young people find and develop their creative talents within.

Karen S. Friend, 41, Executive Director of a Trade Association, Phoenix, Arizona

I graduated from a high school so small that if you wanted to be in the top ten percent you had to be first or second—there were only 23 students in my graduating class. Leona Friermood was our long-standing English teacher and debate coach. Even though we were small in numbers, year after year, Kalama High School in Kalama, Washington, was formidable opposition for any school of any size in the state. It wasn't because of our natural abilities. It was because a teacher understood what the word "educate" means—seeing us not for what we were but for what we were capable of becoming.

Mrs. Friermood constantly affirmed her belief in us. I was very active in high school. I remember her asking me to compose a speech for a United Nations speech contest. I responded, "I'm involved in student government, in band, in sports and in the play. I can't." Her response: "Yes, you can. And you will." And I did! She said, "I'll help you. You need to write a fifteen-minute speech on 'What the United Nations means to me.'" She said, "Bobby, you have great interpretative reading skills. You just need to read your speech in this competition."

So I wrote the speech. She helped me fine-tune it. Then Mrs. Friermood said, "You know all the other students will just be reading their speeches." I said, "Well that's all you need to do." She said, "Well that's all you *need* to do, but what an edge you would have if you memorized yours." I said, "Mrs. Friermood . . ." She said, "You can. And you will." And I did!

She was an amazing person. She reminded me a little bit of Listerine—it didn't taste good but you knew it was good for you. She understood that educate meant to "pull from within" and not to simply transmit information. She was an inspiration to all of us. Many students weren't sure what to think of her because she could be very stern. But after graduating, they'd look back with great admiration. She always had that twinkle in her eyes and was our greatest cheerleader. She'd say, "You beat Castle Rock in football and I'll climb the flagpole." After the win, she'd be sitting on a ladder next to the flagpole for ten minutes during lunch break.

Years later, she was dying of cancer. One of my personal highlights was being asked to be master of ceremonies for "This is Your Life, Leona Friermood." Her students filled the auditorium to honor this amazing teacher. I'll always remember her. She was a great educator, but most of all, she educared!

Bob Moawad, 53, Educator, CEO, Edge Learning Institute, Tacoma, Washington

During my senior year I took an advanced math class with Mrs. Fletcher as my teacher. Because there were only two of us enrolled in the class, she acted as a part-time teacher and only looked in on us occasionally during the year. We were left alone to learn the material and if we had any questions, we had to seek her out and find a time we could get together with her to help us with our questions. Because of this method of teaching we learned how to work on our own, without someone looking over our shoulders. It made me realize the need for honesty. It would have been easy to cheat since there was no one watching, but I know if Mrs. Fletcher could not trust us enough to do the work honestly, the class would not have worked. She had to know that we were going to be doing our best and doing it honestly.

I believe this teacher taught me more about work ethics, and the need for complete honesty with each other in this life than any other teacher I had.

Roger Dexter, 41, Owner of a Sign Shop, Network Marketer, Phoenix, Arizona

One of the most memorable teachers in my life was Clyde Alford, or "Coach," as we knew him. Coach didn't run a big-time outreach program or teach in an inner-city environment. He spent his life helping working-class eighth-graders better understand math—and life—in the small town of St. Albans, West Virginia. Coach must have loved a challenge.

How do you teach algebra to a kid who knows everything about everything important (and math wasn't important); who had emotional problems about which space and time do not allow elaboration; and who had a physical predisposition to weight gain that contributed to his obesity (over 200 pounds at age 13)? Being fat and in middle school is an instant recipe for ostracism a la carte. This was me, floundering and fluctuating, discouraged and uncertain.

I did finally begin to catch on to the algebra, thanks to Coach's persistence. But not before I began to catch on to some other lessons. Coach taught me three lessons. First, I learned that I needed to have something in life compelling me forward. "Let the future pull you forward instead of letting the past push you forward," Coach would say. Second, he taught me that a job is what you make of it. You can enjoy it or dread it—the choice is yours. And finally, I learned to never, never quit. "You will not discover your unrealized resources unless you are tested in some way."

The lessons were not easily learned. But somehow I think that Coach didn't choose his line of work because it was easy. And maybe that's lesson number four: the recipe for happiness doesn't always include happiness as an ingredient. What Coach taught me I imagine he taught to every boy and girl in eighth-grade algebra over the years. By doing so he gave us a foundation for a more successful life. Do you remember this saying: "We can count the number of seeds in an apple, but who can know how many apples are in a seed"?

What I am now in large part is due to Coach. Because of him, all the lives across this country and abroad that I have been privileged to touch have been touched by Coach as well. Thanks, Coach, wherever you are.

Chuck Glover, International Speaker, Instructional Specialist, Chesterfield, Virginia

Mrs. McCarthy, my first-grade teacher, was the first person to validate me as a human being. One day in class, my tooth fell out. Terror! Abject terror! Blood! Kids pointing! Plus the embarrassment of being the center of attention. But Mrs. McCarthy cuddled me up. She took my tooth, taped it to a piece of cardboard and put glitter on it. She put a yarn string about my neck and tied a big bow and made me the proudest kid in first grade!

Academically speaking, I really can't tell you a great story on that level, but practically speaking, she made me feel like a special person, even if it was just for that one day. I fell in love with her that day and to this day I remember her fondly.

I was always a troubled kid—that's a kind way of saying I was really way out there! I stayed by myself a lot. One day, I was standing near the driveway where the custodians had put up wooden barriers to keep people out and keep us kids in. Well, I knew that these barriers were called "horses" and I decided to ride one. Remember, I'm in first grade, five years old, in a private world where horses—the four-legged kind— were tops! Anyway, I decided to play on the damned thing and it fell over and smashed my toe!

The ever-present Mrs. McCarthy saw my catastrophe happen. Off I was whisked to the nurse. Brother, what a mess I'd gotten myself into! I knew I wasn't supposed to take any of my clothing off for strangers, and naturally shoes and socks fit my definition of clothing! Good old (she was probably 22) Mrs. McCarthy! She just held onto me while I screamed my head off at the nurse for trying to take off my shoe and sock, and she made the nurse stop trying to disrobe me. This woman was a saint! Mrs. McCarthy stayed with this half-hysterical five-year-old until my mother came to school.

Boy, was I in trouble! Not only did I have a broken toe, but an angry mother and a very angry nurse all hollering at me. Know what Mrs. McCarthy did? She had me go back to class and told the kids what I did was right! Right, mind you! That I was mistaken about playing on the horses, but not wrong!

She gave me a glitter star to wear for that day because what I did was Very Right, but I had just made a little mistake.

Oh yeah, Mrs. McCarthy ranks up there as one of the most positive of all role models to me! She taught me that I was right even though I was mistaken! She was my candidate for sainthood the entire time I attended J. Huelings Coles School.

Patricia McKeone-Moffatt, W.I.T. (Whatever It Takes),
Cherry Hill, New Jersey

Murray Bolnick was my ninth-grade English teacher at Ditmas Junior High number 62 in Brooklyn, New York. He must have been about 35 years of age back then, in the 1958-59 school year. I have to credit Mr. Bolnick with getting me interested in literature, which, until then, I really couldn't stand. I read and read well, but somehow I just didn't have the patience to sit and read the assigned stories, which seemed to be so boring!

Through the school year, he put his all into the different stories we read. Even then, I felt he was very much into getting us students into the process of thinking about what we were reading. When it came time for our class to prepare for our play, I made some wisecrack about who should play the leading role. Next thing I knew, he assigned me the part! I just about died! I was really scared and could see myself up on stage in front of all the ninth-grade classes not remembering a single line. But I couldn't back down because my buddies would laugh at me.

He put me in a position where I had to rise to the occasion. This was an important lesson to me—sometimes you just have to do what you have to do.

Recent efforts to contact him after 35 years have been futile. Hopefully, he's still around. I'd like to thank him and share with him the things that I'm sharing with you now. The funny thing is, this didn't really click until I was a father in my thirties. It was during this time that I looked back to my youth to see if there was anything I could cull from that time that might help me, along with my wife, in raising our three boys. I began to realize the importance of how something should be taught, as well as the subject matter itself. I would like to thank the man for bringing me to the point that he did, intellectually as well as emotionally.

During the fall semester of 1960 at Erasmus Hall High School, Mr. B.C. Occhiogrosso was my English teacher. You might say that he picked up where Mr. Bolnick left off. At that time, male students did not dress up in suits and ties, but Mr. Occhiogrosso did, of course. One day, he brought up Oxford University and I thought, "Gee, I heard about that place. Very bright students go to learn at that fine, classic, cultured place of higher learning."

I had read about Oxford University from a bound volume of *National Geographic.* I bought it from one of those used book-stores that I started to frequent along Fourth Avenue near Union Square in Manhattan. In this 1929 volume was a story on Oxford University. What gorgeous pictures of a great institution! I brought it to school and was so pleased at Mr. Occhiogrosso's delight in showing it to the class, saying, "Yes, these photographs show fine examples of the University," referring to the many buildings that dated back hundreds of years.

I wanted to emulate the refinement and culture that I perceived in Mr. Occhiogrosso and decided that I, too, would now wear a tie and jacket to school! If Mr. Bolnick had started something with me, Mr. Occhiogrosso gave it a wonderful finish, sort of a seal of approval, saying it was okay to be a polished individual.

I really attribute a lot to these two guys who inspired me the way they did. They helped me stay on a very good path, and I've tried to instill the same things in my kids. Hopefully it's taken—not just about developing a love of reading, but also about just being a decent person.

By the way, I still have that fine, beautifully bound volume of *National Geographic*. Also, I never did find out what the "B.C." stood for in Mr. Occhiogrosso's name, but maybe one day I'll get lucky!

Keith A. Reinsdorf, 49, Staff Assistant, Superior Court, Los Angeles, California

A REALLY GREAT TEACHER IS SOMEONE WHO . . .

. . . organises things after school for the next day.
. . . is responsible for things he does.
. . . is enthusiastic.
. . . believes in what he teaches.
. . . shares things.
> Stacy, 12, Clarkson, Western Australia

. . . is outrageously funny.
. . . always has a positive attitude.
> Josclyn, 11, Clarkson, Western Australia

. . . believes in himself.
. . . sets an example.
. . . thinks positively.
> Natalie, 11, Perth, Western Australia

. . . believes in you and understands you.
> Lisa Ann, 12, Perth, Western Australia

. . . stands up for what she thinks is right.
. . . is trustworthy.
> Joe, 11, Perth, Western Australia

. . . is energetic.
> Siti, 11, Perth, Western Australia

. . . is motivating.

> Jereme, 11, Clarkson, Western
> Australia

. . . is creative.

> Carina, 11, Clarkson, Western
> Australia

. . . gives me a choice of who I want to be.

> Laura, 11, Clarkson, Western
> Australia

. . . has high self-esteem.
. . . exercises.

> Kate, 11, Carabooda, Western Australia

. . . respects what the students have to say.
. . . tells us how to improve our grades.

> Deanne, 12, Perth, Western Australia

. . . is always there for you and helps you solve problems.
. . . you will miss at the end of the year.

> Paul, 12, Perth, Western Australia

. . . cares about your future.

> Rima, 12, Lockridge, Western
> Australia

. . . listens to you when you get in trouble and never tells
anyone.

> Rebecca, 12, Lockridge, Western
> Australia

. . . is not sexist or racist to any student.
. . . is at least an average athlete and a fair judge.
>   Brett, 12, East Victoria Park,
>   Western Australia

. . . listens to students' ideas and considers them
seriously.
>   Sarah, 12, Beckenham, Western
>   Australia

. . . lets us have hugs in the classroom.
. . . lets us drink in the classroom.
. . . tells good jokes.
>   Stephen, 12, Cannington, Western
>   Australia

. . . gives responsibility to his or her students.
. . . gives rewards like free time, games or relaxing
outside when it is sunny when the students listen
well or work in class.
. . . plans exciting excursions.
>   Al, 12, Lockridge, Western Australia

. . . has good manners.
. . . treats people with feeling.
>   Sharidan, 12, East Victoria Park,
>   Western Australia

. . . is considerate of students' feelings.
>   Victor, 12, Bentley, Western
>   Australia

. . . lets us have parties and eat in class.

> Mark, 13, St. James, Western
> Australia

. . . instinctively knows each student's individual needs.
. . . is a model of integrity and dedication.
. . . is overjoyed by achievements.

> La Kisha, 18, Mays Landing, New
> Jersey

. . . inspires you to work rather than forcing you to learn.

> Jennifer, 18, Mays Landing, New
> Jersey

. . . manifests caring of the students in his or her
enthusiasm and the time he or she is willing to
spend with the students.

> Dawn, 17, Egg Harbor, New Jersey

. . . will reach out to help a student, even if the
student doesn't ask for help.
. . . can find ways to incorporate what the students
are into or can identify with to teach a lesson.

> Anthony, 18, Mays Landing, New
> Jersey

. . . can relax and has a good sense of humor.
. . . is able to communicate efficiently with students.

> Melanie, 17, Mays Landing, New
> Jersey

. . . knows the subject matter and really wants others to learn about it.

. . . gets students involved in the lessons because most learn by doing.

> Toni, 17, Mays Landing, New Jersey

. . . not only teaches lessons on the course work, but life lessons as well.

> Colleen, 17, Mays Landing, New Jersey

. . . finds time to work with all the students.

. . . makes sure you understand the work.

> Jessica, 11, Anchorage, Alaska

. . . teaches nicely.

> Lance, 9, Anchorage, Alaska

. . . you can have a friendly relationship with.

. . . you can talk with freely on any subject.

> Tamar, 11, Anchorage, Alaska

. . . helps you solve problems and doesn't get frustrated.

> Darin, 11, Anchorage, Alaska

One day in 11th grade, I went into a classroom to wait for a friend of mine. When I went in the room, the teacher, Mr. Washington, suddenly appeared and asked me to go to the board to write something, to work something out. I told him that I couldn't do it. And he said, "Why not?"

I said, "Because I'm not one of your students."

He said, "It doesn't matter. Go to the board anyhow."

I said, "I can't do that."

And he said, "Why not?"

And I paused because I was somewhat embarrassed. I said, "Because I'm Educable Mentally Retarded."

He came from behind his desk and he looked at me and he said, "Don't ever say that again. Someone's opinion of you does not have to become your reality." It was a very liberating moment for me. On one hand, I was humiliated because the students laughed at me. They knew that I was in special education. But on the other hand, I was liberated because he began to bring to my attention that I did not have to live within the context of what another person's view of me was. And so Mr. Washington became my mentor. Prior to this experience, I had failed twice in school. I was identified as Educable Mentally Retarded in the fifth grade, put back from the fifth grade into the fourth grade, and failed again when I was in the eighth grade. So this person made a dramatic difference in my life.

I always say that Mr. Washington operates in the consciousness of Goethe, who said, "Look at a man the way that he is, he only becomes worse. But look at him as if he were what he could be, and then he becomes what he should be."

Like Calvin Lloyd, Mr. Washington believed that "Nobody rises to low expectations." This man always gave you the feeling that he had high expectations of you and you strived, all of the students strived, to live up to what those expectations were.

One day, when I was still a junior, I heard him giving a speech to some graduating seniors. He said to them, "You have greatness within you. You have something special. If just one of you can get a glimpse of a larger vision of yourself, of who you really are, of what it is you bring to the planet, of your specialness, then in a historical context, the world will never be the same again. You can make your parents proud. You can make your school proud. You can make your community proud. You can touch millions of people's lives." He was talking to the seniors, but it seemed like that speech was for me. I remember when they gave him a standing ovation.

Afterwards, I caught up to him in the parking lot and I said, "Mr. Washington, do you remember me?" I added, "I was in the auditorium when you were talking to the seniors."

He said, "What were you doing there? You are a junior."

I said, "I know. But that speech you were giving—I heard your voice coming through the auditorium doors. That speech was for me, Sir." And I said, "You said they had greatness within them. I was in that auditorium. Is there greatness within me, sir?"

He said, "Yes, Mr. Brown."

I said, "But what about the fact that I failed English and math and history, and I'm going to have to go to summer school? What about that, sir? I'm slower than most kids. I'm not as smart as my brother or my sister who's going to the University of Miami."

And he said, "It doesn't matter. It just means that you have to work harder. Your grades don't determine who you are or what you can produce in your life."

I said, "I want to buy my mother a home."

He said, "It's possible, Mr. Brown. You can do that." And he turned to walk away again.

I said, "Mr. Washington?"

He said, "What do you want now?"

I said, "Uh, I'm the one, sir. You remember me, remember my name. One day you're gonna hear it. I'm gonna make you proud. I'm the one, sir."

School was a real struggle for me. I was passed from one grade to another because I was not a bad kid. I was a nice kid, I was a fun kid. I made people laugh. I was polite. I was respectful. So teachers would pass me on, which was not helpful to me. But Mr. Washington made demands on me. He made me accountable. But he enabled me to believe that I could handle it, that I could do it.

He became my instructor my senior year, even though I was in special education. Normally, special ed students don't take speech and drama, but they made special provisions for me to be with him. The principal realized the kind of bonding that had taken place and the impact that he'd made on me because I began to do well academically. For the first time in my life I made the honor roll. I wanted to travel on a trip with the drama department and you had to be on the honor roll in order to make the trip out of town. That was a miracle for me!

Mr. Washington restructured my own picture of who I was. He gave me a larger vision of myself, beyond my mental conditioning and my circumstances. People are convinced that whatever they've done is all that they're capable of doing. They operate within the context of the vision that they have of themselves, of what they feel subconsciously they deserve. That's what they manifest. Any time what they achieve and acquire in life exceeds that vision or that sense of deservingness of themselves, they will engage in a self-destructiveness to bring themselves back to where they feel they should actually be.

So if you can give them a vision of themselves that goes beyond their circumstances and mental conditioning, you can help them to see themselves differently and get that larger vision. That belief system has been created for them by life, and they're operating within that context of themselves. It takes somebody else from outside to mirror the possibilities back to them. They can't do this for themselves.

Years later, I produced five specials that appeared on public television. I had some friends call him when my program, "You Deserve," was on the educational television channel in Miami. I was sitting by the phone waiting when he called me in Detroit. He said, "May I speak to Mr. Brown, please?"

And I said, "Who's calling?"

And he said, "You know who's calling."

"Oh, Mr. Washington, it's you."

He said, "You were the one, weren't you?"

I said, "Yes, sir, I was."

Les Brown, 50, Author, Speaker, Detroit, Michigan

I stood with the multitudes listening to Mark Antony's impassioned speech at Caesar's funeral. I witnessed, firsthand, the murderous climax of *Lord of the Flies*. I was the object of Heathcliff's undying passion and I lived a lifetime of wicked cunning as Becky Sharp. Actually, I had spent two years in Roberta Redding's English courses at Highland High School in New Mexico. For Roberta Redding, literature was alive!

She relished not only the plot and character development, but the vivacity of the writing itself. She acted out passages from the literature, giving full dimension to every detail, showing how the author uses language to create a scene or impression. It took her three days, I remember, to act out the opening scene from William Faulkner's *Intruder in the Dust.*

She taught us how to read literature by teaching us how to understand the author's tools of expression. We learned how to trace symbolism through a story; what the author portends with foreshadowing; how to recognize and appreciate onomatopoeia, alliteration and other uses of language.

She taught us how to write an essay properly and effectively; how to make a thesis paragraph with a thesis statement; how to support your argument and summarize your thoughts at the end of an essay.

We wrote essays continuously for those two years (no multiple choice exams in these courses). And the rule was: you could give the literature any interpretation you felt valid as long as you could support your argument and write it, of course, in proper essay form.

What freedom! What creative motivation! What greater gift of education than to learn how to express your ideas in clear and powerful terms. The reading, writing and thinking abilities I developed in her classes have helped me in every aspect of my life. In college my professors often returned exams to me saying, "You didn't give the literature the interpretation from the lectures, but you write so well and you made such a good argument, I have to give you an A." It's enabled me to listen carefully and critically to the statements of politicians and to be thorough in examining my own principles and ideas.

I hear too often, "You get out of a class what you put into it." That's not true. You can put a lot into a class and get nothing out of it if the teacher isn't fully engaged in the process of education. Mrs. Redding took two weeks or more to grade the essays. Many times her comments would be as long as the essay itself. Her criticism and feedback were invaluable. And, by the way, if you didn't agree with your grade—you guessed it—you could challenge it if you could support a good argument.

I've visited Mrs. Redding a number of times over the years, as have many of her former students. Each time I make it a point to thank her for teaching me how to write so well that I will never be limited in my ability to express myself. Perhaps it's not a coincidence that I went on to get a bachelor's degree in English, in British literature. I'd always been interested in literature, but she was a main factor in my decision to go on. I live in the U.S., but tonight I will join John Reed at the opening of the Russian Revolution. Thanks for the ticket, Mrs. Redding!

C. Earnshaw, 37, Writer, Albuquerque, New Mexico

At Georgetown, I learned how to think and how to ricochet. It began during my third week on campus, when Professor Roger Slakey returned my premiere freshman English composition assignment—a take on the novel *Lord of the Flies*—with a grade of E-. He expressed amazement that anyone who wrote as badly and carelessly as I had any ideas worth developing—yet, he wrote, he detected the glimmer of one or two actual thoughts buried in my "turgid" prose. I was indignant, crushed, furious, discouraged. I crumbled that typed essay into a ball and threw it across the room. What did Slakey know? He was obviously incapable of comprehending my brilliant and original observations. An hour later I dug in the trash can and smoothed out my pages, ready to retort his every critique. I hated the sight of his angular, pointy handwriting, his brown ink, the procession of irritatingly undotted question marks that decorated my neat margins. I scanned line after line to rebut every blatant misreading. In 15 minutes I had reached the end of the page—"finis" I had written, with what I believed was great flair and sophistication. And there it was, the worst, most enraging thing of all: He had been right.

I still write for Roger Slakey, though he doesn't see the drafts. He perches on my shoulder, crowding the space with other fine, tough teachers, and screams in my ear: "The Text! The Text! If your words and analysis aren't clear to the reader, they're no good." And it doesn't help now, any more than it did then, to argue with him. I've learned to surrender to and make the best of the inevitable rewrites. Professor Slakey's point about literary criticism translates into an approach to life: As artists, as citizens, we must take our opening cues from context; we are wise to listen before we speak, look before we step, think before we act. Such an attitude is "wisdom," but in my own experience, it's seldom automatic—rather, a hard-to-learn response.

Michael Dorris, Author of several books, including **A Yellow Raft in Blue Water, Paper Trail,** *and* **The Broken Cord.**

Since Tom Hanks gave his acceptance speech at the Academy Awards this past March, my life has changed in many significant ways. His recognition on worldwide television of my influence on him was one of the most—if not the most—gratifying things to happen to me in my 30-year career as a drama director and teacher of theater. This event set me to thinking of the people who had influenced *my* life.

Over the years of my directing and teaching, I have often been asked by colleagues, parents and students where I got my training and "know how." Without hesitation, I always replied that I studied with and learned all I know about theater from Dr. Karl C. Bruder. I've had many fine teachers and professors, but Dr. Bruder stands head and shoulders above the rest. I studied and trained with him at Kansas State Teachers College, which is now Emporia State University at Emporia, Kansas.

I transferred to KSTC in my junior year. It was Dr. Bruder's first year at Emporia as well. He came to the campus from Yale and was designated as head of the Speech and Theatre Department. He immediately set about to revamp and improve the training within the department, to benefit prospective teachers going into teaching at the secondary level.

His program was geared to teach us how to teach stage performance as well as the technical and backstage mechanics of theater through practical experience in the productions given on the main stages of the college. He introduced many innovative and creative courses from which I benefited. I found in my first few years of teaching my own students that I continually modeled my work after his work. I received my baccalaureate degree in the spring of 1952 and began my high school teaching career at a new high school in Wichita, Kansas, the following fall.

It was at this time that Dr. Bruder organized a summer theater on the KSTC campus in which there were seven different productions presented in seven weeks. This was for the benefit of all students, especially those of us who wanted to do graduate work toward a higher degree but were busy working and teaching during the regular school year. The program was so geared that a student would be either performing in or working backstage on one show at night and rehearsing or working technical theater during the day of the show for the coming week. This was very intensive training and very valuable when we returned to our secondary schools each fall. I used many of the ideas I'd learned in this intensive training in my own teaching. It took me ten summers to accumulate enough graduate credits, but I received my master's degree in 1962, with a major in theater.

The thing I remember most about Dr. Karl C. Bruder was his great patience, special consideration for each of his students and his professionalism. We all felt we were doing professional work at Emporia. It was here that I learned the importance of always striving for professionalism in any theatrical undertaking, even though you may miss the mark sometimes.

Rawley Farnsworth, Retired Educator, San Francisco, California

Soaring glacier-studded peaks, hungry grizzlies, bugling elk, rare glacier lilies and snowy mountain goats. Four walls could never contain one of my greatest teachers, not when the "classrooms" were Glacier National Park and the Canadian Rockies!

This shy "flatlander" first met Danny On when I took a summer job at a lodge on the east side of Glacier Park. (A tremendous leap of faith considering I had never been west of the Mississippi or seen a mountain up close before.) There I was in a sea of over 500 summer park employees. One day I waited on a friendly smiling Asian-American man, and the rest is history. (Little did I know my "teacher-to-be" was a famous photographer and forester, much beloved in the West!)

After he learned I was a genuine "flatlander," Danny taught me how to see through "mountain eyes," ever patiently opening mine to the majesty of the high country. One of my favorite lessons was on a seemingly blank rock face. "Look at that mountain as a clock," he said. "Go down to about 2:00. Follow the little hand out to the rock outcropping. See it?" Sure enough! There was a tiny patch of snowy white, a sure-footed mountain goat making its way along the rocks. This was truly a special treat I cherish to this day, a treat I never would have seen with my "city eyes."

On our days off, Danny often took a few of us on grand adventures, from hiking up to find a rare red-anthered glacier lily to cross-country skiing in summer clothes high at Logan Pass. He even took a small group of us up to the magnificent Canadian Rockies one color-splashed autumn to see great wildlife, like elk bugling in the frosty morning air or a grizzly rooting for dinner along the road.

Danny would surprise me every now and then with one of his popular 16" x 20" nature photographs. (His snowy mountain goat—my favorite—still graces my wall.) After I returned to Minnesota, he sent me carefully labeled boxes of his breathtaking outdoor slides from Montana to Alaska, to "continue my education."

Danny took such pleasure when he could help me see some facet of nature with new eyes. He was playful and warm, always full of surprises and fun! He taught me how to love the mountains and all their treasures. As I finish writing this tribute, I'm riding the Alaska state ferry up the spectacular mountain-lined Inside Passage on a sunny October day. I recall with a smile Danny's Alaska slides and his great enthusiasm for this vast land.

Sadly, Danny was killed in a skiing accident only a few short years after we met, but his spirit still lives on for me throughout this spectacular trip. He truly inspired me to be a "mountain woman" and wherever my travels take me, from the snow-splashed Alps to the rugged Caucasus Mountains in the Georgian Republic, I'm forever grateful for his patient nurturing of this eager young "flatlander."

Linda Sorenson, Author, Workshop/Retreat Leader,
Traveler, White Bear Lake, Minnesota

As a 59-year-old I still remember vividly my first-grade teacher, Miss Brubeck. From the first day of class we knew that she liked us. I cannot remember her ever raising her voice to anyone in the class, or a time when I felt any kind of fear about anything we did during our first- and second-grade years. I can still visualize in my mind her lessons on Eskimos, Holland and American Indians.

I can picture to this day the igloos and Eskimos we colored and displayed around the room. During our study of Holland, Miss Brubeck invited an immigrant from Holland who lived in our community. He wore his wooden shoes to class and talked to us about Holland. We made windmills and tulips of construction paper.

Miss Brubeck had outstanding penmanship and taught each of us how to write our letters and numbers. Again, I cannot recall a time when she did not view all of us as successful students. She was both caring and competent and was a friend of mine until she died a few years ago.

Another teacher I recall with appreciation was my junior high teacher, Mrs. Bowman. One of my favorite memories is how she would read out loud to us. I can remember as if it were yesterday, and see her in my mind's eye standing before the class reading Mark Twain's *Tom Sawyer*. Keep in mind, we were junior high students, yet on the second day we begged her to continue after the normal reading period ended. She literally read to us the rest of the day, and it was one of my most memorable days in school.

Today, I live within 20 miles of Mark Twain's home of Hannibal, Missouri, and rarely go through that community without thinking of Mrs. Bowman and her understanding of how important it was to teach junior high students the value of quality books.

Gene Simon, 59, CEO of a Child Welfare Agency, Quincy, Illinois

Doug Emery was my daughter's teacher when Kala was in third grade. He's the kind of teacher who looks at each student as a whole person when he's teaching, and he does that in terms of a larger view of the whole class as a community.

I think Kala had some value issues that year. For example, there were a number of handicapped students that she had "adopted" in this class. She was always making sure that they could see or they were in the right place or they had whatever they needed if they couldn't get it themselves. She would explain the assignments to them and help them in all kinds of ways. It seemed like she was more interested in them than in herself. Doug was really aware of this from the beginning of the year. And throughout that year, he helped her to stand up for herself, to acknowledge the reality of her own needs, that she had to take care of herself just like anybody else.

He was really supportive, checking with her on how she was doing to meet deadlines, making sure she knew it was okay for other people to struggle or to have difficulty, reassuring her that she didn't have to take responsibility for their problems. He did this with the other kids in the class, too. He let them know that they could take more responsibility for themselves. They didn't have to depend on Kala and she didn't need to be responsible for other people. He also didn't dismiss or negate her helpfulness. He encouraged it and even commented on both her empathy and her sacrifice and the fact that Kala is a very giving person. He just helped to create boundaries and support reality a little more in terms of what she needed to do for herself.

As a result, Kala started becoming much more confident and much more decisive and, during that year, came to have a much deeper appreciation of herself. She definitely was a changed person, and I feel a large debt of gratitude to him for paying attention to her, for noticing her and for looking at her individually and personally and intimately.

There was a certain amount of vulnerability that he allowed, a certain camaraderie that he was able to create with the students. He was definitely the teacher and the leader in charge, but there was also a certain democracy and equality in the class, and all those things, I think, helped her feel her value and her individuality more.

What is remarkable to me is that she didn't stop being sensitive or empathetic or giving. There's just a better boundary now between taking care of herself and helping others. She still engages people very deeply and is very sensitive, but she also knows what she wants and there's really no conflict for her. She can find a way to do what she wants and satisfy other people's needs simultaneously, whereas before, other people's needs were more important. Now there's a wonderful balance. None of this has anything to do with curriculum. It was a much more holistic approach. It was as important for him to teach personal value and citizenship as it was to teach math or reading.

K.J. Quick, Director of Purchasing, Petaluma, California

In 1974 I was 14, a timid freshman in our small New England town's high school. My first week, miserably overwhelmed by my new environment, I hid in the nurse's office with migraines. I was a model of awkward adolescence: too ashamed to eat my mother's homemade lunches, I left them to rot in my locker; fiercely aware of my every move, I began to walk funny. I brushed my hair several times an hour and compulsively smoked cigarettes in the bathroom between classes.

Mr. Kramer's Spanish I class was sixth period—right after lunch, and sometimes right after a joint shared with friends in the woods surrounding the school. He was a teacher who demanded class participation, and so on my sober days he called on me often as we went around the room reciting vocabulary words. On stoned days, I placed my head on the desk and stared at the wall, and he left me alone.

In the language lab we listened to taped sentence and vocabulary drills through headphones, while Mr. Kramer listened to our repetitions through his own set. At times he would speak to an individual through his microphone to correct a mispronunciation. One day as I fumbled through the repetitions, his voice broke through: he wanted to see me after class. I knew in my bones he'd say I wasn't keeping up. He asked instead if I could take the class earlier in the day, since I was doing so well and the rest of this class was so slow. I was unable to switch, but in one sentence Mr. Kramer altered my perception of myself from that of an awkward, average girl stunted by shyness, to someone with some intellectual capacity, perhaps even a knack for languages. He was the first teacher in eight years to single me out, to treat me as exceptional.

At the end of my junior year I accompanied several hundred American high school students on a month-long sojourn of study and adventure in Spain. Mr. Kramer and his wife went along for the ride (his wife was Spanish). They introduced me to people and slices of Spanish life that I wouldn't have found otherwise: food and wine, restaurants and friends' homes that flavored my stay with an indelible authenticity. For the first time, a teacher regarded me with adult respect.

After graduation I attended the nearby university, where I minored in Spanish. (Mr. Kramer urged me not to declare it as a major, saying it would limit my employability.) I saw him for the last time just before college graduation. My hometown was having some sort of day-long fair, where I'd volunteered to sit at the booth for the local chapter of the National Abortion Rights Action League. This town fostered neither political awareness nor activism, so I expected a light afternoon. Several stalls down from mine, though, sat Mr. Kramer at the Right to Life booth. We exchanged nervous glances for quite some time before I decided to walk over to him and say hello.

"Well, it certainly looks as though a lot of water has passed under the bridge over the years," Mr. Kramer said quietly to me. I nodded and sort of giggled, asking whether he and his wife had gone back to Spain recently. He said that he had, and began a lecture about how Spain had suffered since Franco's demise. My eyes glazed, my smile froze, and I stopped hearing. My teacher Mr. Kramer—the only educator in my seventeen years as a student who had been a true advisor to me—not only opposed my cherished political cause, he supported a despot.

And so he taught me a valued lesson: that authentic caring can cross all boundaries to leave the most lasting of life's impressions.

Joy Jacobson, 34, Massage Therapist, Albuquerque, New Mexico

I had an English teacher in high school named Tom Wehling who gave me the nuts and bolts to express myself in writing. Everything I've done since then, from college to professional work, even writing great letters to boyfriends, all comes from the tools he gave me.

Mr. Wehling took writing out of the realm of the scary and intimidating and made it accessible to me. He showed me that you could have any topic—plumbing, relationships, or Einstein's theories of relativity—and that the important part of writing, regardless of the nature of your topic, is how you go about gathering information, how you organize the information and how you give it back to the person reading it. There is no subject too scary to write about if you have the tools to write.

He taught me this by making me write. Instead of assigning the Big Paper that every kid freaks out about, he had us come in and write papers every two days. These papers would be on almost anything. Sometimes they were on literature or various writers, but other times they were on silly topics, like why we hated doing the dishes. We still had to take the same approach to that kind of topic as we would to writing about a great literary author. It was really cool because we got to flex our writing muscles and just kept doing it and doing it and doing it.

When I arrived at Northwestern University, I was supposed to be among the cream of the academic crop, but I realized that a lot of people didn't have this basic ability to write. The other students would stress out every time they had to write a paper, even if they were very bright. But I had this blueprint in me that said this is how you write. I didn't realize how ingrained that was or what an impression this teacher had made on me until that point. No matter what, I will always know how to write.

I feel as if what he gave me was such a blessing. I guess I really loved him, too, because he had a fun, vivacious, almost earthy way of teaching. He was not lofty or removed. On college breaks, I'd stop by my old English classroom to show Mr. Wehling a stack of A+ papers. I wanted him to know that I never stopped using the gift he gave me.

Brenda Shoss, 33, Owner, Brenda Shoss Advertising and Public Relations, Freelance Writer, Professional Dancer, St. Louis, Missouri

Grade 4 was a time of transition for my family. I was going through a lot of changes and I turned to school as a way of getting away from everything that was happening at home. I don't remember my Grade 4 teacher's name. It was quite a stressful time, and although I do remember the effect that year had on me, my memory is quite poor for details.

My family moved around so much that I was in a different school for each grade—sometimes in three different schools for a grade—so I didn't have much of a social life. In fact, at that time, my social life was pretty much nonexistent. In this class we used to have parties for no special reason that I can recall. These parties helped create a social life for me and gave me a welcome break from the tension at home.

The most important thing that happened to me in Grade 4 was when I was told that I could do a project at the end of the year. This was near summer and it was very hot. I remember in 90-degree weather carrying books home stacked up to my chin and working until very late at night. My mom had to get up and ask me to go to bed. I was so inspired to be able to do a project that I could choose myself. Later on, the same teacher told my mom that I had written a report of university quality, such was the organization and the research. This gave me a great deal of confidence in my ability to learn, to bring together information and organize it, to teach myself and to work independently. It taught me that I can be quite focused and that I do have value. It helped me to believe in myself and showed me that I could be self-directed when I applied myself.

I also had a science teacher in high school who gave us a test that we all flunked. Instead of blaming us, he apologized! It amazed me that he took responsibility for our failing the exam. Over the next two weeks, he went over all the material more slowly and made sure that we understood it. We even had a mock test before the real test to ensure that all students could succeed. He was more concerned about the fact that we had all failed the test than he was about placing blame. I learned that when something goes wrong, sometimes "authority" can be in error. I mean, I grew up in a household where the adults were *never* in error, so this gave me a taste of an adult owning the problem, taking responsibility for a situation that didn't turn out, and doing something about it.

My life was also shaped by a teacher in university who helped me to believe that I could do an honors degree, which was something that I had never dreamed I really could do. When we were studying poetry, she'd ask us what we got out of the poetry. She didn't give us someone else's interpretation or even her own. We had a lot of discussions and everyone's opinion was taken into account. No one's opinion was discredited.

Such is the nature of poetry, I realize, but from my other experiences with literature and instructors, this was a welcome change for me. This professor encouraged me to believe in my own insights, in my own intuition, in my own feelings about words and about language, in my personal mythology, my own symbols and my dreams—things that poetry deals with a lot. Each of these teachers helped me achieve a level of confidence that I've carried with me into adulthood, lessons I've learned about myself that I can use over and over throughout my life.

Roshael Brenna, 35, Speech Assistant and Child Care Professional, Red Deer, Alberta, Canada

I had two teachers who had a profound effect on me. One was Mrs. Brown, who taught Grade 5. Quite often after lunch, we would have long discussions in class on all kinds of different issues that would be important to a bunch of 10-year-old children. We would sometimes talk for a whole half hour or longer. Mrs. Brown seemed really interested in what we had to say. She would also share part of herself with us in these discussions and tell us little stories that went along with the topics. These discussions seemed to make school so exciting. They really put those things into perspective for me and helped me form my own morals and values.

The other teacher was Mr. Nuttle, who taught Social 20, which is Grade 11 social studies. He used to come in and tell us stories and dramatize the events of history to us in class. He was so interesting and so fascinating. I don't ever remember taking a single note in his class, and yet I remember lots and lots of information. I can even remember dates, and I don't have a single date written down in my Grade 11 social studies notebook. He would also share his experiences as a teacher, a lot of good things and some not-so-good things that had happened. He was somebody I felt I knew, and yet I don't ever remember having a one-on-one, personal conversation with him. By sharing himself, he really affected my life.

Pat Brown, 35, Grade 6 Teacher, Calgary, Alberta, Canada

My favorite teacher was one who used to read to us.

Jean M. Auel, Author, Sherwood, Oregon

When Mrs. Banuke taught me in Grade 3, she was 21. It was her first year teaching. I was a real "please me" kind of child: I sat in the back and I did everything to please everybody. I wasn't high academically and I didn't have very many social skills either, but I sucked up to the other kids and was friendly. Once Mrs. Banuke told my mom, "Sally is always a nice person and is always friendly to everyone, and she tries her best to get along." Well, my mom has held onto this comment to this day. At least once a year, she says, "Mrs. Banuke said that little Sally always gets along with other people." She still says this to me, even though I'm now a 28-year-old adult.

This meant so much to my mom that it really influenced my upbringing because it had an effect on my relationship with her. Because my mom is very socially conscious and aware of what other people say, I don't think that she would have recognized on her own the behaviors Mrs. Banuke described—but someone else pointing them out to her was worthy of attention. This statement got me respect from my mom, which was important to me. It gave her something tangible to see as a positive in me.

Sally Bowen, 28, Resource Teacher, Calgary, Alberta, Canada

I went to a very small country school with about 80 other kids, maybe ten kids in my grade. When I was in Grade 6, Mrs. Bey, who was the wife of a Canadian Forces officer, came from Europe and taught at our school for a year. Mrs. Vey would bring in films that she and her husband had made. I'll never forget the film they had taken when they lived in Italy, of Rome and of its people.

She always said to us, "You can go anywhere you want. You can see anything you want. You can go anyplace in the world." Up until that point in time, my world had revolved around my family's small farm. I lived in the country and had never been outside of Manitoba. I thought she was the most amazing woman because it never even occurred to me that I could go anywhere else or do anything else. I never even thought of being able to travel. I was a very shy child and the whole idea intimidated me. Her films, her stories and her encouragement certainly broadened my horizons.

Later on, when I traveled to other places or when I moved to another province, I thought back to Mrs. Vey and thought, "Oh, she would be so proud of me because I actually did what she said: I went out and traveled and I saw things." I could go places. Back in Grade 6, I would tell her, "Oh, Mrs. Vey! You're so wonderful," and she would tell me, "You can do it, too, Karen." And she was right, I could!

Karen Ellefson, 29, Teacher, Calgary, Alberta, Canada

My favorite teacher was not in the school system. She was my piano teacher. I had to walk five miles for my piano lessons. It wasn't just the music that she was giving me—she also gave me courage. She once told me, "What I love about you is that when you make a mistake, you keep on going." Those words have been with me ever since.

Jeannette Vos, 49, Author, El Cajon, California

When I was 16 or so, about to graduate from high school, my best friend and I just wanted to get out of high school and join the service. I guess that was pretty short-sighted, but we thought that was the best way to travel at that time in our lives.

My mother, who never finished college, sat us down one day in the back yard and said, "Okay, why do you really want to join the service? Why not go to college and get an education? That will open up a number of doors and then, hopefully, travel will come out of that." We just dismissed her advice, but during our senior year in high school, we started to really consider it. Did we really want to join the service?

I decided to go to junior college instead. My mother always needled me, saying, "You need to take this college thing seriously." The following year, I got into college. My mother wanted me to major in business. I thought about it for a while. I was only 18 or 19 at this time and I realized that I didn't like business: "What is it that I've done within my life that I really had fun doing?" I thought back to my junior year in high school. I had taken a TV class. I went to a brand-new high school my freshman year. They had a TV studio and the TV instructor really influenced me, got me interested in broadcasting. And as a junior, it was like, "You know, this is really cool. I like this." But I didn't do it my senior year because I just wanted to get a car and work and get money in my pocket, which I did. But here I was, 19, and I had to do something I liked. I chose broadcasting as my profession.

The teacher of this class was Mr. John Stevens. He was a well-known broadcaster who worked with WGN and had strong ties with Columbia College, which is a broadcasting school in Chicago. He made it interesting, he made it challenging and he made it fun, which was a big thing for me when it was time for me to make a decision about a career. Now, 18 years later, I'm in broadcasting, producing live sporting events for ESPN, TBS and everybody else. Today I can wake up every morning to a job I have fun doing. There are no two days ever the same in my profession, and I love it. I love producing television programs and now I travel all over the world! So as I look back on it, my mother is the one that really made the difference in my life by telling me, "Don't sell yourself short. Go get an education and see what happens after that."

Jeffrey Green, 35, Independent TV Producer, Lithonia, Georgia

My favorite teacher kept a message on the board all year long that said, "There is nothing in this world that you may want to know that you cannot find in a book, and all your life you will learn."

This message has stayed with me all my life. It taught me very early on that you never stop learning.

Jacqueline Petrie, 62, Bookkeeper, Grande Cache, Alberta, Canada

Before I started high school, we moved to a new town. I'd been there for about three years, living out in the country. I had no brothers or sisters living at home anymore. At that time in my life, I was a very negative, quiet, "into myself" kind of person. I had few friends at school. I didn't get along with a lot of people. I got my good marks and I lived my own life. But by Grade 10 or so, I got into such a state of depression that I couldn't cope anymore. I didn't want to be at school. Home provided love and shelter but was quite lonely. I didn't care about anything. I started skipping school, spending my time alone, walking around just trying to get away from life and things that were happening.

Mr. Penner, the school counselor and math teacher, never mentioned about my skipping. He just let it go. But after a while, I realized that I had skipped too many of Mr. Penner's math classes and I needed to be there. So one day, I was sitting in this math class and I was supposed to be doing an assignment, which, of course, I wasn't doing because I was just too depressed. I didn't know where life was going or where I wanted it to go.

I started doodling on the back of the assignment paper, drawing a circle that looked like the world, and lines and stars. I had roads that started from home and then went off into space. I had "insanity" written over all these scribbles and squiggles. There didn't seem to be any sense or direction to what I was drawing. But I just kept at it and ended up spending my entire 80-minute math class drawing this picture, coloring and sketching and drawing more and more and more until the whole sheet was covered.

At the end of math period, feeling a little uncomfortable but not really caring a whole bunch, I handed the paper in with my name on it. Math, incomplete as usual. Mr. Penner took the paper and never said anything. The next day when I came back to class, he handed me back my assignment. Of course I had gotten a zero on it because I hadn't done any of the work, but on the back of my drawing he wrote, "Life is trouble. My door is open. You are more than welcome to come anytime." I went later on that day.

He'd been sitting back and watching me for a long time, knowing that I had problems, but he wasn't going to come and ask me to come to him. I guess he knew that if he'd come to me, I would not have responded, but would have blocked him out instead. But because he left it up to me to make this decision and I wanted to talk to somebody, I chose to go to him. I went down to his counselor's office and he said, "Yep. Life is trouble, and I can see that you're having some trouble. Did you want to talk about it?"

At that point I didn't really want to talk, so I just sat there for about 40 minutes. I never really came up with anything to say, and he just sat there and let me sit alone and be quiet. At one point, he asked me if there was anything that I'd like to do in school. "What are you going to do in your career? Have you made any choices?" And I talked to him about maybe getting into physiotherapy and things like that, but he never questioned me about my picture, my marks, my skipping or anything else.

About a month down the road, he called me to his office and he said, "Deanna, I've got something for you." He said, "I think that we're going to make arrangements for you to have a summer job, working as a physiotherapist so that you can decide whether or not you'd like to do this kind of work. I think you'd be really good at it. If you're interested, this is what you can do. . . ."

I did go into physiotherapy that summer and spent a wonderful summer doing it. At the lowest point in my life, Mr. Penner offered me a sanctuary by allowing me to go into his office anytime I got stressed out in class. I had the option to get up and leave and go and sit in his office, whether he was there or not. I went often. He gave me the guidance to be able to make decisions on my own, and made it possible for me to sit in a room quietly and be able to think my problems through. Mr. Penner taught me something very important that year.

I still have that paper and now and then I take it out and look at it, and I remember that there was somebody out there who cared, who would just sit and listen, and who wouldn't judge. I don't know where he is anymore, but he had a tremendous influence on my life, and probably on my four children's lives, as well, because now I can respond to them when they're having a hard time and let them be quiet and sit with their thoughts. I may not say much—I may just sit with them and hold them. But I'm present and I'm there with them, which is really important.

My children often leave me notes that say, "I had a bad day, Mom." And on the back of their notes, I often respond, "Life is trouble. My door is open."

Deanna Ruether, 31, Housewife, Volunteer, Rehab Technician (in training), Bruderheim, Alberta, Canada

Growing up in 1950s America, with the emphasis on uniformity and intolerance of anything out of the norm, being left-handed in grade school was not easy. I learned to write using a desk designed for right-handers and a handwriting chart with an illustration of a right hand forming the letters. When the teacher described how to do the letters, she told the two left-handed kids in the class, "Just do the same thing but with your left hand."

Well, considering I was already twisted halfway out of my seat with my left arm dangling in space, I found "doing the same thing" to be quite a challenge! I eventually did learn to form the letters, and as all left-handers do, I developed a writing style nothing like the "norm." I never earned an A in penmanship or in neatness, but I realized no one who had my affliction did, either.

I grew up in an extended family household with my brothers, parents, grandparents, two uncles and an aunt. We lived in a Polish and German neighborhood in Pittsburgh, Pennsylvania. All the neighbors knew me and assisted in my upbringing as a child, since it was an area with row homes and noisy children living in every one. I was the only left-handed child in the neighborhood, so I learned how to throw a ball by doing the reverse of everyone else. This trick did not work when I was trying to learn how to ride a bicycle, however—I kept applying the brakes by pedaling backwards, and I didn't understand how all my friends would go forward when I would just fall over! My dad and uncles taught me that I had to pedal just like them, and then all that I had to learn was to balance myself. When I finally rode a whole block by myself, the neighbors were all shouting, "Jerry is riding his bike! Jerry's riding his bike!"

However, something that my family could not teach me was how to tie my shoelaces. I could not follow their hands and transpose the movements quickly enough, so they would just tie them for me. When I was in kindergarten and my laces would untie, I would have to ask the teacher to tie them or I would walk the half-mile home with my laces undone. Finally, my first-grade teacher, Miss McKay, discovered that I could not tie my shoelaces. She didn't ridicule me as I had expected, but spent several days slowly tying my shoelaces, over and over again, teaching me as best she could how a left-hander would tie. I eventually learned how to tie my shoelaces, and I noticed that I did get special attention from that point on by Miss McKay, just in case she was teaching in a "right-handed" way.

Now, at 45, I obviously lace in a unique way, since people stare as I tie my laces "like a little kid," as I'm often told. Miss McKay's method works for me, and I have always appreciated that she was willing to "learn" what I needed and to teach me so patiently and in such a caring way.

Jerry Tereszkiewicz, 45, Business Manager, Albuquerque, New Mexico

I sometimes wish that students knew how much of a difference they make in a teacher's life. Let me share a story with you that changed my life and my teaching forever.

During a corporate class I was conducting one evening, a young woman named Jena was sitting in the front row. Jena was home on vacation and her father, part of the corporate group, had brought her with him to the class. As I began my talk, Jena listened attentively to every word I said. Congenitally blind since birth, Jena had finished high school and gone on to college, where she graduated with a B.A. in

French. At 32, she was now working as an English translator in the French courts. She had lived in France for over two years in an apartment with only her seeing-eye dog.

As I began teaching about the Comfort Zone, Jena suddenly lit up. Sitting forward in her seat, she nodded in agreement as I shared how the Comfort Zone is a person's zone of safety. She got more excited as I went on to say that sometimes when we leave our Comfort Zones, we feel a bit anxious and even scared because we are entering new and unknown territories.

Finally unable to contain herself any longer, Jena burst out, "That's it! That's it! That's why I can travel halfway around the world and live by myself with such an unusual job. People always ask me how I do all the things I do with my handicap. They marvel at the fact that I live alone and work in the huge French government system. They are amazed at my distance from my family and my choice of career."

By now, all the attention in the room was riveted on Jena, for we had all silently wondered the same thing.

"As you spoke about risking and getting out of our Comfort Zones, I realized what it is that makes me secure. It's because I carry my Comfort Zone within me," she said emphatically, sitting back in her seat. "I have been able to do all the things that I do because I carry my zone of safety with me wherever I go! I make the world around me safe, because I'm safe within me."

That night we all realized that Jena was not a woman with a handicap. She was indeed a woman who had found peace within herself, in spite of a seeming limitation. The triumphs she experienced in life were a direct reflection of her inner safety and security.

I discovered that the secret to students' success in and out of the classroom lay in helping them strengthen and expand their Comfort Zones, and that I was responsible for creating a safe emotional learning environment for my students. By building their self-esteem through the accomplishment of small goals, students develop a sense of confidence that helps them accelerate their learning. To this day, I constantly see the results of that discovery. My students go beyond the normal educational process and take on goals and challenges at the community level. For example, another student of mine, Lester, was recently asked to speak to his first-grade daughter's class. This would have caused terror in him months earlier; however, with some encouraging, Lester decided to stretch his own Comfort Zone by speaking to the group. He later reported his success. The 30 youngsters were enthusiastic and their teacher took copious notes, so that she could share the information in the years to come.

Thank you, Jena. You have made a difference in this teacher's life. You remain a constant inspiration and reminder that adults have a responsibility to create that safe emotional learning place for our students.

D. Trinidad Hunt, Educator, Author, Keynote Speaker,
Kaneohe, Hawaii

I attended Bantu High School in what was then called Western Native Township near Sophiatown, Johannesburg—later to be indicted by Trevor Huddleston in his book *Naught for your Comfort*, a searing indictment of apartheid's forced population removals policy.

My school was for children coming from South Africa's black ghettos, and it had most of the characteristics of a ghetto school: hardly any facilities to mention. I went to the laboratory only once in my five or six years at school, there was a wholly inadequate library and very few recreational and games facilities. It was a tough school; and the teachers needed to be tough to maintain discipline and be able to teach at all. I recall that the school population was scattered in classrooms and church buildings because we did not even have a decent school campus with adequate accommodation. Our own class, badly overcrowded, was held in a church building. (It was routine to have anything up to 80 students in one class.) We did not have normal classroom desks—we sat on pew benches and when we wrote, we knelt behind the pews and used the seats to write on.

The circumstances were quite grim and made education a thoroughly unpleasant job. But I had good teachers who helped to neutralise all these negative factors. I recall vividly one teacher who came to instruct us in arithmetic, part of mathematics. I can't claim that it was ever my favourite subject; actually I learned it only because it was compulsory.

However, things changed dramatically after Mr. Nimron Ndebele stood in front of the class. He was a middle-sized man with a fine alto voice. He always had a gentle smile playing around his mouth, a very pleasant image, and he made learning his subject so much fun. He always had objects that he used to illustrate what, up to that point, had been cloaked in mystery and unrelieved gloom. He had an extraordinary knack of making the most complicated and abstruse principle seem so straightforward and obvious. Nobody, just nobody, failed his subject in the public state examinations. In fact, many of his students obtained distinctions.

It will not surprise you to learn that Mr. Ndebele never had any problems with discipline in his classes. He hardly had to scold any of his pupils. Everybody was eating out of his hand. He made us all feel like geniuses. He made us feel so special and that was quite something, coming as we all did from an environment that conspired to make us feel utterly dejected, nonentities whose parents counted for nothing in the land of their birth, who themselves counted for nothing and who had an invisible ceiling over their heads beyond which they could not proceed.

I thank God for Mr. Ndebele and for what he meant for so many of us.

The Most Reverend Desmond Mpilo Tutu, Archbishop of Cape Town, South Africa

The teacher that had one of the greatest effects on my life was Marian McNamara, my Latin teacher. Before sixth grade, I went with my parents and talked to all the teachers of languages in my school, and I chose to take Latin because of her, not because of any interest in Latin. Because she was such a good teacher, I stuck with her for three years.

She made us do these written and oral reports all the time on Roman aqueducts, Roman underwear, Roman olive production—you know, whatever she could think of. This was in middle and high school. At the time, it seemed like really tedious work. We had to do one of these reports every couple of weeks. So we did plenty of writing and plenty of speaking.

It's no dramatic story, but I notice that I know how to write, and most of my peers don't. They come to me for advice on how to write. I do a lot of reading, too. This also helped my oral skills. I'm an actor now, and never thought I would be. Because of her I'm more comfortable in front of audiences.

She was also a teacher who believed in sharing her opinions about moral character. She wasn't just teaching Latin; she was teaching us how to be what she thought was good. Her values, her integrity stick with me—things like citing your sources and doing a good job, becoming interested in what you're studying, not just doing it for the grade.

Hugh Fox, 24, Student, Used Bookshop Salesperson, Boulder, Colorado

Like a lot of young girls in the Flatbush section of Brooklyn coming from families of first-generation Americans, I grew up with many of the cultural values that came across the Atlantic along with my grandparents. In my family, one of these values was that an education was not something that young girls should have. Education was really for boys—there was a sense that it was wasted on girls. Because my mother was divorced and there was no money—divorce itself being very, very shameful at that time—I recognized that what was in store for me was, as my mother put it, a "just in case" education, so I could become a teacher or a secretary "just in case" a man didn't take care of me. The idea, of course, was that you were going to be at the mercy or the privilege, depending upon how well you married, of the particular man in your life. Those were the values with which I was brought up: to marry early and to make the best marriage that I could. I remember my mother attempting, at one point, to fix me up with the son of the local kosher butcher because I'd always be in lamb chops. Diamonds no, but lamb chops for sure. Marriage was really going to be pragmatic—that was the whole idea of what this was about.

At 14, I met the man who was to become my husband. He introduced me to his mother and I saw a view of a very different life. From that day forward, I have truly recognized the power of one, the idea that it takes one person to believe in you, one person you're willing to entrust with that inner core of yourself, one person to help you toward a direction that will make a positive dent. And at 14 she completely turned my life around.

What I saw was a woman who had a number of traditional values in terms of her religion and a very centered sense of life, without a lot of regrets about the past or a lot of idealism about the future; someone who seemed to live fairly closely in the present. She's a woman who marched in the first Women's Suffrage march down Fifth Avenue. She had a lot of feelings about women and empowerment, about how you live your life within your own family, and about how you're treated in your family as setting the stage for everything from that point on into the outer world.

She was one of the first female graduates of Columbia who went on to the school of dentistry and became an orthodontist. She had her own practice, with an office in her home and one in Manhattan that she went to on occasion. She kept a beautiful home. She had lovely things. She got an enormous amount of respect from her two children and her husband. She was quite valued and had a great deal to say in her marriage in terms of decision-making.

I remember her as a woman who dressed from the inside out. I never have gotten over this. If she was wearing beige, she wore beige from her lingerie to her stockings to the dress that she wore, and matched it with some jewelry. It was just an absolutely different world from the perhaps well-intended but totally chaotic life in which I lived my daily comings and goings.

What this woman said to me was as follows: "If you're interested in my son, you'd better get yourself a good education, and you'd better have some skills." And I heard that loud and clear. It is so interesting that it is possible to undo the years of your cultural background when you really feel that somebody offers you something more and opens up another window for you. You talk about eternal flames? This is the woman who really lit the flame for me.

So I went to school. In the days that I attended Brooklyn College, a female had to have an 83 average and a male had to have an 81. You could never get away with that now. Think about that. I'm grateful in some ways that I experienced that kind of sexism. A lot of younger women who have never experienced any of these things have no sense of what the generations before them had to do to give them the things that they just take for granted. My mother-in-law was one of the women who were a part of all that. She's alive within me even now, after her death, because I've really taken on a lot of who she was. Whether it's the foods she cooked or a semblance of who she is, there's a lot of her in me.

I went on to get a Ph.D. in psychology and have just had this miracle career, and it's all because of one woman who basically said to me, "If you want my son, go get yourself an education." She really lit the candle that has lighted my path throughout my life.

Sonya Friedman, Ph.D., Former Host, "Sonya Live"
(CNN), Psychologist, Author, Birmingham, Michigan

I grew up in a predominantly Italian immigrant section of Brooklyn. There were nine of us jammed into three rooms, living on a struggling garbage collector's wages. It was a neighborhood of overwhelmingly law-abiding, working-class people, but there were several seedy pool halls, street gangs and hoods. Caught up in the exciting heroics of the street cult, rumbles, building a rep and proving my machismo, I entered the seventh grade at P.S. 259 with a school history that included mediocre grades, atrocious conduct and a flip attitude that was summed up in "School is fa [*sic*] creeps."

But one teacher—a 25-year-old Norwegian-American woman—turned me away from the streets to books. For a long time I was viewed as a hopeless student, until I was placed in her class. Miss Lawsen stationed herself on my desk regularly throughout term. She treated everyone with animated attention, but I was her favorite. I guess it was because I was the only swarthy, black-haired Italian boy with blue eyes in the class. She selected me for all the honors. If I had ever pinned on all the service ribbons and merit badges she gave me, I would have looked like a dictator.

Miss Lawsen made me feel special. Her encouragement and praise inspired me to study. I wanted to excel for her. At night, instead of playing ring-aleavio, buck buck and the other games, I stayed home to read. Since there was no private place in the apartment, I sat in a corner with the couch pulled behind me. Until then I had dreaded books, and thinking about it now, I can understand why. My uncles distrusted book learning and said that too much reading makes a person go crazy. Ma and Dad seldom read anything except *True Confessions* and the

Daily Mirror, respectively. All my friends considered books a gruesome drag. But when I began paying attention to what books said, I started enjoying them. History became as exciting to me as a war movie, and I could remember it as vividly.

As a result of Miss Lawsen's concern and confidence, I applied myself to learning and eventually achieved the highest grade average in junior high school. At the end of the term, I was on the honor roll. Worried that my friends might see my name, I asked the principal's secretary to take it down. Regrettably, peer pressure in high school tipped my inner balance back to destructiveness and street violence, fighting every week, failing all my subjects until I was finally expelled at the end of my freshman year.

For a long time I grinded in back-breaking jobs in warehouses, piers, factories, railroad yards and construction. I tried to climb out through professional boxing, but I quickly grew disillusioned from the sleepless nights caused by internal bleeding and my head throbbing in pain.

At 20, I passed a night school with the sign: Enroll Now. Classes Free. I had failed at four previous attempts at night school, but I was now mature and I had the memory of Miss Lawsen and the academic aptitude she had nurtured in me. Still working days shoveling cement, I attended evening classes with adult immigrants, and with determination forged from years of toil, I completed three years and graduated with the highest average in my class. I went on to college, where I graduated magna cum laude, to UCLA for my master's degree, to Oxford for further study, and finally graduated from Harvard Law School, where I was selected as the class valedictorian.

I know from my own experience that even one dedicated, inspiring teacher can change a young person's life. One-to-one caring is not a Hollywood answer. It is not a script of love merging into trauma and tragedy, of a kid rising from the depths of despair into the sunlight. It is a quieter drama, of real people going through real problems, listening to each other when they need it most. It is one person caring enough about another to help at a crucial point.

Judge Joseph Sorrentino, Criminal Prosecutor, Author, Los Angeles, California

A REALLY GREAT TEACHER IS SOMEONE WHO . . .

. . . lets you work at your own pace.

Ellie, 10, Anchorage, Alaska

. . . knows who you are.

Eli, 8, Anchorage, Alaska

. . . won't be grouchy all the time.

Josh, 9, Anchorage, Alaska

. . . listens to you when you need to tell her something, even if you're interrupting.

Josh, 10, Anchorage, Alaska

. . . listens to you no matter how boring you might get.

Rebecca, 11, Anchorage, Alaska

. . . makes you feel good.

Brianna, 7, Anchorage, Alaska

. . . understands about the different feelings and abilities of his or her students.

Jasper, 14, Surabaya, Indonesia

. . . will make the students learn the lessons without the students ever knowing they are studying.

Thomas, 14, Surabaya, Indonesia

. . . has a sense of humor and is united with the students.

Jordan, 14, Surabaya, Indonesia

. . . can take a walk in his students' shoes and truly understand how a kid might feel when put in a certain situation.

Kasia, 14, Surabaya, Indonesia

. . . always cares and understands you.
. . . tries to look at it from your point of view every time you do something crazy.

Wan Ling, 14, Surabaya, Indonesia

. . . helps you when you need help with homework or something.
. . . is funny and has a really fun way of teaching.

Anna, 12, Boise, Idaho

. . . makes you laugh so you want to go back and see her every day of the year and you never forget her and you even give her a present for Christmas.

Summer, 13, Boise, Idaho

. . . helps you with something you don't understand and keeps helping you till you understand it.

Trevor, 12, Boise, Idaho

. . . teaches you not only about school, but about life in general.

Colin, 13, Mishawaka, Indiana

. . . treats you the way you want to be treated.

Gina, 10, Mishawaka, Indiana

. . . encourages you to try your best in everything.

. . . stays by your side every step you take.

Jonathan, 12, Mishawaka, Indiana

. . . will not get mad if we do not get our work done.

Harsha, 8, Mishawaka, Indiana

. . . lets you move around a lot.

Andrew, 9, Mishawaka, Indiana

. . . won't rush you and lets you go to recess no matter what.

. . . helps people so they won't hurt each other.

A.J., 8, Mishawaka, Indiana

. . . answers all the children's questions.

Allison, 8, Mishawaka, Indiana

. . . likes all the students in her class.

Philip, 8³/₄, Mishawaka, Indiana

. . . understands what it's like to be frustrated.

Sarah, 12, Mishawaka, Indiana

. . . knows how you feel by the way you're acting.

Lauren, 12, Mishawaka, Indiana

. . . doesn't mind when you need to come to them for help.

Sonya, 13, Mishawaka, Indiana

. . . is supportive.

> Trent, 12, Mishawaka, Indiana

. . . teaches you to be positive even when you're in a negative situation.

> Ava, 13, Mishawaka, Indiana

. . . believes in you.

> Katy, 13, Mishawaka, Indiana

. . . works with your parents to find solutions to your problems.

> Anthony, 10, Mishawaka, Indiana

. . . teaches you respect.

> R.J., 11, Mishawaka, Indiana

. . . runs their classroom as a democratic dictatorship.

> Kristofer, 12, Mishawaka, Indiana

. . . will challenge you but not overwhelm you.

> Daniel, 11, Mishawaka, Indiana

CREDITS

Jean Auel, author of the "Earth's Children" series, beginning with *The Clan of the Cave Bear.*

Peggy Bielen, M.A., is the Executive Director of Enhancing Education, a non-profit corporation, and the co-author of *Project Self-Esteem.* She does workshops and trainings in the areas of elementary education, self-esteem and parenting. Contact Peggy at PO Box 16001, Newport Beach, CA, 92659, 714-756-2226.

Harold Bloomfield, M.D., author of *How to Heal Depression* and *The Power of Five.*

Dr. Michele Borba, author of *Esteem Builders Complete Program,* eight components to improve student achievement, behavior and positive school climate (Jalmar Press, 800-662-9662) is also an international consultant who inservices over 250,000 educators each year. To contact Michele: 840 Prescott Dr., Palm Springs, CA, 92262, 619-323-5387

Les Brown, author of *Live Your Dreams.* William Morrow & Company is the publisher and holds the rights to this book by Les Brown, which includes this story.

Leo F. Buscaglia, author of *Love; Living, Loving and Learning* and *Born for Love.*

Glenn Capelli is part of the team that runs the True Learning Centre with membership and programs in Australia and the USA for youngsters, youth, families, teachers and corporations wanting to tap into accelerative learning methods, lifelong learning and self-esteem. His products include *The Magic Brain* music cassette series, *Born to Learn* video program, and *Maximizing Your Learning Potential: A Handbook for Lifelong Learners* (Kendall-Hunt, Publishers). Contact Glenn at Windsor House, 37 Windsor St, East Perth 6004 Western Australia, Phone 011-61-9-2271420, Fax 011-61-9-2271421, E-mail tlcmagic@iinet.net.au.

Michael Dorris, author of several books, including *A Yellow Raft in Blue Water*, *Paper Trail* and *The Broken Cord.*

Donna Evens, co-owner, MarkTel, Inc.

C. Lynn Fox, Ph.D., university professor; author of *Let's Get Together* and *Unlocking Doors to Self-Esteem* (Jal-Mar Press), *Creating Drug-Free Schools and Communities* (Harper Collins) and *The Front 9: Golf Instruction* (Links Publications).

Dr. Sonya Friedman has just completed over seven years as the host of the CNN informational/news program "Sonya Live." One of the most recognized psychologists in the country, she is the author of the books, *Secret Loves: Women with Two Lives, On a Clear Day You Can See Yourself, Men Are Just Desserts, Smart Cookies Don't Crumble* and *A Hero Is More than Just a Sandwich.*

Patricia Gallagher is author of *Raising Happy Kids on a Reasonable Budget*, Betterway Books, $10.95.

Allen Ginsberg is a member of the American Institute of Arts and Letters and co-founder of the Jack Kerouac School of Disembodied Poetics at the Naropa Institute, the first accredited Buddhist college in the Western world. Now a Distinguished Professor at Brooklyn College, Ginsberg is the author of numerous books including *Collected Poems 1947-1980, White Shroud Poems 1980-1985, Howl* (Harper & Row) and *Journals Mid-Fifties* 1954-1958 (Harper Collins).

Carol Greene, creative arts specialist, Moreland School District, San Jose, CA.

David Harp, author of over two dozen books on music (especially harmonica), meditation and health. He also presents "harmonica team building" and "Zen harmonica" seminars to business and church groups.

D. Trinidad Hunt, author of *Learning to Learn: Maximizing Your Performance Potential* (Book, Book on Tape, Audiocassette Series) and *Remember to Remember Who You Are* (Elan Enterprises Press), Elan Enterprises, 47-430 Hui Nene St., Kaneohe, HI, 96744, 808-239-4431.

Eulogio Izaguirre, classroom teacher, fourth-grade, Ben Franklin Elementary, Alamo, TX.

Joy Jacobson is a freelance writer and massage therapist living in New Mexico.

Marcela Kogan is a writer in the Washington, D.C., area.

Mary Ann F. Kohl, author of *Scribble Cookies, Mudworks, Good Earth Art* and *Science Arts*, Bright Ring Publishing.

Shari Lewis, president, Shari Lewis Enterprises, Inc.; star of Lamb Chop's "Play Along," as seen daily on PBS.

Stephanie Marston is the author of *The Magic of Encouragement: Nurturing your Child's Self-Esteem* and *The Divorced Parent: Success Strategies for Raising your Children after Separation* (Pocket Books). Stephanie also does seminars for parents and teachers nationwide.

Mark Medoff is Dramatist in Residence and Professor Emeritus of Theatre Arts at New Mexico State University. He works with public school students and teachers around the country, promoting the notion of full inclusion of all students in the writing and theatrical workshops he conducts. Formerly Head of Theatre Arts and Artistic Director of the American Southwest Theatre Company, Mark is the award-winning author of a dozen plays and half a dozen movies including *Children of a Lesser God, Clara's Heart, City of Joy* and *When You Comin Back, Red Ryder.*

Lee Mirabal, nationally syndicated radio talk-show host, entrepreneur, mother and wife.

Bob Moawad, chairman/CEO, Edge Learning Institute, Inc., President National Council for Self-Esteem, 1994-1995; Author of numerous audio and video-assisted processes focusing on self-esteem, personal accountability, and other potential-releasing insights for both youth and adults. Contact Bob at 2217 N. 30th, Suite 200, Tacoma, WA, 98403, 1-800-858-1484 .

Evelyn Petersen, early childhood consultant, author and columnist.

William Watson Purkey is Professor of Counselor Education, The University of North Carolina at Greenboro, and co-founder of the International Alliance for Invitational Education, a non-profit organization located at UNCG. Dr. Purkey has authored or co-authored nine books, including *Inviting School Success* (Wadsworth Publishing) and *Invitational Counseling* (Brooks/Cole Publishing).

Richard "Rico" Racosky, F-16 fighter pilot, airline pilot, author of children's books on goal-setting and self-esteem *dreams + action = Reality!*, Boulder, CO.

Bob Reasoner is the president of Self-Esteem Resources, the author of *Building Self-Esteem: A Comprehensive Program for Schools* (Consulting Psychologists Press), and has published numerous articles on staff and student self-esteem. He presents keynote addresses and conducts training for schools and parents. He also serves as president of the International Council for Self-Esteem. Contact Bob at 360-437-0300.

Sandi Redenbach, author of *Self-Esteem: The Necessary Ingredient for Success* (Esteem Seminar Programs, Davis, CA, 800-354-6724) and *Innovative Discipline: Managing Your Own Flight Plan* (NEA); motivational speaker and staff development trainer, Esteem Seminar Programs.

Larry Rood, publisher, president of Gryphon House, Inc.

SARK, author/artist.

Dr. Bernie Siegel, surgeon, author of *Love, Medicine & Miracles*.

Gene Simon, head leader, Chaddock School, Quincy, IL.

Judge Joseph N. Sorrentino. Career highlights include Juvenile Court judge (held titles of Municipal Court Judge Pro Tem, Referee); adjunct professor (Pepperdine University; University of Southern California; University of California, Los Angeles); author of books published by Prentice Hall, Bantam, Dell, Manor, Nash-Dutton, Wollstonecraft and Tedco; criminal prosecutor, and national lecturer ranked in Forbes Magazine.

Robert Subby is the Executive Director of Family Systems Center in Minneapolis, Minnesota, and a founding board member of The National Association for Children of Alcoholics. In addition to Bob's full-time clinical practice, he maintains an active schedule of teaching and consulting. He is the author of *Lost in the Shuffle: The Codependent Reality* and *Healing the Family Within* (Health Communications, Inc.).

Sally Templeton-Bowen is a resource teacher and counselor in a Western Canadian elementary school.

Jeannette Vos, co-author, *The Learning Revolution* (Jal-Mar Press).

Sharon Wegscheider-Cruse, president, ONSITE Training and Consulting, Rapid City, SD; author, lecturer, consultant.

Charles Whitfield, M.D., is a physician and psychotherapist in Baltimore and Atlanta. His pivotal books include *Healing the Child Within*, *Boundaries and Relationships* and *Memory and Abuse*.

Anne Wilson-Schaef, author of *Women's Reality*, *When Society Becomes an Addict, Beyond Therapy, Beyond Science* and *Meditations for Women Who Do Too Much*.

Bettie B. Youngs, Ph.D., Ed.D., author, professional speaker and consultant, is one of the nation's most respected voices on the role of self-esteem as it detracts or empowers health, vitality, achievement and performance for both children and adults. Bettie is the author of 14 books published in 27 languages, including *How to Develop Self-Esteem in Your Child* and *Safeguarding Your Teenager from the Dragons of Life.* Her stories are adapted from her book *Values from the Heartland* (Health Communications, © 1995). Contact Bettie at 3060 Racetrack View Drive, Del Mar, CA, 92014. 619-481-6360.

Zig Ziglar, author of *Dear Family* (Pelican Publishing) from which this story was excerpted.

INDEX OF SOURCES

How each story was obtained is shown in parentheses.
Number refers to page on which a story from contributor begins.

ABOUT THE AUTHOR

Jane Bluestein, Ph.D.
President, Instructional Support Services, Inc.
1925 Juan Tabo NE • Suite B-249 • Albuquerque • NM • 87112
1-800-688-1960 • 505-323-9044 • Fax 505-323-9045

Dr. Bluestein has worked in the field of education for more than 20 years. A dynamic and entertaining speaker, she has worked with thousands of teachers, counselors, administrators and parents, presenting keynote addresses, workshops and classes on positive adult-child relationships. She has appeared internationally as a speaker and talk-show guest, including several appearances as a guest expert on National Public Radio, *TalkNews Television, The Vicki! Show* and *The Oprah Winfrey Show.*

Her down-to-earth speaking style, practicality, sense of humor and numerous stories and examples make her ideas clear and accessible to her audiences. Author of *21st Century Discipline, Being a Successful Teacher, Parents in a Pressure Cooker* and *Parents, Teens & Boundaries,* as well as numerous magazine articles, Dr. Bluestein specializes in children at risk and developing healthy, functional relationships and interactions between adults and children.

Formerly a classroom teacher (in inner-city Pittsburgh, Pennsylvania), crisis-intervention counselor and teacher training program coordinator, Dr. Bluestein serves on the board of the National Council for Self-Esteem as well as on the board of *Adolescence Magazine.* Dr. Bluestein works as a volunteer supervisor and instructor at a local middle school and currently heads Instructional Support Services, Inc., a consulting and resource firm in Albuquerque, New Mexico.

Share the Magic of Chicken Soup

Extra Helpings of Chicken Soup

Chicken Soup for the Soul™ Cookbook
101 Stories with Recipes from the Heart

Here authors Jack Canfield and Mark Victor Hansen have teamed up with award-winning cookbook author Diana von Welanetz Wentworth and dished up a delightful collection of stories accompanied by mouthwatering recipes.

Code 3545: Paperback $16.95
Code 3634: Hardcover $29.95

Sopa de pollo para el alma
(Spanish Language Version)
Relatos que conmueven el corazón y ponen fuego en el espíritu

The national bestseller and 1995 ABBY Award winner *Chicken Soup for the Soul* is now available in a lovingly prepared Spanish language edition. The stories found in *Sopa de pollo para el alma* are as rich as mole sauce and as robust and invigorating as café Cubano.

Code 3537: Paperback $12.95

Chicken Soup for the Surviving Soul
101 Stories of Courage and Inspiration from Those Who Have Survived Cancer

For years, the uplifting stories in the *Chicken Soup for the Soul* series have empowered individuals who have serious illnesses. Now Jack Canfield and Mark Victor Hansen have joined with Patty Aubery and Nancy Mitchell for a special batch of *Chicken Soup* devoted to stories of people beating cancer and finding renewed meaning in their lives.

Code 4029: Paperback $12.95
Code 4037: Hardcover $24.00

Available at your favorite bookstore or call 1-800-441-5569 for Visa or MasterCard orders. Prices do not include shipping and handling. Your response code is BKS.

Lift Your Spirits with Chicken Soup for the Soul™ Audiotapes

The Best of the Original Chicken Soup for the Soul™ Audiotape

This single 90-minute cassette contains the very best stories from the ABBY Award-winning *Chicken Soup for the Soul*. You will be enlightened and entertained by the masterful storytelling of Jack, Mark and friends.

Code 3723: One 90-minute cassette $9.95

Chicken Soup for the Soul™ Audio Gift Set

This six-tape set includes the entire audio collection of stories from *Chicken Soup for the Soul*—over seven hours of listening pleasure. It makes a wonderful gift for friends, loved ones or yourself.

Code 3103:
Six cassettes—Seven hours of inspiration $29.95

A 2nd Helping of Chicken Soup for the Soul™ Abridged Version Audiotape

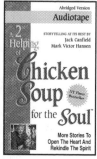

This two-tape volume brings you the authors' favorite stories from *A 2nd Helping of Chicken Soup for the Soul*. Now you can listen to the second batch in your car or in the comfort of your own home.

Code 3766: Two 90-minute cassettes $14.95

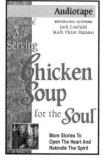

The Best of A 3rd Serving of Chicken Soup for the Soul™ Audiotape

The newest *Chicken Soup* stories on this delightful audio book will uplift and entertain you with their empowering messages of love, hope and perseverance. This scrumptious collection is guaranteed to brighten your day.

Code 4045: One 90-minute cassette $9.95

Available at your favorite bookstore or call 1-800-441-5569 for Visa or MasterCard orders. Prices do not include shipping and handling. Your response code is BKS.

STORY BOOKS TO ENLIGHTEN AND ENTERTAIN

Catch the Whisper of the Wind
Inspirational Stories and Proverbs from Native Americans
Cheewa James

The richness of Native American culture is explored by noted motivational speaker and broadcast journalist Cheewa James. These provocative stories touch the heart and offer deep insight into the soul of the Indian.

Code 3693 ....$11.95

The 7th Floor Ain't Too High for Angels to Fly
A Collection of Stories on Relationships and Self-Understanding
John M. Eades, Ph.D.

In this diverse collection of provocative stories, therapist John Eades helps readers to reflect on how they are living their own lives and invites them to discover the inner resources that lead to true joy and fulfillment. You'll laugh and cry, but you won't be able to put down *The 7th Floor Ain't Too High for Angels to Fly*.

Code 3561 ....$10.95

Bedtime Stories for Grown-ups
Fairy-Tale Psychology
Sue Gallehugh, Ph.D. and Allen Gallehugh

In this witty, fully illustrated book, therapist Sue Gallehugh and her son Allen adapt classic fairy tales to illustrate the fundamental principles of self-love through mental health and psychological growth. This upbeat, entertaining book will leave readers laughing out loud as they explore the value of the serious concept of self-worth.

Code 3618 ....$9.95

Values from the Heartland
Bettie B. Youngs, Ph.D., Ed.D

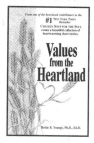

One of the best-loved authors from *Chicken Soup for the Soul* shares uplifting, heartwarming tales, culled from her memories of growing up on a farm in Iowa. These value-laden stories will show you how hard times, when leavened with love and support, can provide strength of character, courage and leadership.

Code 3359: paperback $11.95
Code 3340: hard cover $22.00

Mentors, Masters and Mrs. MacGregor
Stories of Teachers Making a Difference
Jane Bluestein, Ph.D.

Jane Bluestein asked celebrities and common folks around the world the following question: Who is that one special teacher that made a difference in your life? The collected answers to this question make up this truly touching book which will appeal to the student—and the teacher—in all of us.

Code 3375: paperback $11.95
Code 3367: hard cover $22.00

Celebrate *Mother's Day* All Year Long

Lessons from Mom
A Tribute to Loving Wisdom
Joan Aho Ryan

This heartwarming and inspiring collection of short stories, poems and anecdotes illustrates the special bond between mother and child and the lessons in virtues and values that mothers teach. You will cherish the special messages of love, perseverance, courage and hope that only a mother can send. Also included are entries from notables such as Dorothy Parker, Jeff Hostetler, Reba McEntire, Liz Smith and many more.

Code 3863 . . . . **$10.95**

The Essential Grandparent
A Guide to Making a Difference
Dr. Lillian Carson

One in every six people in the U.S. is a grandparent, but there is no ritual of celebration for such a big life passage and no instruction manual for being a grandparent. This comprehensive guide—through anecdotes, quotes and exercises—dispels grandparenting myths and helps readers develop their own grandparenting strategy in order to make the most of this rewarding stage of life.

Code 3979 . . . . **$10.95**

Embracing Our Essence
Spiritual Conversations with Prominent Women
Susan Skog

Embracing Our Essence nurtures and elevates our spiritual awakening as 29 well-known women reflect on their personal spirituality and quest for inner fulfillment. Those featured include Betty Ford, Elisabeth Kubler-Ross, Betty Eadie, Joan Borysenko, Nikki Giovanni, Jane Goodall and Naomi Judd.

Code 3596 . . . . **$11.95**

The Return of Spirit
A Woman's Call to Spiritual Action
Josie RavenWing

This rich book addresses the key issues of women's spiritual growth and offers readers practical steps for finding the conscious connection with the Divine in their own lives. You will learn how to increase personal vitality, deal with male-female balances of power, heal past relationships, interact with the spiritual forces of nature and more.

Code 3855 . . . . **$11.95**

Available at your favorite bookstore or call 1-800-441-5569
for Visa or MasterCard orders. Prices do not include shipping and handling.
Your response code is **BKS**.